Putting this book together was fun, and we hope you find it a valuable guide to making your Dublin experience as enjoyable as possible. If you have any ideas on what we should cover in future additions that are missing here, please e-mail us at afarmar@iol.ie.

the Dublin Bus guide to

Dublin
on a
shoestring

Dublin Bus
Changing With the City

© A. & A. Farmar 2002
ISBN 1-899047-75-1

First edition published 1998
Second edition 2002

Compiled by
Kathy Tynan and Derek Nagle with Matthew Magee, David Houlden,
Sinéad McCormack, K. R. Farmar and loads of others.

Design by Brosna
Maps courtesy of Dublin Bus
Cover photograph by Alice Campbell
Text photographs courtesy Dublin Tourism except pp 46, 78, 134, 167 by Derek Spiers,
p. 234 *Irish Press*
Typesetting by David Houlden
Printed by GraphyCems

Published in Dublin by
A. & A. Farmar
Beech House, 78 Ranelagh Village,
Dublin 6, Ireland
Tel +353 1 496 3625
Email: afarmar@iol.ie
Web: www.farmarbooks.com

Introduction

Dublin is the youngest and most exciting city in Europe: it's young in two ways—its population is young, but also compared with Rome, London or Paris it has not been a city for very long. And that shows in the relaxed, almost casual way that many things are still done.

The economic boom of recent years has left its mark on every aspect of the city's life: a new hedonism, a willingness to stick around Dublin rather than leave the country, an influx of immigrants from all over the world, and, of course, bucketloads of raw cash to buy the funny furniture in the hip nightclubs all mean that the place is buzzing.

A rash of new kinds of shops, cafés and clubs has infested Dublin: literally concrete proof of the vibrancy of the city. Walk the streets, feel the buzz, feel the crackle of ideas sparking off money and youth and pride and innovation.

And since it always has been a place where people talked, strolled around, chatted idly in pubs and did everything they could to have a ball, the combination is electric. Walk around late at night past the 24-hour shops, kebab houses, clubs and coffee-houses and you'll feel the energy suffusing the city and know what an exciting place Dublin is right now.

But Dublin isn't perfect. The new prosperity has infused the city with more life and culture than ever, but it's also raised prices, and not always with good reason. It's easy to throw caution to the wind and spend a fortune on things you could find in any city in the world, but if you take your time you'll get value for money and a truly unique experience.

In truth, the only way to feel the real, the new Dublin is to seek it out in the nooks and crannies of the city, in the little places that the inhabitants know, but guidebooks don't. This is Shoestring Dublin, and wonderfully, this is also the Dublin that doesn't charge you €14 for half a dozen oysters and a pint so that you can feel Authentically Irish.

Contents

The Ha'penny Bridge

A little history

Dublin now contains one-third of the population of the Irish Republic, and a fifth of the island's population. But it was a late starter as a city; when Cromwell paid his memorable visit in the 17th century, it had a mere 20,000 inhabitants. Now it is a city of layers, with a medieval footprint that centres on Christ Church Cathedral, overlaid by a Georgian body filling the space between the canals, and Victorian and modern wings spreading north, south and west of the Liffey valley.

The ancient Irish were not an urban people. They lived in family groups, or sometimes monastic settlements, and were predominantly rural and pastoral. Even today most of the inhabitants of Dublin are only one or two generations away from the country.

This gives Dublin its special character, as of a place inhabited by people who only half believe in where they live. Dublin is therefore a young city in two ways: its population is young, but also it has not been a full-scale city for long.

The first settlement in Dublin proper was a prehistoric huddle of small houses on the ridge above the lowest crossing point of the Liffey. (The ancient settlement of Kilmainham, where the Irish Museum of Modern Art now is, is said to be older still—it was finally incorporated into the city in 1900.)

The centre of the huddle was approximately where the Lord Edward pub is sited. Below this settlement was a rough wicker-work hurdle ford across the river, which since it had not yet been embanked was much wider and shallower than it is now.

Since the end of the 8th century Viking raiders from Norway had periodically plundered the Irish coastline seeking treasure and captives for slaves. In 841 they established a permanent settlement in Dublin as part of a network of trading posts across Europe.

Dublin perched on a ridge twelve metres or more above the Liffey, on a line from the Castle to Christ Church; ancient streets such as Winetavern and Fishamble show the winding way to the river. It was an independent city state, where pagan Vikings and Christian Irish worked and traded together, creating a trading settlement that had dealings as far as the Baltic and Iceland. They traded skins, hides, woollens, and, of course, slaves. In 1171 the Normans came, and Dublin became very much a colony. The new overlords, mostly from Bristol, built defensive stone walls (remnants of which you can see behind the Castle) and the first stone bridge in 1215. Then the centre of Dublin shifted to High Street which now seems nothing much, but throughout the Middle Ages was an intense centre of urban activity.

For the next few centuries, despite further invasions—of Irish, English and Scots—and frequent massacres and plagues, Dublin was little more than a large trading post. The real life of Ireland was still Gaelic and centred on the great clan chiefs. As the English interests in Ireland grew, Dublin became a sort of provincial capital. Its population increased very slowly, being less than 10,000 in 1600, mostly living in the suburbs outside the city proper. Trinity College (founded in 1592) was deliberately placed in the fields, outside the town. St Stephen's Green was still pasture, the site of public executions and a burial place for plague victims.

Medieval Dublin was dirty, quarrelsome, dangerous, and, despite its small population, desperately overcrowded. Animals of all kinds wandered the streets, and were killed and cleaned on the spot in the various markets. As a result public highways frequently became filthy, smelly and even impassable. As well as murderous raids from clansmen in the Wicklow mountains, there was constant fear of plague, fire and hunger. As late as 1575 a third of the population died in an outburst of plague.

> ## THE WALLED CITY
> *To get a sense of Dublin as a walled city, go to St Audoen's church (off High Street, Dublin 2). There's a flight of broad steps going down called the Forty Steps. This was a main thoroughfare of medieval Dublin. It led into the city from Cook Street where the ovens were banished, for fear of fire. Slip through the gate and stand in Cook Street where the city wall (much restored) looms above you. Take a moment to imagine the bustling pack-horses and carts and vendors squeezing through the gate in normal times, or in wartime, the citizenry huddled behind the wall in dread of the 'wild Irish'. (The battlements, by the way, are bogus, a 19th-century fantasy.)*

The glory days of Dublin began in the 17th century. Queen Elizabeth's new policy for the control of Ireland, of 'planting' as many Protestants as possible in rebellious areas, brought a new attitude. The policy was continued by her Stuart successors. Dublin became the social, political and economic focus of these planters in Munster, Wexford and Ulster. From 1660 the city began a hundred and forty years of more or less continual growth. The first stone quays were built along the side of the river, and whereas previous centuries had made do with one bridge (at Bridge Street), now no fewer than four new bridges were thrown across the Liffey in quick succession.

The city finally became the national centre of communications and power; it was the country's leading port, the focus of legal, medical and other professional activity, the place where the landed classes came in winter to disport themselves, financed by their country rents. To house these grandees developers built the squares and townscapes of Georgian Dublin. At the same time great public buildings such as the Four Courts, the Custom House and the Parliament House (now occupied by the Bank of Ireland) were erected. The crooked, twisted medieval roads were refashioned (a hundred years before Baron Haussmann's work in Paris) by the Wide Streets Commissioners.

The militant attempt in the 1790s to secure more independence for Ireland resulted in the opposite—the Act of Union of 1800 and the abolition of the Irish parliament. At war with France, which had already tried to liberate Ireland in 1796, the English were not about to allow Ireland any freedom at all. Now Dublin became a mere political branch office for London; lawyers and clever doctors, such as Sir William Wilde (Oscar's father), rather than aristocratic office-holders dominated social life. Catholic emancipation in 1829 did not mean that Catholics and Protestants mingled socially. The city continued to be split horizontally by class and vertically by religion. As late as the 1960s every firm, every private institution—including banks, breweries, accountancy practices, grocers and charities—was clearly known to be either 'Protestant' or 'Catholic' in orientation. There was little point in an ambitious Catholic applying to join a Protestant firm, or vice versa. The scrupulous took care that the most trivial purchases were made from one of the 'right sort'.

Although the Great Famine of the 1840s had a severe impact on Dublin, the city was in the long run more affected by the railway and steam connection established in the 1850s between London and Dublin. This enabled British manufacturers to pour goods into Ireland, completing the destruction of Dublin's manufacturing base. The city became a storage centre. To run what has been called the 'warehouse economy' you did not need skilled workers—a large body of (Catholic) unskilled labour and a much

4

smaller body of (largely Protestant) clerks and professional men would suffice. This economic divide was quickly represented on the ground as the clerks and the professionals left the city centre and established themselves in townships beyond the canals. The characteristic redbrick of their houses in often tree-lined roadscapes can be seen in the southside villages of Ranelagh, Rathgar and Rathmines, and on the northside in Clontarf and Drumcondra. The new suburbs were leafy and comfortable, although in an effort to keep down the rates the developers often skimped on the pavements and drains.

The inner city dwellers fared less well. Wages were low and intermittent. Since the rich had fled, no one could afford rates and the city became increasingly run-down; housing was poor and getting steadily worse. As a result the tenement slums of Dublin—as written about by Seán O'Casey, James Stephens and others—became some of the worst in Europe, and a scandal that has only been set right within living memory. The Dubliners of Yeats' and Joyce's time inherited almost a century of economic stagnation and squabbling politics. From being the second city of the Empire, 'dear dirty Dublin' had been overtaken by Belfast in size and confidence.

All this was to change with the armed struggle for national independence that ran from 1916 to 1922. Finally, after six years of intermittent but intense fighting, Dublin became the capital city of the first country to break away from the British Empire since 1776. The city still bears the scars of the long struggle —look out for the bullet marks on the front of the Royal College of Surgeons in St Stephen's Green and on the O'Connell statue in O'Connell Street.

Once more Dublin became the political centre, the national focus of commerce, and the legal and professional centre, at least for the 26 counties of the new state.

Dublin's story since 1922 is one of constant expansion as governments strove first to re-house the tenement dwellers and then to build houses for the constant flow of migrants from the country. The city's population rose (and is rising) remorselessly, from the 350,000 or so that Joyce had known, to the 650,000 of Brendan Behan's Dublin in the 1950s, to the 1 million or more of today. Until very recently, the population of the rest of the country went in the opposite direction, falling steadily since the 1840s.

Reshaping the historic centre began in the 1960s, as developers flattened old buildings and erected office blocks and pastiche Georgian terraces. In the 1980s, the Corporation completed the plan to concrete over the ancient Viking core of the city with two blocks known without affection as 'the bunkers'.

For years the Temple Bar area, between Dame Street and the Liffey, had been stricken by planning blight. A great development was planned and not carried through. In the meantime, because of the low rents it became such a lively area of shops and restaurants that the planners accepted the inevitable. They formed the once dingy streets (where the brothels and drinking dens of 18th-century Dublin had traded) into a bustling district of restaurants, arts centres, pubs and smart apartments. Plans for the refurbishment of O'Connell Street, which has been sadly neglected since independence, are well advanced.

Dublin is enjoying both the benefits and some of the perils of prosperity. There certainly is more money around, and a general 'feel-good' buzz. On the other hand, the money is not fairly distributed, and there are still too many beggars on the streets, and too many pockets of urban poverty, especially in north and west Dublin. The country's new reputation has attracted people from all over the world, giving the city a more cosmopolitan air; unfortunately this has exposed a nasty strain of racism that the Travellers have long experienced. Rising incomes mean rising house prices, making it difficult to buy a home on ordinary wages, and making the renting sector very difficult indeed. Another of the perils of prosperity can be seen on the roads. The increasing congestion has made driving very uncomfortable, and has generated a new type of driving aggression that Dubliners had hardly known outside films before.

Compared to most cities, Dublin is friendly, is easy to live in, and is buzzing with a kind of youthful exuberance. Let's hope prosperity doesn't take too much of its charm away.

Getting your bearings

Dublin is built in the dip of a valley, where the Liffey runs from the Dublin mountains into the sea. The best way to get a sense of this ancient valley is to look south as you come in from the airport on the northside. You can look straight across to the looming Wicklow mountains, which are older than the Himalayas, and the city is quite invisible, buried in the valley below.

As in most European cities Dublin's streets follow an irregular, often winding pattern, with the oldest (around Wood Quay) being directly traceable to Viking days. The typical height of a Dublin building is four storeys; church spires are still prominent objects on the skyscape, though large office buildings are beginning to compete. To get your bearings we recommend you identify a number of **landmarks**, and use them as a focus. The oldest parts of Dublin are neatly enclosed by two canals, the Grand Canal and the Royal Canal. The **old city** lies inside the oval shape defined by the two canals. Down the middle of the oval runs the river Liffey, Joyce's Anna Livia Plurabelle. This runs from the Dublin mountains to the sea. Good **landmarks** on the Liffey are (running west to east, towards the sea) the Four Courts, the Ha'penny Bridge, O'Connell Bridge, Liberty Hall, the Custom House and the Point Theatre.

South from the Liffey are Guinness' Brewery, Christ Church Cathedral, Dublin Castle, Trinity College, St Stephen's Green and the National Gallery.

For most visitors the axis across the Liffey to know is from the Parnell Monument (next to the Rotunda Hospital and the Gate Theatre) down O'Connell Street, past Henry Street and its shops, the GPO, over O'Connell Bridge, past Trinity on your left and down Grafton Street to St Stephen's Green.

North/south
Dubliners are convinced that there is a noticeable difference in character and style between those who live on the north of the river and those who live on

Dublin's postcodes

15 Blanchardstown Castleknock Clonsilla	**11** Cappagh Finglas	**9** Drumcondra Santry DCU	**17** Darndale Riverside	**13** Baldoyle Sutton Howth

7
Arbour Hill
Cabra
Phibsboro
Four Courts

5 Artane
Raheny

3 Clontarf
Dollymount
Marino

1 Abbey St
Amiens St
Henry St
Montjoy Sq
North Wall
O'Connell St

20
Chapelizod
Palmerstown

8 Kilmainham
The Coombe

2 College Green
St. Stephen's Green
Harcourt St
Merrion Sq
Pearse St

10
Ballyfermot

12 Crumlin
Walkinstown

6 Ranelagh
Rathmines
Rathgar

4 Ballsbridge
Donnybrook
Ringsend
Sandymount
Belfield

22
Clondalkin

6W
Kimmage
Harold's Cross
Terenure

14 Dundrum
Goatstown
Clonskeagh

Booterstown
Monkstown
Blackrock
Stillorgan
Deans Grange
Sandycove
Dun Laoire
Glenageary
Dalkey
Killiney

16 Ballinteer

24
Tallaght
Firhouse

18 Foxrock
Sandyford
Stepaside

the south. This difference is officially recognised by the fact that all odd-numbered postcodes are northside and even-numbered are southside. Thus in the city centre, Dublin 1 is north of the river, Dublin 2 is south.

Nowadays the southside is pictured as richer, but effete; the north as rougher, but at the same time more 'authentic'. 'Be proud the northsiders are the blacks of Dublin' as Roddy Doyle put it in *The Commitments*. From time to time politicians and others mutter darkly about how the opinions of 'Dublin 4'—in particular the 'trendy liberals' of RTÉ and University College Dublin—are swamping the honest instincts of the plain people of Ireland.

Because of the way the city developed in the 19th century, accommodation and facilities generally are more expensive on the southside, so *Shoestring* readers would be advised to suss out any northside possibilities first.

UPPER AND LOWER

Many Dublin streets are divided into two, and called Upper and Lower—thus Leeson Street, Baggot Street, Mount Street, Dorset Street. Generally, the Lower is the nearer to the mouth of the Liffey, the Upper further away. This is not, however, the result of a deep plan, as the exception, Dorset Street, clearly shows. It seems that the streets called Lower were simply built before those called Upper (though of course there are exceptions to this too).

Dublin for people with disabilities

Dublin is a welcoming place for most visitors but, unfortunately, it is not particularly well adapted for people with disabilities. However, things are gradually improving, with new regulations as well as increased competition in the tourist industry. If you have a disability, the best advice is to plan ahead as far as possible and check all facilities in advance—even those billed as wheelchair-friendly or offering full access for disabled people. People are generally very friendly and approachable when you need help for any reason, so don't hesitate to ask. It is typical of Irish people to be especially apologetic to visitors for shortcomings in services although they rarely campaign for a better deal for themselves.

The national agency, **Comhairle**, 44 Nth Great George's St, Dublin 1, tel 874 7503 provides information and support services. It can give you general information regarding facilities and equipment or personal rights and entitlements. If staff there cannot help you directly, they will refer you to the relevant organisation that can. Its National Disability Resource Centre is open Mon–Fri 10.00–13.00, 14.00–16.00.

Comhairle also still supply the old NRB-published guide to Dublin for people with disabilities who are seeking information on accommodation and facilities. While this guide is by now somewhat out of date, it is still quite useful and contains plenty of general advice as well as listings for both the tourist and the long-term resident. It also includes a list of wheelchair-accessible public toilets.

Staff at **The Irish Wheelchair Association**, Blackheath Drive, Clontarf, Dublin 3, tel 833 8241, are currently compiling a comprehensive county-by-county guide to accessible tourist accommodation and facilities in Ireland. They hope to publish it first on the Web, and eventually in book format. While it may be some time before the guide is complete, staff are more than happy to send out whatever information they have to anyone planning a trip, and will also give advice over the phone. Anyone with a disability considering moving to Ireland long-term can apply for membership of the Association; its range of services covers everything from counselling and housing to equipment sales and repair. A very useful service they offer is wheelchair hire.

Responsibility for meeting the needs of **air travellers** with disabilities is normally shared between the airline and the airport authority at the point of arrival or departure. It is an offence for an airline not to facilitate a passenger with a disability. It is, however, always necessary to inform your airline of your needs when booking your flight. You will often be asked to check-in, and sometimes board, earlier than other passengers, so always arrive in good time.

During the peak season, **Dublin Airport** can become extremely crowded and is not always easy to negotiate independently, particularly for the sensory impaired. All services and facilities at Dublin Airport are, however, fully accessible to people with disabilities. If you have any particular queries about these, contact **Aer Rianta** (airport management) tel 844 4900.

If you have any special needs and are arriving by **ferry**, it is always advisable to give your ferry company about three days' advance notice. Despite the ongoing development of ferry technology and accommodation, some areas of vessels are still awkward to access and, in general, the ferry companies prefer to offer assistance in all cases, for reasons of safety. The terminal buildings in both of Dublin's ports are fully accessible but getting from the building to the ship via the ramps will probably require assistance.

When travelling by **train**, the best advice is to contact the station at least 24 hours in advance, and to arrive at the station with half an hour to spare so that staff will be better able to provide whatever assistance is required. **Iarnród Éireann/Irish Rail** produces a useful free booklet for rail passengers called *Guide for Mobility Impaired Passengers*. This is available through the Access and Liaison Officer at Connolly Station, Amiens St, Dublin 1, tel 703 2634, and at all InterCity and suburban stations. Details are also given on Irish Rail's website www.irishrail.ie.

Not all **DART trains** are directly accessible to wheelchair users, so it is essential to check ahead and it is usually advisable to have some assistance, as access to the stations can be difficult. Also, depending on the station, there can be a gap between the platform and the coach so assistance is often needed.

Mainline and suburban trains require a portable ramp to enable wheelchairs to enter the carriages. A dedicated space in the dining car of each train is available and if several wheelchair users wish to travel together, staff (if informed in advance) will remove seats and tables from the dining coach to make room. There are wheelchair-accessible toilets at most mainline termini and efforts are also gradually being made to upgrade facilities for people with visual and hearing disabilities. As many old stations are being gradually refurbished and some new stations have been built, (namely on the Connolly–Maynooth line at Drumcondra and on the DART line at Clontarf Rd on the northside and Barrow St on the southside) the situation is starting to improve. It is a slow process, however, and smaller stations are not often as well equipped.

Assistance will be required to use most of the **buses** in Dublin as, generally, passengers with wheelchairs are expected to sit in the standard seats, stowing the chair in the space provided. Seats near the door are designated for use by the elderly or mobility-impaired. Happily, Dublin Bus have been purchasing buses that are fully accessible. Features of these new buses include: low floors, single-step entry, kneeling suspension to further reduce entry-step height, retractable ramps at the entrance door, priority space for wheelchair users, wider gangways, improved grip bars, palm-activated bell pushes and high-visibility, electronic destination displays.

The following bus routes are now operated using fully accessible vehicles (new routes are introduced from time to time so check the Accessibility tab in the website www.dublinbus.ie).

Fully-accessible Dublin Bus routes

1	Parnell Sq East–Poolbeg Extension
2	Parnell Sq East– Sandymount
3	Larkhill–Sandymount
11/11A/11B	Wadelai Pk–Belfield/Kilmacud
32/32A/32B	Lr Abbey St–Malahide
32X	Malahide–Belfield and Beresford Pl–Malahide
42	Beresford Pl–Malahide
51B	Aston Quay–Clondalkin (Dunawley)
59A	Dún Laoghaire–Mackintosh Pk
65/65B	Aston Quay–Citywest/Blessington
90A	Heuston Rail Station–IFSC
103/104	Clontarf DART Station–Omni Shopping Centre/Finglas and Marino–Drimnagh Rd
123	Marino–Drimnagh Rd
127	Donaghmede–Leeson St Bridge
129	Baldoyle–Leeson St Bridge
747/748	Dublin Airport–Busáras–Heuston Station

Accessible buses operate sporadically on other routes but, as yet, there are not enough to guarantee the service across the entire network.

If you intend departing from Dublin to travel the rest of the country by bus, you will definitely require assistance. The central station, **Busáras**, Store Street, Dublin 1, is where all of the **Bus Éireann** national bus network routes depart from. Unfortunately, while the station itself is fully accessible, the coach-style buses used on most routes are not. Passengers travel high off the ground above the large, but necessary, luggage compartments. In general, if you wish to travel this way, you will have to fold and stow your wheelchair with the luggage under the bus, and bring someone to assist you with embarking and disembarking via the steep steps. Added to that, as these are provincial bus routes which penetrate every rural area in the county, the stops on the route are often quite awkward to negotiate; these can occur at the side of almost any road, and, in small towns, are sometimes blocked by illegally parked cars. In defence of Bus Éireann, however, it must be pointed out that the services they operate within other cities (Cork and Galway, for example) are generally better equipped and do provide a certain number of ramps and designated wheelchair spaces. For journeys to and from Dublin, however, the bus is an awkward option at best. General information on Bus Éireann services can be accessed at tel 836 6111, website www.buseireann.ie.

If you can transfer from your wheelchair, most **taxis** should be able to transport you with your wheelchair stowed in the boot. A better option, though, is a wheelchair-accessible taxi and, over the past few years, there has been an increase in the number of these operating in Dublin, although many of the independent operators still opt for the smaller, non-accessible vehicles. It is now an offence for a driver at a taxi rank operating a wheelchair-accessible taxi to refuse to pick up a disabled passenger. However, most of these taxis cannot be booked more than an hour or two in advance, which is a real problem in many cases. The following taxi companies have vehicles in their fleets which will accommodate wheelchair passengers: **National Radio Cabs**, tel 677 2222; **Radio Link Cabs**, tel 478 1111; **Blue Cabs**, tel 676 1111.

A service specifically designed for disabled people is **Vantastic**, tel 833 0663. It has a number of minivans fitted with ramps and offers a door-to-door service at a government-subsidised charge (cheaper than a taxi). Most of their work is with their registered members who use the service to get to work, clinics and so on, but they will also take bookings from individuals for single journeys. To avail of this service you need to give 24–48 hours' notice.

In this guide we have indicated where wheelchair access is possible, but not all such places are *fully* accessible—toilets may not be accessible, for instance, so do always check. However, wheelchair users have assured us that the following were fully accessible at the time of going to press:

Thunder Road Café Fleet St, Dublin 2, tel 679 4057

Trastevere Restaurant Temple Bar, Dublin 2, tel 670 8343

Templar's Bistro Clontarf Castle Hotel, Dublin 3, tel 833 2321

Dollymount House Clontarf Rd, Dublin 3, tel 833 2492

Mario's Restaurant Sandymount Green, Dublin 4, tel 269 5992

Rook's Restaurant Regency Hotel, Swords Rd, Dublin 9, tel 836 7333

TGI Friday's Restaurant Blanchardstown SC, Dublin 15, tel 822 5990

Joel's Restaurant Newland's Cross, Naas Rd, Dublin 22, tel 459 2968

The Coachman's Inn Cloghran (adj. Airport), Co. Dublin, tel 840 1827

The Chapel, Trinity College

Other basic stuff

Stuff we thought you might find useful, but couldn't think where else to put.

Accidents and emergencies

If you cannot find a garda (police officer), dial 999 from the nearest telephone (no charge). You will be asked whether you are reporting a fire, medical or police emergency. You will also be asked to give a clear indication of your location. Normally this will be clearly written up in the telephone booth; check this before you dial and if not, make sure you can describe exactly where you are by a local landmark (e.g. a pub) so that the emergency service can find you.

The main accident and emergency departments are at the following hospitals:

Beaumont Hospital Beaumont Rd, Dublin 9, tel 809 2714
Mater Hospital Eccles St, Dublin 1, tel 803 2000
St James' Hospital James St, Dublin 8, tel 410 3000
St Vincent's Hospital Elm Park, Dublin 4, tel 209 4358
Tallaght Hospital Dublin 24, tel 414 3500.

Be prepared to queue. Payment is €31.70 unless you have a referral note from a GP or a medical card. Emergency treatment is free to citizens from other EU countries who present an E111 form stamped in their own country.

Bank holidays

There are nine bank holidays. They fall on 1 January, 17 March (if falling on a weekday, otherwise next weekday), Easter Monday, the first Monday in May, June and August, the last Monday in October, Christmas Day if on a weekday, otherwise the next Tuesday, St Stephen's Day (26 Dec) if on a weekday, otherwise the next weekday. Good Friday is not a bank holiday, though many businesses treat it as if it were.

Dental

Emergency dental care is available at the Dublin Dental Hospital in Lincoln Place, Dublin 2 (just next to the back entrance to Trinity College) tel 612 7391. The emergency charge of €31 covers x-rays and subsequent treatment for three months.

For standard dental work it is possible to opt for treatment at the Dental Hospital by a student under supervision. This saves 25 per cent of the not-extortionate charges.

Drugs

If you are going to use any drugs that you suspect may not be legal, then you should be aware of the stringent laws against the misuse of drugs.

The Public Order Act (1998) grants powers to the Gardaí so wide ranging as to be considered an infringement of civil liberties. The Act created fourteen new crimes, covering noise and boisterous acts at night as well as public protest. Most relevant here, though, are the rights it grants the Gardaí in relation to the drugs laws.

Any garda is entitled to detain and search you on reasonable suspicion that you are in possession of or involved in the supply of illegal drugs. You can be detained without charge for up to seven days, and can be strip searched.

This is a very serious situation to be put in, particularly if you are in a foreign country: that length of time in prison without charge or court process will frighten the life out of anybody. Ironically, these were the very powers that caused most protest in Ireland when the UK Prevention of Terrorism Acts gave them to the British police.

The use of drugs is governed by the Misuse of Drugs Act 1977 and 1984. Drugs made illegal under the Act are known as 'controlled substances' and a distinction is drawn between those that do have some medical use and those that don't. Distinctions are also drawn between acts relating to controlled substances: unlawful supply, intent to supply, import or export and production of controlled substances, the growing of substances, forging of prescriptions, occupying of premises knowingly allowing their use in the traffic in drugs are all specified offences relating to supply or obtaining of controlled substances. Another category is possession, which is divided into possession for personal use and possession with intent to supply. The latter carries a far more severe penalty.

The penalties are different for all these offences. It is down to the judge's discretion whether to impose the full penalty. First-time conviction for possession of cannabis and/or Ecstasy for personal use carries a fine of €200 in the District Court. Jail is automatic for second and subsequent offences, together with a fine. Possession of heroin, cocaine etc. incurs a penalty of €500–€700 or 12 months in jail or both; before a judge and jury there is no maximum fine and you can be fined or sent to jail for up to ten years, or both.

The sentencing is far stricter for any crime involving *supplying* drugs, and whole squads of gardaí are employed to find you if you offend.

IRISH ATTITUDE TO THE WEATHER

To celebrate the 1,500th anniversary of St Patrick, in 1932 a mighty Eucharistic Congress was held in Dublin. Thousands of visitors came from all over the Catholic world to join in the celebrations, many of which were to be held in the open air. Ireland being Ireland, there was some anxiety about the weather. G. K. Chesterton reports that a poor, threadbare, working woman was hear to say to her friend: 'Well, if it rains now, He'll have brought it on Himself.'

Euro currency

Since 1 January 2002 the Irish currency has been the euro, as in most of the rest of the EU. 1 euro is divided into 100 cent. At the time of going to press €1 was worth Stg62p and 88 US cents.

Fax

Faxes can be sent from shops that sell stationery and photocopying services.

Gay Dublin

While Dublin's gay scene cannot be compared to those of, say, London or San Francisco, it is nonetheless vibrant, broad and growing. It was, of course, given a big boost by the liberalisation of the law relating to homosexual activity between consenting males over 18 in 1993. The monthly freesheet *Gay Community News* website www.gcn.ie is the basic start point for gay Dublin; its fat pages are crammed with information. Available from Waterstone's, Books Upstairs, Tower Records, Juice and other city centre cafés.

If you are looking for a gay place to stay, try
Frankie's 8 Camden Place, Dublin 2, tel 478 3087
Inn on the Liffey 21 Upr Ormond Quay, Dublin 7, tel 677 0828

There are some specifically **gay pubs** in Dublin—**The George**, 89 Sth Great George's St, Dublin 2 tel 478 2983, **Out on the Liffey**, 27 Upr Ormond Quay, Dublin 7, tel 872 2480 and the newest the **Wig and Pen** 131 Thomas St, Dublin 8; however, lots of others are gay-friendly, in particular **Gubu**, Capel St, Dublin 1, tel 874 0710, and **The Front Lounge** 33 Parliament St, Dublin 2, tel 670 4112 (memorably described in *Gay Community News* as 'conversationally swanky'). The **gay club** scene is moving fast, so you're best to make a bee-line for the listings in *In Dublin* or *Gay Community News* to find a place that suits your taste and pocket.

Medical

A medical card, which entitles you to free medical attention, is available to residents (including students) earning between €88 and €114 a week. For details contact the **Eastern Regional Health Authority** (formerly the Eastern Health Board) tel 1 800 520 520.

Muggings, robberies

The relaxed atmosphere is certainly nice but there *are* muggings and robberies in the street particularly after the pubs close, and opportunistic robberies in public places. A large proportion of crime is driven by alcohol and drugs, which means muggings and thievery are not necessarily rationally calculated. If in doubt, stick to the rule—if you wouldn't do it at home, don't do it here.

Keep away from murky streets at night, from groups of youths (who will probably do more damage to themselves than you, but it's wise to keep clear); keep valuables tightly under control; keep bags and wallets out of sight (don't, for instance, be lulled by the atmosphere into leaving valuables on a table in the pub while you go to the toilet): don't flash cash at an ATM machine; don't wear 'rob-me' jewellery; if you are out late at night, stay in groups; be aware that young men are more likely to be attacked at random than young women.

Some places are more risky than others: queues at chippers after the pubs close are particular flashpoints; it is probably best to keep clear of O'Connell St late at night.

If you are robbed or injured, report the crime to the gardaí. If you need to replace passports, or have money sent from home ask the gardaí for a referral to **Tourist Victim Support,** tel 478 5295, who will help you to contact embassies, banks etc. The line is open Mon–Sat 10.00–18.00 Sun, bank holidays 12.00–18.00. **Victim Support** tel 1800 661 771, is a 24 hr helpline for victims of crime.

Newspapers and magazines

There are three daily Irish broadsheets *The Irish Times*, the *Irish Independent*, and *The Irish Examiner* and an evening paper, the *Evening Herald*. The *Times* is your standard AB journal of record, middle-class, middle-age paper, published by a Trust. Its website, www.ireland.com is a mine of constantly updated information, free at the moment but likely to be charged for soon. The *Independent* with higher sales, is a rougher, job. It is owned by *Sir Anthony* O'Reilly (or as the man in the bar said 'sure didn't I know him when plain Tony was good enough!'), as is the *Evening Herald*, the key venue for all sorts of small ads, from houses and cars to computers. *The Irish Examiner* has good political and books coverage. If you want to check up on the news from home, a wide selection of international and country papers are on display at Easons in O'Connell St, Dublin 1. For free reads, many pubs and cafés carry customer copies of these papers—it's worth asking.

There is one truly essential **listings mag** for Dublin, and that is the fortnightly *In Dublin*. It's good value, giving details of pretty much everything that's going on in the city, including theatre, clubs, restaurants, gigs, and sex industry stuff at the back. Features and columns are hugely entertaining, but it helps to be clued in on the past twenty years of Irish popular culture.

If you'd rather not shell out €1.95, there's *The Event Guide*, available free in many city centre bookshops, pubs and cafés which offers much the same as *In Dublin* without the strange editorials, the satirical columns, or the exotic ads. *The Event Guide* is well worth checking out for the interviews and reviews, which are often longer and more detailed than you'd find in a mainstream magazine.

Hot Press also gives listings, but is better known for its unique mixture of music, politics and opinion.

Other mags that are worth a glance on the newsagents' shelves are *Magill*, which every few issues has a riveting insider piece on a current political scandal, and *Phoenix* (a wannabe *Private Eye*), required reading in stock market circles for its business revelations.

Opening hours

BANKS Mon–Fri 10.00–16.00 (Thur 17.00). There are numerous 24-hour Automatic Telling Machines (ATMs) in the city centre.

PUBS Mon–Wed 10.30–23.30 Thur–Sat 10.30–00.30 Sun 12.30–23.00 with variations for individual pubs.

PUBLIC AND BUSINESS OFFICES 09.00–17.00.

RESTAURANTS 12.00–14.30 for lunch, dinner 18.30–23.00. Cafés, café-restaurants all day.

SHOPS Mon–Sat 09.00 or 09.30–18.00 Thur 20.00 in the city centre and some shopping centres; Sun (many, but by no means all) 12.00–18.00. 24-hour convenience stores are increasingly common. Smaller shops, especially the interesting ones run by free spirits, don't open till 10.00.

Post

Letters and cards can be posted (already stamped) in postboxes on the street and in post offices marked *Oifig an Phoist*. The postboxes are emptied several times a day.

Stamps are only obtainable from post offices. Post offices and postboxes are all painted bright green so are easy to spot.

Shopping bags

Ireland's green and pleasant land was, until recently, in danger of being strangled by plastic. So the Minister for the Environment has slapped a tax of 15c on every plastic shopping bag used. This is, incidentally, one of the very few taxes hardly anyone objects to. Dubliners are slowly getting into the habit of bringing their own bags out shopping.

The GPO (General Post Office), O'Connell Street

Telephone

Eircom dominates the landline service and hence public telephone services. Phone booths mostly take phonecards rather than cash; pubs usually have a telephone available for public use, and these generally take cash. Phonecards are available from newsagents in denominations ranging from 10 units (where 1 unit represents a 3-minute call) to 50 units. Local calls from payphones cost a minimum of 30c for a local call, although pubs and other places may charge you 50c. Local calls from a private phone costs 5c per minute.

Unfortunately, Eircom telephone directories are not easy to get hold of outside private homes; the public phone in the nearby pub *might* have one, but it will be extremely tatty and very likely missing crucial pages; the local library will have a set, and the library in the ILAC Centre, Henry St, Dublin 1 has a fine collection of overseas directories. The cheapest directory enquiry service is from Eircom, tel 11811 for Irish and British numbers at a cost of 35c, 11818 for international numbers, at a minimum cost of 58c.

Time

Although the sun rises in Dublin some twenty minutes later than in London, the time used is the same Greenwich Mean Time. Summer time, when the clocks are put forward an hour, runs from the last Sunday in March to the last Sunday in October.

Tipping

Tipping is much more casual in Dublin than other European or American cities. The main place for tipping is in restaurants and hotels. Nowadays many upmarket restaurants automatically add a 'service charge' to the bill; however, this often goes to the restaurateur, so staff still hope for a tip of 10 per cent or more. Hairdressers, taxi-drivers and others appreciate a tip of 10 per cent or so.

Toilets

There are some public toilets in Dublin, marked **MNÁ** (for *women*) and **FIR** (for *men*) which can be embarrassing if you assume M stands for male and F stands for female. Dubliners generally prefer to use the toilets in pubs, cafés and hotels. Toilets in large department stores are open to the public.

Traffic

The boom has brought more people into the city and more cars to roads in a system ill-adapted to modern urban living. The public transport system has not been given priority and the result is choked streets and angry and frustrated travellers.

Road usage by both motorists and pedestrians is erratic and often individualistic. The most obvious example is at traffic lights, where the orange light, intended as a warning to slow down, is often treated as a signal for the driver to hurry so as not to be caught by the red. (This attitude to road safety is regarded as one of the main contributors to Ireland's appalling toll of road fatalities: the death rate per head is double that of the UK.) Seeing a gap in the traffic, pedestrians will happily surge across the road regardless of the state of the lights.

For those unused to these conditions, Dublin traffic can be unnerving. However the good news is that traffic in the city does not generally move very fast, and motorists are generally considerate to other road users, even philosophical, though the increasingly crowded conditions have given rise to a new strand of aggression among some frustrated motorists. If you're a pedestrian trying to cross the road without the benefit of a pedestrian crossing (too few) be sure to watch out for cyclists whizzing along in the cycle lane.

Weather

The most notable thing about Dublin's weather is its variability. (Hence the view that Ireland has no climate, only weather.) A day that starts bathed in brilliant sunshine is likely to be overcast by noon, experience a quick shower of rain an hour later and then be sunny again in mid-afternoon. This variability provides a useful conversation opener: 'It's a grand soft day' (meaning 'it's pouring'), says one. 'But it's not cold, thank God', says another. And then they can embark on other topics.

Average temperature in summer ranges between 10°C and 19°C, and in winter between 3°C and 8°C. There is considerable variance around these figures: in a heatwave temperatures can reach 30°C. It is, however, rarely very cold, and there might be no rainfall, especially in summer, for two or three weeks in succession.

Generally Irish rain is unaggressive—but it *will* rain, so be prepared. It's often a good idea to carry an umbrella, but serious wet-gear isn't required. The best clothing solution is to dress with lots of light layers that can be readily peeled off and slipped into a bag as occasion requires.

Tourist Information and Bookings

By phone, e-mail or online from anywhere in the world:

Bord Fáilte
website www.ireland.travel.ie
tel +800 668 668 66 (+ denotes international access codes)
e-mail reservations@gulliver.ie

Dublin Tourism
e-mail information@dublintourism.ie
website www.visitdublin.com

Somewhere to sleep

Somewhere to stay

Dublin offers a huge choice of good-value, high-standard accommodation in hotels, guesthouses, townhouses/B&Bs, tourist hostels, self-catering apartments and university campuses. The number of available tourist beds in the city has increased dramatically over the past few years, giving visitors more than ever to choose from. However, tourist numbers have also increased hugely, so it can still be difficult enough to find a place to stay if you have not booked in advance.

Most premises that are approved by Bord Fáilte/Irish Tourist Board display the shamrock sign and are included in the computerised booking system used by tourist offices throughout the country. Some premises operate outside the remit of Bord Fáilte and these can be worth investigating, but remember, if something goes wrong, you cannot then use the official Bord Fáilte channel for complaints.

The *Dublin Accommodation Guide* contains an extensive listing (all Dublin Tourism members) of registered and approved hotels, guesthouses, town and country homes, hostels and self-catering accommodation in Dublin city and county. Complete with photographs, it outlines the details of prices and facilities. The guide is available for €4 from any Dublin Tourism office or by post.

Our recommendations (listings by area start on p. 33) range in price from approximately €11 pps (per person sharing) in a tourist hostel to about €55 in top-quality guesthouses or good-value hotels. These are a selection of the most comfortable, convenient and best-value places in the various categories of accommodation available in April 2002. Hotels, B&Bs and guesthouses usually include breakfast in their prices—a full Irish breakfast of fruit juice, cereal, bacon, eggs, sausages, black pudding, brown bread, toast, tea or coffee (vegetarian variations are usually available) is a substantial meal in itself. It's a bit heavy for some tastes, though.

One thing to bear in mind when booking your stay in Dublin is that, when times are quiet, the normally expensive **hotels** often do very good, room-only, discount rates. It is therefore often worthwhile ringing up, particularly mid-week or off-season, to see what's on offer. If you want to try for a hotel bargain, one place that gives an instant idea of whether you are likely to get one (*and* save you from making repeated phone calls all over town) is **Central Reservations at Jurys Doyle Hotels**, one of Ireland's largest and most established hotel chains, tel 607 0000, www.jurys.com. This group has a selection of 3-, 4- and 5-star hotels, either within walking distance or a short bus ride from Dublin city centre, as well as the two centrally-located budget Inns, listed below. Their 4- and 5-star premises normally charge around €250–€350 per room but some can be booked for €150 or less when business is slow. Jurys also have a selection of solid 3-star business hotels in which rooms are available from €149 or less—a very good deal for two or more people or even families with children willing to share. Many other hotels offer similar discounts all year round if they experience a temporary slackening off in demand for any reason.

Guesthouses, which are much like small hotels, and **townhouses/ B&Bs**, which are usually family homes and are smaller than guesthouses, nearly always include a full breakfast in the price and this is worth taking into account when you're working out your budget. There are not many B&Bs within walking distance of the city centre but most are only a short bus ride away. Style and size vary hugely, but standards (in most cases monitored by Bord Fáilte) are generally very high, and the proprietors are usually friendly and welcoming.

Most of Dublin's **hostels** have long shed their old image of scruffy, communal living and strict rules and curfews. Almost all have private *en suite* rooms—some doubles as well as the usual dormitories. All the tourist hostels supply bedlinen either free or for hire, but you usually have to bring your own towels, soap and so on. Guests of all ages are welcome, including families with children. As a rule of thumb, the more people you share a room with, the less you pay per head. So, while a twin or double room in a hostel may cost as much as a B&B/townhouse in the suburbs, a night in a city centre dormitory can cost as little as €11, depending on the time of year.

The hostels recommended here are all cheerful and busy, and although not luxurious in style, they are clean and cosy enough for most tastes. All offer secure facilities for luggage—particularly important when you're sharing with strangers—and most keep comprehensive information on local events. Some have foreign exchange facilities and Internet access as well as self-catering kitchens and laundry facilities all of which help to save money.

All in all, hostels offer the best value around, from the most basic to the best equipped. There are well over 100 independent holiday hostels in Ireland, including around 20 in Dublin (most of those we recommend), and a listing of these is available for 50c from: **Independent Holiday Hostels of Ireland**, 57 Lower Gardiner St, Dublin 1, tel 836 4700, fax 836 4710, e-mail info@hostels-ireland.com, website www.hostels-ireland.com.

Self-catering studios, apartments or houses are a good option, particularly for a small group or a family. From about €360 per week, you can get a very comfortable, centrally-located, one-bedroom apartment for two people. If you are prepared to stay a short bus ride from the city centre, there are plenty of options to sleep groups of four, six and more from €350. A good selection of the above is listed in the *Dublin Accommodation Guide*. You can also contact the **Dublin Self-Catering Accommodation Association**, tel 269 1535, fax 283 7915, e-mail info@dublin-accommodation.com, website www.dublin-accommodation.com, which has a further listing of properties in Dublin that have been inspected by Bord Fáilte. They will advise you what is available at any particular time and you then book directly with the owner. The standard let is from Saturday to Saturday, but some owners are prepared to let for weekends, or by the night. It is also worth checking the **small ads** in *The Irish Times*.

From mid-June to mid-September **university accommodation**— either B&B or self-catering—becomes available. The three main university campuses with accommodation—Dublin City University (DCU), University College Dublin (UCD) and Trinity College Dublin (TCD; also, occasionally and confusingly, known as Dublin University)—are located in the north, south and centre of the city, respectively. The Royal College of Surgeons, also in the city centre, has student accommodation available during the summer at its Mercer Court apartments.

Camping in any of Dublin's fine parks is neither allowed nor advisable —the parks are not safe at night. The two official campsites nearest to the city, although still a long way from the centre if you are backpacking, are listed on page 51.

Many of the modern hotels and hostels cater for **wheelchair users**, at least to a limited extent, but access to older buildings is sometimes awkward, if not impossible. Townhouse/B&Bs don't usually have wheelchair facilities, but guest rooms on the ground floor may be accessible with some assistance. Always book in advance and check the exact nature of the facilities offered.

Single rooms can be difficult to find. Off-season or mid-week it is usually possible to negotiate a fair price for single occupancy of a larger room. However, at peak times expect to pay a substantial supplement and sometimes nearly the full price of a double if you are not sharing. **Family rooms** are widely available.

If you **book from overseas** through the Bord Fáilte international reservations centre, there is a €4 booking fee (see p. 26 for tel no. and website.) You also pay a non-refundable deposit of 10 per cent of the total charge, paying the balance to the premises on arrival. Booking is by credit card only. You can also book via the Dublin Tourism website

www.visitdublin.com for the same fee. If you book directly with the provider by phone you may be able to negotiate the price, and there is no booking fee, but of course you have to pay for whatever calls you make.

If you're already in Ireland you could call in to a **tourist office** for free information. For a booking fee of €4 a travel advisor will make reservations for you. You pay 10 per cent deposit and receive detailed directions to your chosen abode for the night (very valuable to the weary traveller!). If you have a credit card, you can also use **the 24-hour, touch screen, self-service units** located out-side each tourist office. This facility is free to use but the 10 per cent deposit is still payable by credit card, with the balance payable in the normal way on arrival at the accommodation.

Family Homes of Ireland, tel (091) 552 000, fax (091) 552 666, e-mail info@family-homes.ie, website www.family-homes.ie, operates outside the remit of Bord Fáilte and lists a selection of B&Bs throughout the country, including Dublin city, all of which can be booked directly. The brochure costs €6.35 and is available from Family Homes of Ireland or in many local newsagents. You can also book ahead, within Ireland, using your credit card by dialling a central number, tel 1850 226 321. For this centralised reservation service, you pay a booking fee of 10 per cent.

Credit cards are accepted in most premises, apart from B&Bs which usually accept a deposit sent in advance as a booking. Visa and Mastercard are the most widely accepted cards though American Express and Diner's Card are accepted in many places. A room booked by credit card is usually held until noon of the day after the arrival date. In the event of a no-show, it will then be released and the card charged for one night's accommodation. However, cancellation policies vary so it is wise to check. Also check if there is a cut-off time for arrivals as many guesthouses and B&Bs are family-run and do not have night-porters—it is wise to phone ahead even if you are arriving during the day to ensure that there will be someone on the premises to let you in. In high season, B&Bs may stipulate that you check in at a reasonable hour, or at least telephone to confirm that you are on your way.

Dublin Tourism Centre, in the converted church in Suffolk St, Dublin 2, offers the most extensive services, including a café, a bookshop, Internet access points and various accommodation and ticket-booking facilities; however, it tends to become very crowded in the summer months. The full reservation system is also available in the other city-centre offices at Baggot St Bridge, Dublin 2, which is always much quieter, and at 14 Upr O'Connell St, Dublin 1.

Listings by postcode area

The Postcode map is on page 8. Entries within each area are in alphabetical order.

City centre: Dublin 1

The area north of the river surrounding O'Connell St has an air of jaded grandeur, having long-since fallen from its 18th-century status as Dublin's most sought-after address. It has lately been home to bargain accommodation as it includes several points of entry to the city: Dublin Port (North Wall), Busáras (central bus station) and Connolly Train Station (Amiens St). In addition, it has recently undergone considerable residential and commercial development, particularly around Capel St and the International Financial Services Centre, and has also become home to an ever increasing number of young professionals as well as a burgeoning immigrant population. A walk along Gardiner St will, however, still take you past a lively mixture of small hotels, comfortable guesthouses and large tourist hostels. Many of these rely almost solely on the passing trade, although the better ones tend to book up in advance.

What is on offer here, more than anywhere else in Dublin, however, is a very mixed bag. There are some downright unpleasant places which thrive on the droves of gullible and weary who, fresh off the boat/train/bus, take the first thing offered. This area can become quite deserted at night so it's best not to wander around alone—stick to the obvious tourist and shopping routes.

Abbey Court Hostel, 29 Bachelor's Walk, Dublin 1, tel 878 0700, fax 878 0719, e-mail info@abbey-court.com, website www.abbey-court.com Situated right beside O'Connell Bridge, the Abbey Court is probably one of the easiest hostels to locate in the city centre, as well as being one of the cleanest! Standard and *en suite* rooms (with power showers) ranging from double to 10-bed dorms with additional facilities on each corridor. Well-equipped, self-catering kitchen as well as large dining area and patio barbecue area in summer, two cosy TV lounges/common rooms (one smoking, one non-smoking), Internet access, bike hire. High level of security with video cameras on all corridors just in case any undesirables get past the constantly-monitored front door.

€17–25 pps dorm €76–88 pps double or twin *en suite* room. Breakfast included.

Abraham House Hostel, 83 Lr Gardiner St, Dublin 1, tel 855 0600,
fax 855 0598, e-mail stay@abraham-house.ie,
website www.abraham-house.ie

More basic in style than some of the newer hostels in Dublin, but all of the standard facilities as well as a few extras such as laundry and parking. Relaxed and friendly atmosphere, helpful staff. Specialises in group bookings and will organise events and evening meals for groups on request.

€13–17 pps dorm €30–46 pps private room. Breakfast included.

Castle Hotel, 3–4 Great Denmark St, Dublin 1, tel 874 6949, fax 872 7674,
e-mail hotels@indigo.ie

Situated just off Parnell Sq in a mid-18th-century building, the Castle is one of Dublin's oldest hotels. Traditional decor and atmosphere, basic but homely comfort and friendly service. All rooms *en suite* with telephone, TV and tea/coffee-making facilities. Singles welcome. Bar and restaurant. Car parking.

€42.50–60 pps €55 single. Breakfast included.

Charles Stewart Budget Accommodation Centre, 5–6 Parnell Sq,
tel 878 0350, fax 878 1387, e-mail cstuart@iol.ie

Something between a hostel and a budget hotel and located in the Georgian building that was the birthplace of the writer, Oliver St John Gogarty. The original architecture has been largely restored and some rooms have exquisite ceiling decoration but much of the accommodation is in small modern additions that have little character. All private rooms, many *en suite*,

from singles to 4-beds, some with views over the square. Comfortably furnished to a high standard for the price with TV, tea/coffee-making facilities and an iron provided. One double room on ground floor with ramps and fully adapted bathroom for wheelchair users. However, there are steps to be negotiated at the entrance.
€35–44.50 pps €57–63.50 single. Full breakfast included. Limited wheelchair access.

Clifden Guesthouse, 32 Gardiner Place, Dublin 1, tel 874 6364, 874 6122, e-mail bnb@indigo.ie, website www.clifdenhouse.com
Restored Georgian townhouse with 14 rooms. Comfortable, well-equipped accommodation and very friendly service. Close to the very centre of town, all rooms *en suite* and—very unusually—provides free parking for guests.
€32.50–70 pps €40–80 single.

Comfort Inn, 95–98 Talbot St, tel 874 9202, fax 874 9672, e-mail info@talbot.premgroup.ie, website www.premgroup.com
Large purpose-built guesthouse tucked away in the middle of a row of busy shops on lively Talbot St and recently taken over and entirely revamped by the Choice hotel chain. Unassuming exterior offers no clue to the pleasant, quiet haven inside which is now decorated with bright, up-to-date style to maximise light and space. Small rooms (the best on the fourth floor), all *en suite*, comfortable and well-equipped with telephone, TV, tea/coffee making facilities and hairdryers. No specific wheelchair adapted rooms but the bigger ones might be manageable and there is a lift from the ground floor. Cosy lounge and breakfast room. No bar or restaurant but reception open 24 hours and friendly staff will direct you to the city's nearby nightspots. Limited private parking available.
€45–95 pps, depending on the time of year. Full Irish breakfast included. Possible wheelchair access.

Globetrotters Tourist Hostel, 46 Lr Gardiner St, Dublin 1, tel 873 5893, fax 878 8787, e-mail gtrotter@indigo.ie, website www.iol.ie/globetrotters
The Globetrotters is close to O'Connell St. It adjoins The Townhouse (see below) and is run by the same people. The price includes an enormous breakfast and this is served in the great dining room which is shared by the two establishments. Comfortable and very well laid out with thoughtful touches in the dorms, like individual lighting for each bed and floor lighting in each room, all of which help to maintain maximum privacy within the shared areas. No self-catering facilities but meals available.
€16.50–21.50 pps dorm. Breakfast included.

Hotel Isaac's, Store St, Dublin 1, tel 855 0067, fax 836 5390, e-mail hotel@isaacs.ie
Converted from a wine warehouse and located just a stone's throw from Busáras and Connolly Station, Hotel Isaac's offers bright, comfortable rooms though without exceptional style. All rooms *en suite* with telephone, TV and tea/coffee-making facilities. The hotel also houses a quirkily decorated, Italian-style restaurant which is open daily for lunch and dinner. Limited parking available if you book in advance (€6.35 per day).
€55–95 pps €90–160 single. Breakfast included.

Hotel Saint George, 7 Parnell Sq, Dublin 1, tel 874 5611, fax 874 5582, e-mail hotels@indigo.ie
The Hotel Saint George is along the same lines as the Castle Hotel (see above) with comfortable, if not fashionable, rooms at a reasonable price. All *en suite* rooms with telephone, TV, tea/coffee making facilities and hair dryer. Bar and private parking on site. Breakfast is served in the restored basement room that would have housed the original kitchen in Georgian times.
€45–65 pps €57–75 single. Breakfast included.

Isaacs Hostel, 2–5 Frenchman's Lane, Dublin 1, tel 855 6215, fax 855 6574,
e-mail hostel@isaacs.ie, website www.isaacs.ie
A little more basic than its sister hostel, Jacobs Inn, (see below) which offers
every modern tourist comfort, this long-established hostel is a favourite with
backpacker types looking for atmosphere and chat above state of the art
facilities. Nonetheless, it has a good range of services and facilities including a
great café serving breakfast and lunch as well as Internet access.
€10.75–22 pps dorm €26–38 pps private room. Breakfast available for
€3.80–5.80.

Jacobs Inn Hostel, 21–28 Talbot Place, Dublin 1, tel 855 5660,
fax 855 5664, e-mail jacobs@isaacs.ie, website www.isaacs.ie
Situated beside Busáras, this modern, purpose-built hostel has dorms that
sleep 10 people as well as double and family rooms. Sparsely decorated, but
very clean and spacious. All rooms *en suite* with storage facilities. All of the
usual hostel facilities including a café which is open for breakfast and lunch,
as well as Internet access. Wheelchair access to two dorms, lifts to all floors.
€13–25 pps dorm €30–40 pps private room. Breakfast not included but
available for €4–6 in the café. Wheelchair access.

Jurys Custom House Inn (hotel), Custom House Quay, Dublin 1,
tel 607 5000, fax 829 0400, e-mail customhouse_inn@jurysdoyle.com
This hotel is very popular with holiday-makers and business people on
budgets. It is situated on the waterfront, beside the International Financial
Services Centre, only a short walk from O'Connell Bridge. All the usual
facilities of a 3-star hotel. No great atmosphere but good, solid, modern
comfort. All rooms *en suite* with telephone, TV, tea/coffee-making facilities.
Informal restaurant and bar. Early booking essential.
€105 per room. Breakfast extra. Full wheelchair access; some rooms with
specially adapted facilities.

Litton Lane Hostel, 2–4 Litton Lane, Dublin 1, tel 872 8389, fax 872 0039, e-mail litton@indigo.ie, website www.irish-hostel.com
Just off Bachelor's Walk and about 2 minutes' stroll from O'Connell Bridge, Litton Lane is one of the newer hostels on the northside of town, and one of the best. Housed in a former recording and rehearsing studio once used by the likes of U2, Van Morrison, Sinéad O'Connor and Boyzone, the hostel makes the most of its historic associations and has painted the walls of its cosy lounge and dining areas, as well as the corridors, with funky colourful murals of rock icons. Mix of dorms and private rooms, self-catering kitchen which is very small but not often crowded due to the choice of local eateries at this location. All of the usual facilities of a top-class hostel plus Internet access, parking and bike storage.
€16–23.50 pps dorm €32.50–35 pps double/twin room. Breakfast included.

Mount Eccles Court Budget Accommodation, 42 Nth Great George's St, Dublin 1, tel 873 0826, fax 878 3554, e-mail info@eccleshostel.com, wesbite www.eccleshostel.com
Mount Eccles Court is a long-established, family-owned hostel that is popular with backpackers. It spans three converted buildings on one of Dublin's most intact Georgian streetscapes and, like many of the neighbouring houses, it is somewhat run down. However, the splendid proportions of the original architecture and the warm welcome make up for what it lacks in modern conveniences and decor. Mix of private rooms and dorms, some *en suite*. Good self-catering facilities.
€12–14 pps dorm €25–34 pps private room. Light breakfast included.

The Townhouse (guesthouse), 47–48 Lr Gardiner St, Dublin 1, tel 878 8808, fax 878 8787, e-mail info@townhouseofdublin.com, website www.townhouseofdublin.com
A convenient stroll from O'Connell Bridge and one of the great surprises of the northside. Run by the same people as the adjoining Globetrotters Hostel,

The Townhouse offers stylish, superior accommodation for the price. Choice of room styles from the sumptuous, old-world feel in the original Georgian building to the very modern chic design of the newly-built extension.
€47.50–55 pps double/twin €125 for a 3-bed room €127 for a 4-bed room. Lavish breakfast included.

Walton's Hotel, 2–5 North Frederick St, Dublin 1, tel 878 3131, fax 878 3090, e-mail waltons@eircom.net
Another converted Georgian building, situated around the corner from the Castle Hotel and part of the same group. Walton's was only recently opened as a hotel and shares the same building that houses Walton's Music Store, a family-run musical instrument shop that has been there since the 1920s. The Hotel offers all of the same basic facilities as its sister establishment but, due to its more recent renovation and its location, it has just a shade more comfort and a slightly better view. Rooms *en suite* with telephone, TV, tea/coffee making facilities. There is no bar but there is a restaurant and parking is also available. €45–65 pps €52–75 single. Breakfast included. Limited wheelchair access.

City centre: Dublin 2

Home to Temple Bar and some of Dublin's best and busiest bars, hotels, shops and restaurants as well as cultural institutions, Dublin 2 is much livelier at night than its neighbouring area across the river. This is great for anyone who wants to dance the night away and then safely walk back to their lodgings, but the same liveliness can become a pain if, when you eventually turn in, the noise from the streets keeps you awake. In recent times, many people have been put off the nightlife scene in Temple Bar partly because of its popularity among the rowdiest of visiting groups such as stag and hen parties. If you are a light sleeper, Temple Bar is not the place for you, so you should look at a wider area. Much of the accommodation in Dublin 2 is very expensive, but there is still plenty of choice for the budget traveller.

Finding a bed at weekends

- This can be a big problem. Many places are booked up well in advance so try to book. If you arrive on spec on a busy Friday in summer, consider going out of town for the weekend and returning on Sunday or Monday when the rush is over. You'll have a greater choice midweek and may pay less as many places increase their rates at weekends.

- If you have the time and energy and are prepared to take a risk, the best deals are found by calling in person and bargaining. You won't get a discount well in advance but many places offer very good deals on the night rather than have empty rooms.

- Last minute cancellations create vacancies at any time. It is always worth walking in off the street if time allows.

Ashfield House (hostel), 19–20 D'Olier St, Dublin 2, tel 679 7734, fax 679 0852, e-mail ashfield@indigo.ie, website www.ashfieldhouse.ie
Very central, modern hostel located between the river and Trinity College, and an ideal base for going out at night. Relaxed atmosphere with spacious common area. All rooms *en suite*. Lift to most rooms and one specially adapted for wheelchair users. There is a self-catering kitchen on the ground floor where guests converge to cook, eat or just hang out. Extensive facilities, including fax/e-mail service for guests and Dublin Bus ticket sales.
€13–27 pps dorms €38–44 pps private. Light breakfast included. Wheelchair access.

Aston Hotel, 7–9 Aston Quay, Dublin 2, tel 677 9300, fax 677 9007,
e-mail stay@aston-hotel.com
Situated in a hard-to-beat location, beside O'Connell Bridge and backing onto
Temple Bar, the Aston Hotel is a well-designed, modern-style hotel which
makes a change from the 'classic' look of a lot of the others. Lovely bright
foyer—ideal for sitting and relaxing with a drink. Rooms are simple but
comfortable and well-equipped; many have fine views over the Liffey.
€32–83 pps single €50–166. Full Irish breakfast included. Wheelchair access.

Avalon House (hostel), 55 Aungier St, Dublin 2, tel 475 0001, fax 475 0303,
e-mail info@avalon-house.ie, website www.avalon-house.ie
Provides almost 300 beds set out in private rooms and dorms of every shape
and size—all within ornate Victorian walls. Spotlessly clean, well thought
out and professionally run, with a very high level of service and a great buzz.
Avalon House has its own restaurant on the ground floor which is very
popular and is also open to the public. Offers very good, useful information
about the city and its ongoing events, as well as tailor-made group services.
€15–24 pps dorm €30–38 pps private room.

Barnacles Temple Bar House (hostel), 19 Temple Lane, Temple Bar, Dublin 2,
tel 671 6277, fax 671 6591, e-mail tbh@barnacles.ie, website www.barnacles.ie
Easily among the best of the modern crop of tourist hostels in Dublin—
perfectly situated for easy access to all the entertainment the city has
to offer. Rooms all *en suite*; these are very small but attention to detail
compensates. Bright, stylish decor with ample under-bed secure storage as
well as wardrobe space for each guest. All the standard facilities. Very security
conscious, like most central premises. Also a great place for a night in—
well-equipped kitchen for preparing gourmet meals, cosy common room
with TV, stereo and open fire from which to watch the world go by outside.
€13–19 pps dorm €31–44 pps private room. Light breakfast included.

Fitzwilliam Guesthouse, 41 Upr Fitzwilliam St, Dublin 2, tel 662 5155, fax 676 7488

Very comfortable old-world guesthouse in the heart of the Georgian southside, 5-minutes' walk from St Stephen's Green. All rooms are *en suite* and, for the price, are very well-equipped and spacious. Restaurant, overnight parking. €50.80–69.85 pps €76.20 single. Breakfast included.

Harding Hotel, Copper Alley, Fishamble St, Christchurch, Dublin 2, tel 679 6500, fax 679 6504, e-mail harding.hotel@usitworld.com

The Harding Hotel is situated in the historic heart of the city. Some of its rooms have views of Christ Church Cathedral and all are *en suite*. Offers the usual comforts of a basic 2-star hotel. Good bar and restaurant, plus great local cafés. Wheelchair accessible with ramps on the ground floor. Run by USIT, the same people who run Kinlay House Hostel (see below) and UCD campus accommodation (see below).

€28.33–57.50 pps €60–75 single. Wheelchair access.

Kilronan Guesthouse 70 Adelaide Rd, Dublin 2, tel 475 5266, fax 478 2841, e-mail info@dublinn.com

Very comfortable, long-established, 3-star guesthouse that prides itself on being a cut above the rest in the city centre. Situated in a quiet area, the Kilronan is excellent value if you are looking for good-quality accommodation that is in town but away from the real bustle. Well-equipped and offers elegant bedrooms, some of which are very large. Parking available.

€50–76 pps €50–76 for singles. Breakfast included.

Kinlay House (hostel) 2–12 Lord Edward St, Dublin 2, tel 679 6644, fax 679 7437, e-mail kinlay.dublin@usitworld.com, website www.kinlayhouse.ie

One of the best of the more established hostels in Dublin, particularly popular with groups and full of life at all times of the year. Choice of room types from single to 6-bed dorms all housed in a very large, old building. Accommodation rather basic, but excellent facilities include self-catering kitchens, laundry, bike hire and various special services for groups. Free hand towel and soap provided. €12.50–18.50 pps dorm €24–31.50 pps private room. Continental breakfast included, as is bedlinen.

Leeson Inn, 24 Lr Leeson St, Dublin 2, tel 662 2002, fax 662 1567, e-mail leesonin@iol.ie
Located just off St Stephen's Green, the Leeson Inn offers good-value, hotel-style accommodation in a recently-restored and very elegant Georgian house. (It is not officially a hotel as there is no bar or restaurant on the premises.) Top location, although the area changes dramatically on weekend nights. Many of its basements turn into very late opening nightclubs and the street becomes thronged with queues of desperadoes in search of some post-pub action. Small but very well-equipped rooms, all *en suite*.
€50–70 pps. Breakfast included.

Mercer Court, Royal College of Surgeons Campus Accommodation, Lr Mercer St, Dublin 2, tel 478 2179, fax 478 0873, e-mail sales@mercercourt.ie
Located close to St Stephen's Green and Grafton St, the Mercer Court offers 110 *en suite* bedrooms, with TV and telephone, from late June to late September. Parking on request.
€41–52 pps. Light breakfast included. Well-equipped, self-catering apartments sleeping 4–5 people are available for €785–918 per week. Limited wheelchair access.

Oliver St John Gogarty's (hostel) 18 Angelsea St, Temple Bar, Dublin 2, tel 671 1822, fax 671 7637, e-mail info@gogartys.com, website www.olivergogartys.com
Next door to one of Temple Bar's most popular pubs, this hostel really is in the middle of the action. Mixture of small private rooms and dorms without

much space but all *en suite*. Very good facilities including restaurant, Internet access and bike storage. 24-hour reception.
€18–23 pps dorm €23–28 pps private room.

Trinity College Campus Accommodation, College Green, Dublin 2,
tel 608 1177, fax 671 1267, e-mail reservations@tcd.ie
A 400-year-old oasis in the city centre with over 500 rooms to let each summer. Not cheap, but probably the best location in Dublin. Some rooms are in the charming old buildings around the squares of the college, and range in decor from the seriously basic to the 'tastefully refurbished'. However, many rooms are in the modern apartment blocks on the edge of the campus and overlook the very un-charming Pearse St, so check what you're being offered before booking. For the best views, ask for rooms in the Graduates' Memorial Building overlooking the campanile. Facilities are extensive and largely unnecessary due to the central location. Some rooms are adapted for wheelchairs but access can be awkward across the cobblestones. Free parking at the weekends (unheard of on the southside).
€37.50–59.50. Includes continental breakfast.

North city: Dublin 3, 7 and 9
These residential areas to the north of the city are only a short bus ride from the centre and are full of reasonably priced good-quality B&Bs (we have listed a selection) as well as hostel and campus accommodation.

Dublin City University Campus Residences, DCU, Ballymun Road/Collins Avenue, Glasnevin, Dublin 9,
tel 700 5736, fax 700 5777, e-mail campus.residences@dcu.ie
Offers 522 bedrooms, double and single, in modern apartment blocks from mid-June to mid-Sept. Rooms are either *en suite* or share a bathroom between two. All have access to cooking facilities. Campus bar, restaurant and

sports complex open to guests. Served by Dublin Bus nos 11, 11A, 11B, 13, 13A, 19A, 40N, 46X, 58X, 77B, 103, 105, 116.

€35–41 pp. Full wheelchair access.

Dublin International Youth Hostel, 61 Mountjoy St, Dublin 7, tel 830 1766, fax 830 1600, e-mail dublininternational@anoige.ie, website www.anoige.ie
An enormous hostel housed in a former convent and the only Dublin hostel member of An Óige, the Irish Youth Hostel Association (IYHA). The accommodation is simpler than in many of the newer hostels and consists mainly of dorms, though some private rooms are available. Excellent facilities include a games room, comfortable common areas, laundry and parking. The sense of a busy community makes it ideal for people travelling alone looking to meet up with others. Open to members of the IYHA and Hostelling International, also welcomes non-members. Dublin Bus nos 10, 38.

€11–17 pps dorm. Includes breakfast (supplements apply for the private rooms and non-IYHA members pay €2 extra).

Egan's Guesthouse, 7–9 Iona Pk, Glasnevin, Dublin 9, tel 830 3611, fax 830 3312, e-mail info@eganshouse.com
Located halfway between the city centre and the airport, in a quiet suburb. Elegant, comfortable, well-equipped rooms. All have armchairs or sofas to allow guests to lounge in private in front of their own TV. There is also a public lounge on the ground floor where guests can enjoy a glass of wine by the open fire (Egan's have their own wine licence). Parking outside. Dublin Bus nos 13, 19, 19A, 40N, 134.

€44–59 pps €49–69 single. Breakfast extra.

Errigal House, 36 Upr Drumcondra Rd, Dublin 9, tel/fax 837 6615, e-mail errigalhouse@e-merge.ie
Very comfortable and reasonably-priced B&B situated on the airport road. All rooms *en suite* with telephone, TV, tea/coffee making facilities and hair dryer

provided. Member of the Family Homes of Ireland group. Dublin Bus nos 3, 11, 11A, 13A, 16, 16A, 41, 41A, 41B, 41C, 41N, 51A, 746 pass the door. €35 pps, single supplement €10. Full Irish breakfast included.

Janice Conboy, Autumn Leaf, 41 St Lawrence Rd, Clontarf, Dublin 3, tel 833 7519, fax 833 7506
Very welcoming B&B in an attractive restored Victorian home situated in a lovely, quiet neighbourhood close to the sea. Four bedrooms, three *en suite*. TV in rooms, parking available. Dublin Bus nos 31N, 103, 104, 130.
€29–44 pps €38–57 single. Breakfast included.

Maureen and P. J. Dunne, Tinode House, 170 Upr Drumcondra Rd, Dublin 9, tel 837 2277, fax 837 4477, e-mail tinodehouse@eircom.net
Top-quality B&B in a comfortable and stylish Edwardian home on the main airport road, close to the city centre. Excellent and varied breakfast menu. Non-smoking house. Dublin Bus nos 3, 11, 11A, 11B, 13A, 16, 16A, 41, 41A, 41B, 41C, 41N, 51A, 746.
€30–35 pps €52–70 single.

Myra O'Flaherty, Sea Breeze, 312 Clontarf Rd, Dublin 3, tel 833 2787
Comfortable, very homely B&B situated on the sea front. All rooms *en suite*. Dublin Bus nos 103, 104, 130.
€31.79–34.29 pps €44.44 single. Full Irish breakfast included.

Sunnybank Hotel, 68–70 Botanic Rd, Glasnevin, Dublin 9, tel 830 6755, fax 830 6726, e-mail info@sunnybank.ie
Small, family-run hotel with bar and restaurant and situated a short bus ride from the city centre. All rooms *en suite*. Not exceptionally stylish but

well-equipped. Parking available. Good value if you prefer a hotel option.
Dublin Bus nos 13, 19, 19A, 40N, 134.
€44–57 pps €57–69 for single. Breakfast included.

North city: near the airport

As Dublin Airport is not very far from the city centre, there is really no need
to book special accommodation there. However, if you are worried about
missing your flight or if you simply want the extra time in bed, staying in the
area between Drumcondra and Santry would give you a far shorter journey
to the airport. B&B signs can be seen along most of the main roads between
the city and the airport. The following is just one fits the bill—the are
plenty of others.

The Airport Lodge 322 Swords Rd, Dublin 9, tel/fax 842 4848
Situated on a direct bus route from the city to the airport, The Airport Lodge
offers comfortable, well-equipped rooms with TV and tea/coffee making
facilities. Dublin Bus nos 3, 16, 16A, 33, 41, 41A, 41B, 41C, 41N, 104, 746.
€32 pps €38 single. Full Irish breakfast included.

South city: Dublin 4, 6 and 8

The accommodation in the south city is mainly concentrated in the expensive
Ballsbridge area, though it is well worth looking elsewhere. Dublin 4, Dublin 6
and 8 all have their own charms and are very close to town, some parts being
within walking distance of the centre.

Belgrave Guesthouse, 8–10 Belgrave Sq, Rathmines, Dublin 6,
tel 496 3760, fax 497 9243
Comfortable, homely accommodation housed in two early-Victorian houses
that are interconnected. The location is superb and rooms overlook either the
large garden at the back, or the square to the front. All rooms *en suite*,

tea/coffee making facilities and even a chocolate! Parking available to guests. Only 15 minutes from St Stephen's Green by Dublin Bus from Ranelagh or Rathmines.

€55–60 pps €55–65 single. Full Irish breakfast included.

Brewery Hostel, 22–23 Thomas St, Dublin 8, tel 453 8600, fax 453 8616, e-mail breweryh@irish-hostel.com, website www.irish-hostel.com

A very comfortable hostel in an old public library building with lots of light and real character. Located in a charming part of the city that is characterised by the rich aromas from the Guinness brewery next door. Excellent service and facilities, including Internet access, barbecue area and secure car parking. Free shuttle service between the airport and the hostel available for groups. Dublin Bus nos 51B, 51N, 78A, 123, 206.

From €11 pps dorm, from €28 pps private room. Breakfast included.

Carmel Chambers (B&B) 25 Anglesea Rd, Ballsbridge, Dublin 4, tel/fax 668 7346

Offers simple and good-value accommodation in a welcoming home in Ballsbridge. Serviced by Dublin Bus nos 5, 7, 7A, 7N, 18, 45 and close to DART train (Lansdowne Rd station). Also within walking distance of the city centre.

€32–40 pps €45 singl. Full Irish breakfast included.

Colette Carter, 32 Annesley Pk, Ranelagh, Dublin 6, tel 496 6039, e-mail colettec@bigfoot.com

Offers three rooms—a double, twin and family—all *en suite*. Very homely, relaxed and welcoming, smoke-free home. Special diets catered for at breakfast by the hostess who is a cordon bleu cook. Lovely, quiet location close to Ranelagh village and the city. Dublin Bus nos 11, 11A, 11B, 13B, 44, 44N, 48A, 48N, 86 pass nearby.

€40 pp including single occupancy. Full Irish breakfast included.

Four Courts Hostel, 15–17 Merchant's Quay, Dublin 8, tel 672 5839,
e-mail info@fourcourtshostel.com, website www.fourcourtshostel.com
This large, very well-equipped hostel is served directly by Dublin Bus No. 748
from the airport and is within 10 minutes' walk of O'Connell Bridge. While
perhaps not the warmest in atmosphere or traditional welcome, it is very clean,
modern and secure, with every facility you could want. Many of the rooms overlook the Liffey and the architectural splendour of Gandon's Four Courts and
there are two that are fully-accessible for wheelchair users. Also easy to find on
the quays due to the colourful but hideous cartoon-style window decoration.
€15.50–21.50 pps in dorms €22.50–32.50 pps in a private room. Breakfast
included. Wheelchair access.

Jurys Christchurch Inn, Christ Church Place, Dublin 8, tel 454 0000,
fax 454 0012, e-mail christchurch_inn@jurysdoyle.com
The original in the Jurys Inn chain. Great location (if you don't mind church
bells)—directly opposite Christ Church Cathedral and around the corner from
St Patrick's. All the facilities of a 3-star hotel with good, solid, modern comfort
though no great atmosphere. All rooms *en suite* with telephone, TV and tea/
coffee-making facilities. Informal restaurant and bar. Early booking essential.
€105 per room. Breakfast extra. Wheelchair access; some rooms with specially
adapted facilities.

A QUESTION OF PRIORITIES

When John F. Kennedy, then a US Senator, visited Ireland in
1957, he stayed with his wife Jacqueline at the Shelbourne
Hotel. Jacqueline rang the Irish Independent to offer an
interview, but the journalist decided to take the details over
the telephone. 'It was Sunday,' he later explained, 'and three
fellows were waiting for me on the golf course.'

Tavistock House, 64 Ranelagh Rd, Dublin 6, tel/fax 496 7377,
e-mail info@tavistockhouse.com
Very homely and impressively well-equipped B&B situated in a Victorian
house on the city-side of Ranelagh village. Seven rooms, all *en suite*. As
comfortable as any hotel, but retains a welcoming, family atmosphere in the
bustling suburb of Ranelagh, which is within walking distance of Stephen's
Green. Facilities for pets available.
€48.50–54 pps €60–65 single. Full Irish breakfast included.

UCD Village Campus Accommodation, Belfield, Dublin 4, tel 269 7111,
fax 269 7704, e-mail ucd.village@usitworld.com
Well-equipped, modern apartments located in the landscaped setting of
Dublin's largest university. Rooms are let either individually or as complete
apartments and are open to guests from mid-June to early September. The
accommodation is well-equipped and is near all the campus facilities which
include a bar, restaurant and café. Dublin Bus no. 10 to city centre.
€33 single room €127 per night for 4-bed apartments. Wheelchair access.

Waterloo House (guesthouse), 8–10 Waterloo Rd, Ballsbridge, Dublin 4,
tel 660 1888, fax 667 1955, e-mail waterloohouse@eircom.net
Very luxurious guesthouse within walking distance of St Stephen's Green. Offers
seventeen *en suite* rooms in two restored, Georgian houses. Lift and car park.
€57.50–80 pps €41–65 single. Wheelchair access.

Out of town: Dún Laoghaire

This busy ferry port is full of good-value B&Bs for anyone just off the boat
from Holyhead. As it is linked to the city centre by the DART train and Dublin
Bus nos 7, 7N, 46A, 746 it is quite convenient for getting in and out of town.
There are also lots of lovely places to stay in all of the seaside areas between
here and the city. The hostel below is near the port.

Marina House (hostel), 7 Old Dunleary Road, Dún Laoghaire, Co. Dublin, tel 284 1524, e-mail info@marinahouse.com

Small-scale, friendly hostel in a restored stone building by the sea. Close to the ferry terminal and DART. Offers seven private rooms and one dorm. Parking available.

€18–21 pps dorm €22.50–27 pps private room. Includes continental breakfast.

Tourist Information and Bookings

By phone, e-mail or online from anywhere in the world:

Bord Fáilte
website www.ireland.travel.ie
tel +800 668 668 66 (+ denotes international access codes)
e-mail reservations@gulliver.ie

Dublin Tourism
e-mail information@dublintourism.ie
website www.visitdublin.com

Camping out of town

Camac Valley Tourist Caravan and Camping Park, Naas Rd, Clondalkin, Dublin 22, tel 464 0644, fax 464 0643, e-mail camacmorriscastle@eircom.net, website www.irishcamping.net

Located 35 minutes south-west of the city on the N7, Dublin Bus no. 69, with facilities which include showers, toilets, full washing, TV, 24-hour security and waste disposal.

€6–7 per night per backpacker, €13–19 per night for families with a tent, caravan or motor-home.

Shankill Caravan and Camping Park Shankill, Co. Dublin, tel 282 0011, fax 282 0108, e-mail shankillcaravan@eircom.net

Approximately 16 km south of the city centre and about 20 minutes from Dún Laoghaire ferry port by bus or DART train, this park is served by frequent

Dublin Bus nos 45 and 84 to and from the city centre and also by DART train from nearby Shankill station. Facilities include showers, toilets, washing and waste disposal.

€8–9 for backpackers €11–12 per caravan or tent and car. No advance booking.

TOURIST OFFICES IN THE CITY

Dublin Tourism Centre: Suffolk St, Dublin 2

Open June–Sept: Mon–Sat, 09.00–17.30, Jul–Aug: Mon–Sat, 08.30–18.30, Sun, 10.30–15.00.

14 Upr O'Connell St, Dublin 1

Open Mon–Sat, 09.00–17.00 (closed 13.30–14.00)

Baggot St Bridge, Dublin 2

Open Mon–Fri, 09.30–17.00 (closed 12.00–12.30)

Arrivals Hall, Dublin Airport

Open June–Sept: Mon–Sun, 08.00–22.00, Jul–Aug: Mon–Sun, 08.00–22.30

Dún Laoghaire Ferry Terminal

Open Mon–Sat, 10.00–18.00

The Square, Tallaght, Dublin 24

Open Mon–Sat, 09.30–17.00 (closed 12.00–12.30)

Somewhere to live

Cheap, long-term accommodation is hard to find in Dublin. The rate of home ownership in Ireland is far higher than that in most other European countries and, although there have been some recent administrative attempts to slow down the booming property market for the sake of first-time buyers, the rental sector continues to be neglected by policy makers. House prices have rocketed over the past few years resulting in a serious housing crisis for the less well-off. This is, of course, more marked in Dublin than anywhere else in the country.

The warrens of cheap flats and bedsits in the traditional student and low-rent areas such as Rathmines, Ranelagh and Drumcondra are almost entirely gone as property owners cash in on the economic boom. The result is an acute shortage of affordable accommodation to rent in, or near, the city. It is very much a seller's market. Current sample rents are as follows:

Rents

room in large house on the Naas Rd, Dublin 22	€100pw
bedsit in Synge St, Dublin 8	€110 pw
bedsit in Clontarf, Dublin 3	€140 pw
3-bed house in Dublin 3	€1,100 pm
3-bed townhouse Stoneybatter, Dublin 7	€1,400 pm
2 bed penthouse in Dublin 1	€1,600 pm

You may get lucky and find a suitable place for less but, as a rule, the only way that you will get cheaper rent is to move well out into the suburbs and/or house-share with several people.

Many landlords, particularly in the lower-rental bracket, like to avoid the paperwork and taxes entailed in renting a premises through the official channels. It is common enough for rental agreements to be either exclusively verbal, or at least not entirely above board. This *can* result in a satisfactory arrangement all round, but may also leave the tenant very vulnerable.

A legal leasing arrangement clearly defines your obligations and entitlements. Essentially, every tenant is entitled, by law, to a rent book or a written letting agreement that contains basic details on the premises, the names and addresses of any parties involved, the term of the tenancy, the amount and method of payment of rent, the arrangements for paying for light, heating and so on, the amount of, and conditions of, any deposit paid, and a statement on basic rights and duties of both landlord and tenant.

Threshold (advice office tel 874 9750), a voluntary organisation supported by the Department of the Environment, is the acknowledged authority in the area of tenants' rights and even provides a model rent book suitable for most lettings. Threshold's leaflets, *Renting for the First Time* and *Renting a Home from a Private Landlord*, are full of useful advice and tips that outline your basic obligations and entitlements as a tenant. See also the organisation's very handy *Guide to Using the Services of Estate Agents and Other Accommodation Agencies* and, if you are claiming unemployment or other state benefits, the leaflet on *Calculating Rent Supplement*.

Even if you don't think you'll have any difficulty in finding (and holding on to) a suitable place to live, it is worth browsing through Threshold's information simply for helpful tips. If you do need to discuss a particular problem or if you have a specific query, the staff there are extremely well-informed and sympathetic.

Threshold is currently without a drop-in centre but hope to have a new one in Stoneybatter open by the end of 2002 where people can actually call in for advice. In the meantime, however, information can be obtained by telephone or post.

You may well find that you need Threshold's service since tenants' rights are flimsy, the law being weighted in favour of landlords. Long-term leases are rare, allowing landlords to hike the rent up year-on-year, and if you jib at the rise, they can simply get another tenant. Be under no illusions, even if you finally find a place, you are vulnerable at all times even when you have a lease. Landlords will rarely renew a lease after a year and this can leave you even more vulnerable than before.

If you are claiming social welfare, on a FÁS scheme or working part time and finding it difficult to make ends meet, you may qualify for help towards your rent. Apply to the Community Welfare Officer at your local health centre. The amount granted is calculated to leave a minimum 'after rent' income. Assistance is occasionally also given towards deposits on rented property. Assessment is quite rigorous, however, and you can be refused rent allowance if your flat is considered unnecessarily large or expensive, for example.

The method and time span for payments vary considerably from office to office, so be prepared for some unsympathetic responses from landlords who, when asked to complete the required application form, are less than delighted to help. Unfortunately for all concerned, many offices are slow in making the payments, leaving landlords temporarily out of pocket. Fortunately, however, many landlords in the lower-rental bracket are quite used to dealing with rent allowance payments and are happy to plan around them.

If you ever find yourself in a serious housing emergency in Dublin, there are a few organisations which may be of use to you. If you are having landlord/tenant problems regarding your letting arrangement, whether it is written or verbal, then Threshold is the place to go for advice. If you need specific legal advice, your local **Citizens Information Bureau** may be able to help, but Threshold is generally considered the best.

If your emergency leaves you with literally no roof over your head and no money to do anything about it, the place to go is **Focus Ireland**, an organisation specifically set up to deal with the problems of homelessness in Ireland. It is located at 15 Eustace Street, Dublin 2, tel 671 2555 or 677 6421, and offers the services of a trained crisis worker, as well as a low cost meal, to anyone in need. It also has a range of day services for homeless people.

Finding a flat or bedsit

The best flats and bedsits are always passed on between friends, so ask anyone you know in Dublin if they have heard of anywhere suitable. Check the notices in local shop windows, and on their notice-boards inside. You can also keep a look out for 'To Let' signs in the neighbourhood you want to live in.

Looking for a place through an estate agent or accommodation agent can be a useful way to save time and legwork but, as a rule, these organisations tend to focus on the higher end of the rental market rather than the budget end. The most important thing to remember if you are using their services, however, is to be absolutely clear about what is on offer, i.e. whether or not there is a charge to tenants and, if there is, what you are entitled to for this fee. Estate agents are required by law to be licensed and bonded and many also belong to professional institutes with their own rules of conduct. The exact legal position regarding other accommodation agencies is not as clear, so it is important to be aware of the type of organisation you are dealing with. If you do pay anything out to one of these companies, always get a receipt and check first whether you are entitled to a refund if they fail to find you a suitable place within a reasonable time.

Looking online for a place to live is an increasingly popular choice as it takes a lot of the expense and hassle out of the process for both landlords and potential tenants. Most of the major estate agents and letting agents have websites (e.g. **www.gunne.ie**, **www.mannion.ie**, **www.homelocators.ie**) where you can check out their lists of properties for rent, without the need to call to their offices. There are also a number of other useful sites to check and these are being added to daily, it seems; so again, ask around if you know anyone who has recently used one to find a flat.

Shaw's birthplace—a typical Georgian Terrace, no. 33 Synge St, Dublin 8.

One popular site is **www.daft.ie**, which has lists of houses, flats and sharing arrangements. Potential tenants and people with property to rent can make direct contact with other parties by using this free service. Another useful site is **www.myhome.ie**, which lists all kinds of properties. It has pictures of each premises and provides all the details together with a number at which you can contact the relevant estate agent. Some sites, such as **www.a1brokers.ie**, charge tenants a €90 registration fee if after a preliminary chat they think it likely they can find what you want. This site sources its extensive list of properties through estate agents, letting agents and private landlords and offers a sort of 'one-stop' service to potential tenants. Another site that operates in a similar way is **www.findahome.ie**, which also has a special section for students. A €10 registration fee is charged. **www.letbynet.com** is a free advert site with lettings all over Ireland and Britain.

The *Evening Herald* is the best newspaper for small ads and has columns of 'houses to let', 'apartments and flats to let', and 'house/flat sharing'. Buy it as soon as it hits the shelves—usually around 12.00, daily, except Sundays—and start making appointments to view immediately. Competition is fierce, and it is not unusual to have to queue with hordes of other flat-hunters even to get a look at a place. Another publication worth keeping an eye on is *Buy&Sell*. While this may not have as extensive a list as the *Herald*, it does carry a good selection of accommodation listings that are generally in the reasonably-priced bracket. It is published twice a week, on Wednesdays and Saturdays, and contains small ads for just about everything. It is also one of the best places to source cheap furniture and appliances once you have moved into your flat. The *Buy&Sell* website which has all the ads in the paper is **www.buyandsell.net**.

When viewing a property, always arrive early for appointments and bring some cash for a booking deposit. Regardless of your place in the queue, most landlords will respond more favourably to someone with money in hand. Don't forget to get a receipt if you do part with any money on the spot.

September and October are traditionally the worst months of the year for flat-hunting, as students are returning to every part of Dublin in search of a cheap place to live. It is slightly easier to find somewhere in May and June when students disappear for the summer holidays but even then it is neither a simple nor enjoyable task. The situation for returning students has reached such crisis proportions in recent years that some are now forced to pay rent for the whole summer on a flat they do not occupy in order to guarantee that they will have a place to return to when term begins.

Student accommodation

All of the major colleges have their own campus accommodation, but enough for only a small proportion of their students. Therefore, demand is very high. Information is sent out when university places are offered and the criteria governing who qualifies for accommodation varies from college to college. Even overseas students are not guaranteed places but, generally, the colleges are very helpful to students unfamiliar with Dublin and keep listings of accommodation that is available only to their students. If you are coming to study at any of the main universities, advice on both campus and other accommodation is available, for students only, from:

DCU Student Services Accommodation Office, tel 700 5344

DIT does not have any campus accommodation but provides incoming students with lists of digs before term starts. Available through Student Services, tel 402 3000.

Royal College of Surgeons Student Services Office, tel 402 2294, offers advice to its own incoming students. Campus accommodation (limited) at its Mercer Court apartments, tel 474 4120.

Trinity College Accommodation Office, tel 608 1177

UCD Student Accommodation Office, on-campus tel 716 1034, off campus tel 716 8750.

Sharing

Sharing a house or flat makes a lot of sense if you find that even a one-bedroom flat is out of your price range. Apart from the obvious advantages of getting more for your money by pooling resources, sharing can be great for anyone who doesn't want to be tied to a full year's lease.

As in other cities, house or flat shares are often advertised by students living together who need a quick replacement for someone who's left. They generally don't expect a huge commitment from a new tenant as they'll probably only remain for the academic year themselves. First-time home buyers also often take in tenants to help with mortgage payments.

In Dublin, young working people, not yet in the market to buy a house, often share for a few years. There are always plenty of ads for house/flat shares in the daily papers from people who, for example, have rented a three-bedroom place between two on the assumption that they can advertise for a third person to share.

Other places to check are the extensive notice-board in the headquarters of **USIT**, the student travel agent, at Aston Quay, beside O'Connell Bridge, in

HOW DUBLIN GOT ITS NAME

The naturalist Robert Praeger once met a Cavan man, a civil engineer, who pooh-poohed the traditional theories of how Dublin got its name.

'Before there was e'er a bridge over the Liffey,' he told Praeger, ' there was a slip on either side, near the Castle, and a ferry, and beside each slip there was a pub. That's how the name came—Double-inn. How many know that now?'

R. PRAEGER THE WAY THAT I WENT

Dublin 2, and university notice-boards (in Trinity turn right inside Front Gate and go into House 6—the board is directly opposite the door). During September, Trinity also has a special extra accommodation notice-board and office for incoming students, which is located in the Arts Building.

Hostels

With a number of the agencies listed above catering to tenants from overseas via their website listings, it is increasingly possible to find a place to live before you arrive and this is certainly an advisable strategy. However, if you cannot get a place before you move, and you do not have friends to stay with temporarily, you will need somewhere affordable to stay while you search. Hostels (see Somewhere to stay) are about the best option but unfortunately, with the increased demand from tourists for short stays, most hostels are reluctant to take a reservation for more than a week. Some are more flexible than others, however, so it is worth trying to strike a deal, particularly at less busy times of year.

Lodgings/digs

Another short term possibility for anyone new to Dublin is to take lodgings (also known as 'digs') in a family home where, from about €95 a week, you can get a warm room in someone's house with breakfast provided and sometimes an evening meal.

Digs can be found in the 'Accommodation Offered' column in the newspapers, and the universities also compile lists of digs for their students that are generally made available before term starts. This is ideal accommodation for anyone who does not feel capable of fending entirely for themselves in a new city, and the sheltered atmosphere of an established family home means guaranteed security.

However, it does not generally offer the same independence as your own flat or house. It is usually expected in 'digs' that due consideration is given to the fact that you are in someone else's home and therefore should play by their rules, at least to some extent. Also, many people offering this sort of accommodation do so an a Monday to Friday basis, which only suits students or long distance commuters from the rest of Ireland who are travelling home for the weekend. While it is a very sound and relatively inexpensive option, especially for the newcomer, it is not the sort of arrangement that would suit everyone.

Getting around

Into the city centre

From the airport

Dublin Airport is about 12 km north of the city centre. Due to the recent economic boom, it is growing at a very rapid rate and ongoing development work means that it seems quite chaotic all year round. Despite this, its facilities for passengers are quite good, (but see 'Dublin for people with disabilities'). The **tourist office** in the Arrivals Hall gives free information and directions and will also make various types of reservations for a small charge. It's open daily from 08.00 to 22.00 (22.30 during July and August).

For shoestring travellers the bus service is a must, so it's as well to start as you mean to go on. The airport bus, the **Airlink** (Dublin Bus nos 747 and 748), stops outside the Arrivals Terminal and goes direct to the city centre. Route 747, which runs every 10–15 minutes, starting at 05.45, stops at

O'Connell St, then at the central bus station, Busáras, then at Connolly Railway Station. The service operates until 23.30, Mon–Sat. On Sundays the service starts at 07.15 and runs about every 20 minutes until 23.30. Route 748 starts at 06.50 and runs twice an hour until 21.30. It stops at Busáras, Tara St DART train station, Aston Quay in the city centre and finally Heuston Railway Station. Both routes cost €4.50 and take about 30 minutes to the centre (an extra 15 minutes to Heuston Station).

Cheaper options are **Dublin Bus nos 16A** which goes from the Arrivals Hall to the city centre and as far south as Ballinteer, Dublin 16, and **41** which goes to Swords, Co. Dublin as well as the city centre, both for €1.45. These run three or four times an hour between 06.00 and 23.30 and are ideal if you are staying on the northside of the city as they are normal suburban bus routes and stop off everywhere along the way. However, journey time to the city centre can be an hour or more, depending on the number of stops and the traffic.

Another option within the normal city service is **Dublin Bus no. 746**, which links the airport to the south city. Starting from the airport from 09.15, it means you can get to areas like Donnybrook, Stillorgan and Dún Laoghaire without having to stop off in the city centre. This is a long route so the fare depends on how far you travel but at a maximum of €1.45 it is still cheaper than the private Air Coach service.

Air Coach, tel 844 7118, www.aircoach.ie, operates from the airport to Donnybrook, Dublin 4 for a flat fare of €6 single and €10 return. Children under 12 with two adults go free.

There is a **taxi** rank outside the Arrivals Terminal. Expect to pay at least €15 to the city centre, and €20 to Ranelagh, Dublin 6. There are extra charges for more than one passenger and for extra luggage.

Most of the major international **car rental** companies have desks in the Arrivals Hall, but car rental can be a very expensive option in Ireland due to the high cost of insurance. It always pays to shop around as, even in high season, rates can vary hugely from company to company. Spend a euro or two ringing around when you get to Dublin and you could save yourself up to €15, but when things are busy, it can be difficult to get a car at all. Pre-booking through a travel agent usually costs more, but you are at least guaranteed a car. If you are staying in Dublin, a car may turn out to be more of a hindrance than a help, anyway, so don't bother with one unless you intend to go further afield.

Aer Rianta, the airport management authority, has a 24-hour information line for all queries relating to services at the airport, tel 814 1111 and their website, www.dublin-airport.com, gives a good account of the facilities on offer as well as timetables of scheduled flights and 'real time' information on arrivals and departures.

THE UNIQUE IRISH STYLE OF GREETING . . .

. . . a little nod allied to a slight inclination of the head, as if trying to touch the left shoulder with the right cheek, together with a wink . . . usually accompanied by 'Hawaya' (How are you?) or 'Hayadone' (How are you doing?) or 'Hazagone?' (How is it going?). This requires years of training.

FROM DUBLIN: LE GUIDE AUTREMENT

From the ferry ports

There are two ferry ports in Dublin. The port of arrival normally depends on the ferry company you sail with. **Dublin Port**, also known as 'the North Wall,' is about 2 km from the city centre. It is served by Dublin Bus no. 53 which goes direct to the city centre. This is a roughish area so don't linger, especially at night.

Dún Laoghaire Port is about 10–12 km to the south of the city centre, but is served by the DART train as well as Dublin Bus nos 7, 46A and 746, making it reasonably convenient to the city. Dún Laoghaire Port has its own **tourist office** in the terminal building which opens for information and reservations Mon–Sat 10.00–18.00.

Busáras, the central bus station

> Busáras, the central bus station, is the main bus terminal for all Bus Éireann buses, i.e. those serving all regions outside Dublin. It is across the road from Connolly Station—5 minutes' walk from O'Connell Bridge.

From the railway stations

If you are coming to Dublin by train from the south or west you will arrive at **Heuston Station** (the old Kingsbridge), on the south bank of the Liffey. The city centre is a short bus (on the Railink service, Dublin Bus nos 90, 90A) or taxi ride away, or 15 minutes' walk down the quays.

If you are coming from the north, north-west or south-east you will arrive at **Connolly Station**, also known as 'Amiens St,' on the north bank of the river. Connolly is 10 minutes' walk from O'Connell Bridge.

Getting around the city

Central Dublin is quite a small area: it is possible to walk from one side to the other in less than 30 minutes. A **good street map**, however, is a must to find the minor alleys and laneways etc. which is where some of the most interesting shops, cafés and pubs are, and signposting is patchy. Our map (inside the front cover) is fine for the city centre, but for more extensive wanderings, you will need something more elaborate. **Free maps** are available from the

Dublin Tourism centre, Suffolk St, Dublin 2, among others. The best commercial map for exploring the city, at least inside the canals (see Getting your bearings), is the handy spiral bound pocket edition of the *Dublin City Centre Pocket Atlas* published by the Ordnance Survey Ireland, price €4.44, widely available in bookshops or directly from the Ordnance Survey map sales office tel 820 6100, www.irlgov.ie/osi. If you are going to spend a lot of time in the city, you may like to get a copy of its big brother publication, the larger format spiral bound Ordnance Survey Ireland *Dublin City and District Street Guide*, price €10.15. *The Independent Directory* (delivered free to households) contains detailed street maps of every part of the city and has the added bonus of loads of money-off coupons for restaurants and videos stores etc. They will post one to any address in Ireland for free, tel 411 2222.

Walking

Depending on the time of day and, of course, the completely unpredictable weather, walking around the city is the best way to get to know it. In the last edition, we warned visitors that a new law had been passed which outlaws jay-walking, a favourite habit of Dubliners. As predicted, however, this has proven either too difficult or too ridiculous to enforce, and dashing in front of the eternally gridlocked traffic or crossing without pedestrian lights is still a widely practised, if dangerous, phenomenon.

Cycling

If walking does not appeal to you, but you are fit enough to propel yourself to your chosen destination, cycling is the other option to consider. Although cycle lanes are increasing cars very firmly rule the roads in Dublin, therefore this is an option only for the brave. Cycling has some marvellous advantages, though, if you have the stomach for it. It's probably one of the fastest ways to get around the city as most traffic jams can be avoided or bypassed on a bike and you can stop wherever you like.

Bicycle theft is big business in the city centre. Dublin is very short on secure bike parks at the moment due to the rocketing price of retail space so at least try to leave your bike somewhere highly visible and use a good lock (locks and advice available in bike shops). Also, for your own safety, wear a helmet and some high visibility clothing. Many drivers seem to think that cyclists are an unwanted extra hazard on the roads. Don't give them the excuse to blame you!

If you're only in Dublin for a short stay, **renting a bike** is a cheap and easy option. There are lots of outlets around the city that rent out bicycles, particularly during the summer months when demand from tourists is high and when the Dublin weather is a little more likely to suit this mode of transport. Some hostels also offer this service to their guests. Since 11 September 2001 insurance rates have gone through the roof, so several operators have left the bike rental market. However, you could try your luck with: **Cycle-Ways** at 185 Parnell St, Dublin 1 (directly opposite the ILAC Centre), tel 873 4748, which sells bikes, cycle clothing and equipment. and also rents bikes during the summer season for a rate of €15 per day or €50 per week.

Square Wheels Cycleworks which specialises in the sale of customised bikes and tricycles, is a funky looking place at 21 Temple Lane Sth in Temple Bar, Dublin 2, tel 679 0838, and a good central address for bike repairs. They also have a small selection of secondhand bikes for sale or hire and a secure bike park for 50c per half day €1 per day. Opening hours are generally Mon–Fri 08.30–18.30 but these are subject to change according to the whim of the proprietor!

The **Golden Pages** classified telephone directory is a good source for **bike sales** and hire outlets. If you are buying a bike, there are lots of shops in the suburbs, particularly on the northside, so it pays to shop around a bit. Secondhand bikes can be had for around €150 but you will normally have to pay more for something of good quality.

A great source for secondhand bikes is the **Garda auction** held twice a year (usually March and September/October) at Kevin Street Garda station near St Stephen's Green in Dublin 2. Here, all the unclaimed and stolen bikes which the police have held for more than a year are auctioned off for half nothing to the public who can view them the day before. For further details, tel 475 2693.

Dublin Bus Head Office

59 Upr O'Connell St, Dublin 1, tel 873 4222, website www.dublinbus.ie

Open Mon–Fri 09.00–17.30, Sat 09.00–14.00 for general information, route maps, timetables, ID cards and information on tours.

The information and customer service line tel 873 4222 is open Mon–Sat 09.00–19.00.

The website www.dublinbus.ie is a really comprehensive site with timetables, details of services and fares.

On the buses

The bus system operated by **Dublin Bus** is the mainstay of the city's transport system. Buses are a great way to see the city, and with a little gentle eaves-dropping you can learn something about real Dubs. All parts of Dublin and the surrounding suburbs have at least one Dublin Bus route going through them and many areas have several. Outer suburban routes extend as far north as Balbriggan, as far south as Newtownmountkennedy and as far west as Kilcock. When choosing where to stay or live in Dublin, try to find somewhere served by several bus routes.

Bus stops carry the relevant **time-tables** for each bus route (a stop may serve several routes) on a revolving carousel. (Some bus stops are set down only: these are clearly marked.) Due to the chronic traffic problems in the city, however, only the time of departure from the terminus is listed, not the time

of arrival at each stop so the timetable is only a guide to the likely frequency of the service. Canny bus-users estimate the likely wait by the number of people waiting—a crowd means a relevant bus hasn't been by in a while.

The bus stops also carry some limited information about the routes served by the buses stopping there. However, not all stops on the route are listed so if in doubt ask the driver. Once on the bus, if you're not sure where to get off, ask the driver to let you know when the bus gets to your destination. The driver will be only too happy to oblige.

Buses are not of a single type so as well as the standard double decker with the Dublin Bus logo, remember that others like the 'CitySwift' buses and the mini-bus style 'City Imp' are also part of the network. All display a route number as well as a logo anyway.

Scheduled bus services operate from 05.30 throughout the day with the last bus leaving the city centre at 23.30 (but see Nitelink below) with an average of under 10 minutes wait between buses, depending on your route. The **XPresso** service, designed with commuters in mind, is an express version of the outer suburban routes which bypasses many of the intermediate stops. XPresso buses are recognisable by the X added to their usual route number. Tickets paid for individually on the bus cost a little more than for scheduled services, but weekly and monthly tickets can be used on them for no extra charge (see below for more details of fares and tickets).

● ●

Using the buses like a Dubliner

■ It probably doesn't seem that there's a queue at the stop. This is because there isn't. There is a collection of individuals waiting for the same event.

■ When the bus arrives, the first person to get on is not the first person who arrived at the stop but the person nearest to the door when it opens. Everyone else gets on in whatever order eventually establishes itself.

■ Pushing and shoving is frowned on but moving in front of people isn't, unless the bus is so crowded that very few people will be let on.

■ Smoking is not allowed anywhere.

■ Sticking chewing-gum on the seats is not technically illegal but it damn well ought to be.

■ Talking loudly is not polite unless your conversation is fascinating and unusual.

■ There are signs on the bus saying 'Exit through centre doors'. The driver will ignore these. So should you. Effectively, the centre doors do not exist.

■ And finally: say 'Thank you' to the driver as you get off. Most Dubliners do and the drivers like it.

Nitelink is a Dublin Bus **late night service**. All Nitelink services have a number of intermediary pick-up points. These buses have an 'N' after the number. Buses depart nightly from the city centre at D'Olier St, College St and Westmoreland St, all Dublin 2, depending on the direction of travel, and serve most of the suburbs around the city for a flat fare of €4 (it's €6 to the outermost suburbs on the network up to 20 km away), making them a cheap and handy alternative to getting a taxi. See pages 74–75 for a map of the Nitelink Services.

TICKETS AND FARES

Tickets for most scheduled services can be bought on the bus from the driver. Each bus route is divided into stages and fares are calculated according to the number of stops passed. For up to 3 stages the fare is 75c; 4 to 7 stages cost €1.05, 8 to 13 cost €1.30 and any more than 13 cost €1.45 (that's for quite a journey—there are 14 stages, for instance between the Airport and the city centre). These fares are for single journeys up to the outer suburban boundary.

A special city centre **shoppers' fare** of 40c is available inside the area bounded by St Stephen's Green, Dublin Castle, Parnell Square and Connolly Station Mon–Sat 10.00–16.30.

If you are in the city for a short stay the seven-day **Short Hop ticket** is valid for unlimited bus and suburban rail/DART travel and costs €24.00. This ticket does not cover the Airlink or Nitelink services

Rambler tickets come in all shapes and sizes, including those which combine bus, DART and suburban rail access. For example, unlimited travel on Dublin Bus for 1–7 days costs €4.50–€16.50.

All of the above tickets can save you money, how much depends on how often and how far you travel. Further reductions on weekly and monthly tickets are available to students with an **ISIC (International Student Identity Card)** and **Travelsave stamp**.

VALIDATION

If you have bought a ticket in advance board the bus on the right hand side and pass your ticket through the machine. Otherwise board the bus on the left hand side of the entrance and state your destination. The driver will tell you how much the fare is. For security reasons drivers are not allowed to handle money, so you must have the exact fare in coins only. If you pay more than the exact fare you will be given a change ticket which can be exchanged in Dublin Bus Head Office (see p. 69).

Fare dodging is almost impossible as you pay for or validate your ticket on the way in. It is certainly not an advisable practice anyway, as fines are on-the-spot and the process is utterly humiliating. Inspections are random, but relatively frequent. Besides, the price of bus travel in Dublin is good value when compared to other European cities like London, for example.

Tickets, route maps and timetables are also available from many newsagents and *The Independent Directory* contains comprehensive Dublin Bus timetables.

One of Dublin's most elegant churches, nicknamed 'the pepper canister', in Upper Mount Street.

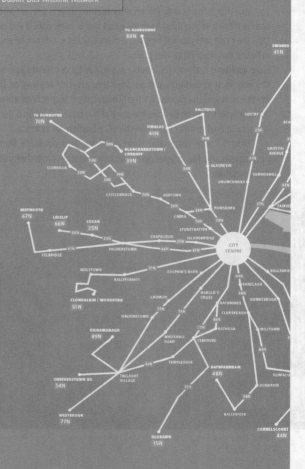

Dublin Bus Nitelink Network

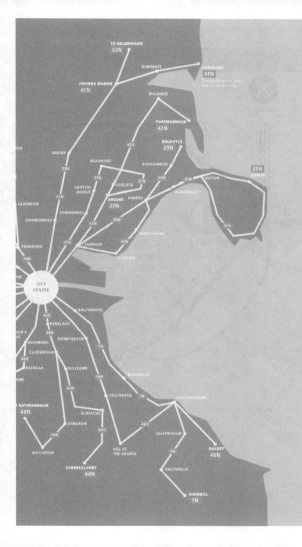

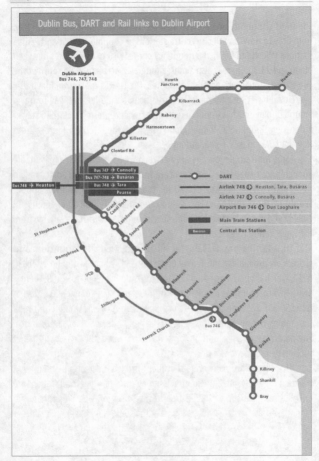

Dublin Bus, DART and Rail links to Dublin Airport

Dublin Airport
Bus 746, 747, 748

Howth Junction
Bayside
Sutton
Howth
Kilbarrack
Raheny
Harmonstown
Killester
Clontarf Rd

Bus 747 → Connolly
Bus 747·748 → Busáras
Bus 748 → Tara
Pearse

Bus 748 → Heuston

Grand Canal Dock
Lansdowne Rd
Sandymount

St Stephens Green

Sydney Parade

Donnybrook

Booterstown
Blackrock
Seapoint
Salthill & Monkstown
Dun Laoghaire
Sandycove & Glasthule
Glenageary
Dalkey

UCD

Stillorgan

Foxrock Church
Bus 746

Killiney
Shankill
Bray

○—○   DART
         Airlink 748 ⟷ Heuston, Tara, Busáras
         Airlink 747 ⟷ Connolly, Busáras
         Airport Bus 746 ⟷ Dun Laoghaire

         Main Train Stations
Busáras   Central Bus Station

Trains

The DART's sprightly green electrified trains run the length of Dublin Bay, from Bray to Howth with city centre stations at Connolly, Tara St and Pearse Stations (Westland Row) at a frequency of every 10 to 15 minutes between 06.30 and 23.30. There is also a more limited service extending south of the city to Greystones and north to Malahide. The DART (apart from inevitable overcrowding at rush hours) offers an efficient and pleasant way to travel around Dublin which is useful to remember when choosing a place to stay or indeed live. Running as it does along the coast, the full DART journey from Howth to Bray makes a great outing.

Fares for a single journey are between €1.05 and €2.95, a reasonable enough price to pay for a good service. A **family day ticket** (2 adults and up to 4 kids) costs €10.15 or €10.70 for the combined bus and rail option. **Weekly tickets** (rail only) cost €18.40 and **monthly** (rail only) €66.00. All weekly and monthly tickets require special photo ID which is available from the Travel Centre (see below).

Timetables are available at all train stations. **Information and tickets** are available at the **Travel Centre** at 35 Lr Abbey St, Dublin 1, tel 836 6222, which is open Mon–Fri 09.00 to 17.00 and Sat 09.00 to 13.00. There is also a low cost number to call from within Ireland daily from 09.00 to 19.00, tel 1850 366 222, and they have a useful website, www.irishrail.ie, with full timetables, details of facilities and services and a selection of sample fares. The timetable for all suburban rail services is a good buy, as it gives lots of subsidiary information on tickets etc.

Tickets are normally bought at the station, but can also be bought on the train or at the end of the journey as some suburban and rural stations are only staffed part time. While a free trip is sometimes possible, there are random checks on trains and procedure at the stations is never predictable, so do not be tempted to think that because someone else got away with it the last time you will not be caught.

Taxis

Taxis are a great if more expensive way to get around the city when you can get one, but there never seems to be enough of them, despite a recent controversial attempt by the authorities to deregulate the whole scene and allow hundreds of new license plates to be issued. Don't be surprised to see huge queues at taxi ranks during the evening rush hour or on any given Friday or Saturday night. It may be wise to call one in advance if you can, but if not, try hailing one on the street—it usually takes less time than queuing although it is not standard practice.

Taxi ranks are located at various points around the city centre, including O'Connell St, Dublin 1 and College Green and St Stephen's Green in Dublin 2. The Dublin taxi meter area extends to quite a distance from the city centre and the following fares apply within it. If you are going further, negotiate with the driver first.

- For a distance not exceeding 9/10 km (5/9 mile) or 3 minutes 20 seconds minimum fare €2.75
- For each additional 1/5 km (1/9 mile) or 30 seconds, 15 c (20 c between 22.00 and 08.00 am and on Sundays and holidays)
- For each additional animal, passenger or each piece of luggage, 50 c.
- And, if the worst really comes to the worst, there is a standard soiling charge of €25.

The **Garda Carriage Office**, tel 666 9850, is the place to call with any queries. If you leave something behind in the taxi, or if you have a complaint, tel 666 9851, quoting the roof sign number.

Hackney cabs offer a call out service only: they do not have roof signs like the other taxis and cannot be hailed on the street or hired at a rank. They can be booked to call for you on both the outer and return journey. Around Christmas there is a huge demand for taxis and hackneys—so many people are partying and therefore not driving so booking is often essential.

Getting out of Dublin (if you must)

The normal suburban bus and train services actually extend quite far into the countryside and tend to offer better value the further you go, so always check first to see if your destination is served by them. If it isn't, you have lots of other options for leaving the fair city.

In such a small country, it is never too expensive to get around anyway, and **provincial buses** are amazingly good value. The main towns and cities are served by regular and frequent bus schedules, and even the furthest away backwaters generally get a good, if roundabout service. Students with an ISIC card and Travelsave stamp get significant reductions. The provincial buses run by **Bus Éireann** (Irish Bus), tel 836 6111 or www.buseireann.ie, all depart from Busáras, the central bus station, Store St, Dublin 1. Tickets and information can be got at Busáras, or from the Bus Éireann desk in the Dublin Tourism Centre, Suffolk St, Dublin 2.

A number of **private bus companies** compete with Bus Éireann on the provincial routes (e.g. CityLink and Nestor's serving the Dublin–Galway route). Most are based outside Dublin and have local operations as their main business, but many of them also run regular scheduled services to and from Dublin. They mostly operate from the quays around O'Connell Bridge and sometimes offer cheaper fares than the equivalent Bus Éireann routes. Information on these services is usually passed on by word of mouth as many of the companies are not in the Dublin area phonebook, so if you are planning a trip to anywhere outside Dublin, ask friends or your accommodation provider at the other end to advise on the best option. Also, keep an eye out as you see their coaches in the street—they normally display a destination and a contact telephone number.

Getting a **train** is certainly one of the more pleasant ways to get out of Dublin, but it is much more expensive than the buses in most cases and not much faster. If you are not a full time student but are lucky enough to be under 26 years of age, you can get an **EYC (European Youth Card)** from USIT for €8.89. While you don't get bus discounts with this, a **Fair Stamp** which costs an extra €8.89 will get you very good deals on all Intercity train services.

Those with USIT cards and the saver stamps get great discounts, but as they also get them on buses, they will still pay almost twice the price for a train journey. The other disadvantage to travelling by train is that the network is not really all that extensive, and while it covers most city to city journeys, it goes no further. To see most of the west of Ireland, for example, you'll still have to transfer to a bus at some point.

There are two main stations for the Intercity trains: Heuston Station which serves Cork, Galway and Limerick, and Connolly Station which serves Sligo, Wexford, Rosslare and Belfast. The standard of these services varies quite a bit (the Belfast route is the best, most of the others are being slowly upgraded) but they are generally quite regular, although drastically reduced on Sundays.

For information on all **Iarnrod Éireann (Irish Rail)** services, consult www.irishrail.ie, call to any station or telephone 836 6222 (within Ireland tel 1850 366 222). The telephone books and *The Independent Directory* also list the numbers for talking timetables on all Intercity routes.

Hitch-hiking is not really practised in the Dublin area but becomes more acceptable further out into the country. In a lot of rural areas, it is common for local people to thumb a lift, but usually this will be from a fellow local who is known to them and therefore does not constitute any risk. In summer, backpackers hitchhiking are a regular sight in or going towards the more popular tourist destinations, and getting a lift is usually easy enough. However, crime takes place in rural Ireland like everywhere else. Unless you are travelling with someone else, hitching is never worth the risk. **Never hitchhike alone**.

It is possible to get a **domestic flight** to a surprising number of destinations including Galway, Cork, Kerry, and Shannon, and Donegal from Dublin Airport, but these tend to be expensive (approximately €95 to Cork, €73 to Galway) and hardly worth the hassle, when very few places are more than 4 or 5 hours drive from Dublin anyway. Consult the Aer Rianta timetable for details of scheduled services, tel 814 1111, www.dublin-airport.com.

Shopping without a gold card

When it comes to shopping 'on a shoestring' you need to be prepared to use energy and ingenuity. Follow our tips and you'll be well-dressed, well fed, well-read and ... you get the picture.

Clothes

It cannot be said that Dublin is an effortless paradise for shoestring shoppers in search of cheap clothes. It is, rather, a cornucopia of exciting challenges for the dedicated bargain hunter. The economic boom has not been kind to those on a budget but it *is* possible to look stylish and chic without spending a fortune. The main shopping areas are O'Connell St, Henry St and Mary St in Dublin 1 and Grafton St and St Stephen's Green in Dublin 2. If you don't venture beyond the plastic frontages of these streets you'll be very disappointed. However, if you're prepared to stalk the backstreets, tracking down low-price finery, you'll be well rewarded for your canny combing of charity shops, secondhand shops and the cheaper end of the high street market.

Charity shops

The huge variety of charity shops means that the city's pool of cast-off garments is spread very thinly indeed. The advantage of living in a buoyant economy, however, is that those with the money can tend to tire quickly of their expensive designer clothes. So, to make room in their bulging wardrobes and possibly to assuage their guilty consciences, they donate some really great items to charity shops. The rewards for those prepared to rummage are enormous and whole outfits can be put together for under €20. This is not in the interests of recycling or hippie frugality: the less you spend on each garment, the more goodies you'll have to squash into your wardrobe. Not only can you find fairly ordinary next-to-new clothes, but also brand names and luxury garments for a fraction of the original price. It is insanity to approach more expensive shops without having totally exhausted the charity options first.

Synonymous with charity shopping, **Oxfam**, with its main branches in Sth Great George's St, Dublin 2, and Rathmines, Dublin 6, commands a good selection of standard charity shop fare. Next to its George's St branch is **Enable Ireland** (aka **Cerebral Palsy**) which is a slightly more upmarket version on the same theme. These shops can suffer from their location near the student vultures of Trinity College, DIT and DBS and many of the best clothes are snapped up in seconds. For this reason, it is well worth heading north of the Liffey to the home of one of the best stocked and least well known charity shops in Dublin, **CASA**. A ten-minute walk up Parnell Sq and onto Dorset St will bring you to the **Mater Hospital Shop**, another well organised and well stocked charity shop which can occasionally have designer outfits at reasonable prices and is frequently overlooked. Close by is **Mrs Quinn's Charity Shop**, which also stocks shoes, books and a large selection of bric à brac.

Away from the city centre, almost every large suburb will be home to yet more diverse and obscure charity shops. Rathmines alone, in Dublin 6, a short distance from the city centre by Dublin Bus nos 14, 14A, 15, 15A, 15B, 15C and 83 has several, but wherever you happen to be, to pass one without going in for a browse misses the point of bargain shopping entirely.

CASA 26 Capel St, Dublin 1, tel 872 8538
Open 09.30–17.00
Enable Ireland 28 Lr Camden St, Dublin 2, tel 478 0647
Unit 8, Sth Great George's St, Dublin 2, tel 478 2763
Open Mon–Sat 09.30–17.30
Mater Hospital Shop 17 Lr Dorset St, Dublin 1, tel 878 7801
Open Mon–Fri 10.00–16.00 Sat 10.30–16.00

Mrs Quinn's Charity Shop 21 Lr Dorset St, Dublin 1, tel 874 5421
Open Mon–Sat 10.00–16.45
Oxfam
204 Rathmines, Dublin 6, tel 496 4181
Open Mon–Sat 10.00–17.00
2 Wicklow House, Sth Great George's St, Dublin 2, tel 478 0777
Open Mon–Sat 10.00–17.00

Secondhand

A couple of absorbing hours spent in the city centre's small but interesting range of secondhand shops means going up several notches in style while spending significantly less than you would on the high street. So, if you're aiming for something smart, glamorous or retro-chic, these are the shops for you. Bargain hunters would be well advised, though, to retain a sense of healthy scepticism and to keep a keen eye out for plain rubbish. Don't assume that a garment's presence in a cool secondhand clothes shop guarantees its place in fashion history's roll of honour.

The gentrification of trendy Temple Bar, formerly the bastion of secondhand chic, has meant that many of the truly great secondhand shops are now located elsewhere. Some remain, however. **Eager Beaver** spreads its huge range of cheap and functional trousers, jackets, jumpers and shirts, as well as a few more glamorous items, over two floors on Crown Alley. They offer a 10 per cent student discount, so bring your ID card. Just down the road on Upr Fownes St, you'll find **Flip** which provides a more customised and well presented stock of trendy trousers, jackets, jeans and shirts, (though they can tend to be a little bit more expensive).

Moving up to Sth Great George's St, you'll encounter **Wildchild**, (twice! there are two outlets on the street, make sure to visit both). Possibly the best secondhand outlet in the city centre, Wildchild caters for both girls and guys and stocks a wide range of secondhand and new funky, retro clothes and shoes, not to mention a variety of somewhat unusual (and often useful) objects.

Ensconced on Market Arcade is the original and interesting secondhand clothes shop for women **Jenny Vander**. Stock comprises a luscious array of genuine period clothes and accessories from the 1920s to 1960s. Strictly speaking this is indeed a secondhand shop, but it can't be classified as cheap, in fact some of the dresses can be very expensive and may make the more financially embarrassed bargain hunters weep. Upstairs from Jenny Vander is **Rufus the Cat**, which houses a broad selection of men's secondhand clothes, including interesting ties, scarves and belts and with an emphasis on 70s kitsch style.

Completing this geographical triangle is **Harlequin**, on Castle Market across the road from Market Arcade. As its name suggests, it has a vibrant and eclectic mix. Its selection of men's shirts in the basement is beyond compare and the occasional bargain rail is always worth a look. Male secondhand dandies can complete their look at **Bogart** menswear, five minutes' walk away on Aungier St, where genuine wool suits are mostly under €80. Representing a fraction of what men would pay for a new suit, this shop makes it a joy to fulfil their order of 'Wear it again, Sam', emblazoned in gold on the shopfront.

Bogart 25 Aungier St, Dublin 2, tel 478 4861
Open Mon–Sat 10.00–18.00
Eager Beaver 17 Crown Alley, Temple Bar, Dublin 2, tel 677 3342
Open Mon–Fri 09.30–18.00 (Thur 20.00) Sat 09.30–19.30 Sun 13.00–18.00
Flip 4 Upr Fownes St, Temple Bar, Dublin 2, tel 671 4299
Open Mon–Sat 09.30–18.00 (Thur 19.00)
Harlequin 13 Castle Market, Dublin 2, tel 671 0202
Open Mon–Sat 10.00–18.00 (Thur 19.00)
Jenny Vander Market Arcade, Sth Great George's St, Dublin 2, tel 677 0406
Open Mon–Sat 10.00–18.00 (Thur 19.00)

Rufus the Cat Market Arcade, Sth Great George's St, (above Jenny Vander)
tel 677 0406
Open Mon—Sat 10.00—18.00 (Thur 19.00)
Wildchild
    71 Aungier St, Dublin 2, tel 475 7177
    Open Mon—Sat 10.00—18.00 (Thur 19.00)
    61 Sth Great George's St, Dublin 2, tel 475 5099
    Open Mon—Sat 10.00—18.00 (Thur 19.00)

New clothes

Of course, it makes sense to shop around and exhaust your secondhand options first, but it is possible to shop quite cheaply and for a quick hit of consumerist trash, real shops with new clothes cannot be beaten.

    Dunnes Stores is unshakeable in its position as the place to go for cheap, sensible, mass-produced clothes. If you need T-shirts, underwear or any other wardrobe staple, join the rest of the Irish population in one of the many branches, the main ones in town being in St Stephen's Green Shopping Centre, Dublin 2 and in the ILAC Centre, Dublin 1. **Penney's** of O'Connell St and Mary St, Dublin 1 and many of the major shopping centres is similar, although it nods more in the direction of 'youth fashion'. Still it is useful if you want a bright new outfit for a night out and have limited financial resources.

    Upstairs in the St Stephen's Green Centre, a visit to the huge, strip-lit, **TK Maxx** for knockdown prices on designer shoes and clothes and sportswear and shoes is a must. Because of its 'bazaar' quality you can be fairly sure that your outfit will be original but this is not a shop for the lighthearted bargain hunter. You may have to search hard through the seemingly endless rails before you find anything you like. **Guineys** on North Earl St, Dublin 1, is also worth a browse especially for jackets, jeans, bed linen and towels.

    The massive penetration of the British chain stores has made shopping for low-cost women's clothes something of a giddy treat. **Dorothy Perkins** and **Debenham's** can be found in the Jervis Centre and Henry St, Dublin 1, and in the St Stephen's Green Centre, Dublin 2. **Clery's** department store on O'Connell St, Dublin 1, houses **Miss Selfridge**, **Warehouse**, (both are also on Grafton St, Dublin 2), **Bay Clothing Co.**, **Angel**, **Karen Millen** and **Dolcis Shoes**—to name but a few—within its doors.

Shopping centre and department store opening hours

Arnotts Dept Store, Henry St, Dublin 1, tel 805 0400
Mon–Sat 09.00–18.30 (Tues 09.30) Sun 12.00–18.00

Clery's Dept. Store, O'Connell St, Dublin 1, tel 878 6000
Mon–Wed 09.00–18.30 (Tues 09.30) Thur 09.00–21.00
Fri 09.00–20.00 Sat 09.00–18.30

Guineys Dept Store, 11–12 Nth Earl St, Dublin 1 tel 872 4347
Mon–Sat 09.00–18.00 (Thur 20.00) Sun 14.00–18.00

ILAC Centre Henry St, Dublin 1, tel 704 1460
Mon–Sat 09.00–18.00 (Thur 19.00) Sun 12.00–18.00

Jervis Centre Mary St, Dublin 1, tel 878 1323
Mon–Sat 09.00–18.00 (Thur 21.00) Sun 12.00–18.00

Penney's Dept Store O'Connell St, Dublin 1, tel 872 0466
Mon–Sat 08.30–18.30 (Thur 21.00) Sun 12.00–18.00

Market Arcade Drury St/Sth Great George's St, Dublin 2
Mon–Sat 10.00–18.00 (Thur 19.00)

St Stephen's Green Shopping Centre, St Stephens Green, Dublin 2, tel 478 0888
Mon–Wed 08.00–19.00 Thur 08.00–20.00
Fri, Sat 08.00–19.00 Sun 11.00–18.00

As you make your way up Henry St a handful of really cheap and cheerful women's shops such as **Japan** and **Extrovert** and **Miss Moneypenny** on Liffey St belt out chart hits in competition with each other. It is worth elbowing your way through the gaggles of teenage girls to see what you can pick up in these shops, particularly Extrovert. Staying on Henry St, take a wander into **A-Wear**, (also on Grafton St, and in many of the satellite shopping centres); it's worth checking out but if you're on a strict budget, avoid heading into their in-house designer range, Quin and Donnelly, which tend to be more expensive. And don't forget the various branches of **Oasis** which stock clothes, shoes, bags and accessories but tend to be a little overpriced.

Tips for saving money

- Shop around. It can get boring but you will save tons of money if you look for the shop with the lowest prices and not just the first one you come across. Be ruthless!

- Treat each shopping excursion like a mission. Wear comfortable clothes and shoes, be aware of what you are looking for, try not to make impulsive purchases and always get a receipt.

- When it comes to food, eating in will always save you money—unless you buy ready-meals at Marks & Spencer's. Buying a roll and some salad at the nearest supermarket will be cheaper than buying a ready made sandwich. What you pay for in a restaurant is service, atmosphere, and having your meal made for you, more than the food itself. Sometimes this is worth the extra, but not always.

- Buy secondhand whenever this is feasible. But beware: one of the contributors once bought a beautiful velvet jacket secondhand for €40 and saw an identical one (new) on sale for €30 in Miss Selfridge the next day. That said, secondhand usually does mean cheap, especially with books and records and the like—it's just not a universal law.

Staying on Henry St, **River Island** (downstairs in Arnotts department store) stocks fashionable shoes, clothes and accessories for both sexes (but is a little pricey). And further down the street in the Jervis Centre **Top Shop** sells high street fashions at reasonable prices. **Arnotts** is also home to a wide range of high fashion shops stocking clothes, shoes, accessories, for men and women, in-store shops including **Mango**, **Esprit**, **Levis**, **Pepe**, **Benetton** . . . the list goes on.

Men tend to do badly in Dublin's fashion mainstream. The range of shops is more limited and none occupy the cheap and cheerful spot that Miss Selfridge does for women; however **Top Man**, part of Top Shop in the Jervis Centre comes close. **Next** of Grafton St and Jervis Centre, are worth a look, they provide a non sporty, casual yet stylish look. The Next chain also stocks reasonably-priced women's clothes and houses a selection of native designers' diffusion ranges for both sexes. For the chaps **Unique Discount Menswear** and **Hairy Legs**, across the road from Miss Moneypenny on Liffey St, don't deserve their local reputation as the pariahs of the men's clothing market. Their honest value in fairly trendy clothes should be checked out.

Independent shops range from the very expensive to the very cheap. **Urban Outfitters** in Temple Bar seeks not only to clothe you but to accessorize an entire lifestyle. It seems to be targeted to appeal to the 20–30s funky, intelligent urban dweller demographic. It's fairly expensive but worth a browse. **Hobo** of Trinity St and Exchequer St is a shrine to street and skater style; laid back clothes for laid back people, and because it stocks its own brand is a little cheaper than other similar shops.

A-Wear Henry St, Dublin 1, tel 872 4644

—also on Grafton St, tel 671 7200, and in many of the satellite shopping centres

Open Mon–Sat 09.00–18.00 (Thur 20.00) Sun 12.00–18.00

Extrovert

    St Stephen's Green Shopping Centre, Dublin 2, tel 478 1097

    21 Henry St, Dublin 1, tel 873 5186

    Open Mon–Sat 09.00–18.00 (Thur 20.00)

Hairy Legs Liffey Street, Dublin 1, tel 8727106

Open Mon–Sat 09.30–18.00 (Thur 20.00)

Hobo 6–9 Trinity St, Dublin 2, tel 670 4869

Open Mon–Sat 09.30–18.00 (Thur 20.00) Sun 12.00–18.00

Japan

    16 Henry St, Dublin 1, tel 872 3193

    St Stephen's Green Centre, Dublin 2, tel 475 4199

    Open Mon–Sat 09.00–18.00 (Thur 20.00)

Miss Moneypenny 13 Liffey St, Dublin 1, tel 872 9440

Open Mon–Sat 09.00–18.00 (Thur 20.00)

Next

    67 Grafton St, Dublin 2, tel 679 3300

    Jervis Centre, Dublin 1, tel 878 1406

    Open Mon–Sat 09.30–18.30 (Thur 20.00) Sun 12.00–18.00

Oasis

    45 Henry St, Dublin 1, tel 873 0876

    3 St Stephen's Green, Dublin 2, tel 671 4477

    Open Mon–Wed 09.30–18.00 Thur 09.30–20.30 Fri, Sat 09.30–18.30

    Sun 14.00–18.00

Unique Discount Menswear 19 Upr Liffey St, Dublin 1,

    tel 873 3823

Open Mon–Sat 09.30–18.00 (Thur 20.00) Sun 12.00–18.00

Urban Outfitters 4 Cecilia St, Temple Bar, Dublin 2, tel 670 6202
Open Mon–Wed 10.00–19.00 Thur, Fri 10.00–20.00 Sat 10.00–19.00 Sun
12.00–18.00

> *If you feel like seeing how the other half lives, take a stroll
> around Brown Thomas on Grafton St which stocks just about
> everything you will need when you finally get that solicitor's
> letter regarding the Will of the unknown distant relative
> who's just bequeathed you their massive fortune.*

Shoes

The only way to survive shoe shopping in Dublin without spending frightening
amounts of money is to join a religious order that forbids the wearing of shoes.
Failing that, **Barratt's** and **Korky's** of Grafton St and Henry St, stock low-cost,
low-quality footwear that will at least be fashionable, although the Grafton St
branch of Korky's does not cater for men. **Schuh** on O'Connell St, stocks a
massive amount of shoes and trainers for men and women at fairly affordable
prices and **Arnotts** has an extensive selection of shoes at varying prices. The
Simon Hart chain (Henry St, ILAC Centre) also has a wide selection of shoes
and boots for women and men and they frequently have discounted stock. It's
also worth checking **Zerep** of Henry St and Grafton St, particularly for men's
footwear. If you do have some money to spend, you should make a beeline for
Nine West on Grafton St, which stocks lovely shoes, sandals, bag and jackets
for women. Keep an eye out for its sales and you may get lucky. The days when
every Dublin teenager made a pilgrimage to the shoe stalls 'round-the-back-of-
the-Lilac' to buy the regulation Doctor Martens, on the Parnell St side of the
ILAC Centre are over. A visit to the last vestiges of Dublin street trade is well
worth while, however, and you may be able to pick up a bargain.

Barratt's Henry St, Dublin 1, tel 872 4033
Open Mon–Fri 09.00–18.00 (Thur 20.30) Sat 09.00–18.30 Sun 14.00–18.00

Korky's

    47 Grafton St, (women only) Dublin 2, tel 670 7943 4

    GPO Buildings, Henry St, Dublin 1, tel 873 1359

    Open Mon–Fri 09.00–18.00 (Thur 20.30) Sat 09.00–18.30 Sun 14.00–
    18.00

Nine West Grafton St, Dublin 2, tel 677 0445

Open Mon–Sat 09.30–18.30 (Thur 20.00) Sun 12.00–18.00

Schuh

    47–8 Lr O'Connell St, Dublin 1, tel 804 9420

    Jervis Centre, Dublin 1, tel 873 0433

    Open Mon–Sat 09.30–18.30 (Thur 20.00) Sun 12.00–18.00

Zerep

    31A Henry St, Dublin 1, tel 873 1644

    57 Grafton St, Dublin 2, tel 677 8320

    Open Mon–Sat 09.00–18.00 (Thur 20.00)

> *Be a pioneer, check out all the shops even the ones that look
> distinctly dodgy. You never know where you'll find something
> fabulous. And always to try clothes and shoes on before you
> head for the cash register. Don't despair if it can't find
> anything you like. They're just material possessions after all.
> Remember, it's what's inside that counts!*

Books

Dublin is well-supplied with bookshops, both new and secondhand, especially
in the city centre, with wide stocks of Irish- and British- published books, some
US, (see Murder Ink below) but very few books in other languages. Most have
a prominent Irish interest section, and the main ones stock some Irish
language books. For information about current Irish-interest books watch out
for *Books Ireland*, sold in the bigger bookshops. For further information on

bookshops in Dublin, try looking up David Havelin's web guide to Dublin bookshops at www.twocultures.org/dublin/books. This is a personal site and makes no claims to objectivity in its descriptions of the shops, but the basic information is sound and seemed to be reasonably up to date at the time of going to press.

The Irish Historical Picture Co.

5 Lr Ormond Quay, Dublin 1, tel 872 0144

For those who like nostalgic old photographs (and who doesn't?) this is a real treat. Situated just by Grattan Bridge it has over 17,000 photographs of Irish life from the late 19th and early 20th centuries. The owner, who has been collecting these for 35 years, reckons that 70 to 80 photographers' work is represented. You can buy an A4 print of the ancestor's home town for a mere € 15.15.

Open Mon–Fri 09.00–18.00, Sat 09.00–17.00.

Nearly all bookshops take credit cards and are open at least between 10.00 and 17.00 on weekdays and Saturdays. The bigger city-centre ones have longer opening hours.

Resale price maintenance for books was abolished in Ireland at least ten years ago, but the vast majority of books are sold at the price suggested by the publisher. It's worth shopping around for 'big' books, especially best-selling fiction, memoirs and glossy coffee table books which are often heavily discounted. Promotional offers—3 for the price of 2—are often available.

Genuine bargains are available at the various remainder bookshops, notably **Chapters** 108–109 Middle Abbey St, Dublin 1, tel 873 0484, and remainders are also sold in some of the main bookshops, but since many are the books nobody wanted when they were first published the experience is often similar to that of rummaging through the bargain bin in a record shop and finding nothing but old Barry Manilow tapes. The secondhand shops and stalls are the places to go for real value.

The House of Astrology

9 Parliament St, Dublin 2, tel 679 3404

> The name says it all really. Everything the amateur astrologer needs, and more: crystals, Tarot cards, incense, candles—plus books to tell you what to do with them.

THE BIGGIES

The Dublin Bookshop Grafton St, Dublin 2, tel 677 5568

The liveliest of the city centre bookshops, smack in the middle of Grafton Street. It's moving at the beginning of June 2002 from no. 24 to a spacious new spot a few metres up the street. The bookshop is part of a chain which also has shops in Rathmines, Stillorgan and Bray. It has upscale, carefully chosen stock (not as much about Dublin as you'd think from the name,) including greeting cards and wrapping paper.

Open Mon–Wed 09.00–19.00 Thur, Fri 09.00–21.00 Sat 09.00–18.00 Sun 11.00–18.00

Easons 40 O'Connell St, Dublin 1, tel 873 3811, website www.eason.ie

A major importer and wholesaler of books, newspapers and magazines, this is the biggy, with shops all over the country. The O'Connell St branch has a surprisingly wide range of books given its equally wide range of newspapers and magazines.

Open Mon–Wed 08.30–18.45 Thur 08.30–20.45 Fri 08.30–19.45 Sat 08.30–18.45 Sun 13.00–17.45

Eason Hannas 27–29 Nassau St/1 Dawson St, Dublin 2, tel 677 1255, e-mail info@hannas.ie website www.eason.ie

This was formerly the independent bookshop Fred Hannas. There are comfortable sofas and a small (but perfectly formed) café on the upper floor, and the stock is still respectable and interesting enough to merit attention;

but a lot of the charm has gone, and the shop no longer sells secondhand books. Still, a good selection is a good selection, and Eason Hannas has it.
Open Mon–Sat 08.30–18.30 (Thur 20.00) Sun 13.00–17.30

Hughes & Hughes St Stephen's Green Centre, Dublin 2, tel 478 3060
With branches at Dublin Airport and Blackrock, Hughes & Hughes fills the 'we try harder' slot. It concentrates on bestsellers—no surprise given its locations.
Open Mon–Sat 09.30–18.00 (Thur 20.00) Sun 12–18.00

Hodges Figgis 56-8 Dawson St, Dublin 2, tel 677 4754,
website www.hodgesfiggis.com
This is the oldest surviving bookshop in Dublin, tracing its history back to the 18th century. Large, solid, well-diversified stock of new books on multiple floors; also a big remainder and bargain books section in the basement. A favourite target for book thieves, so staff will sometimes prevent you from sitting on the floor. A café on the first floor, however, provides comfortable chairs where you can mull over your potential purchases in comfort with coffee and scones, and if you decide not to buy after reading half the book, you're only doing what most of the patrons do so nobody will complain.
Open Mon–Fri 09.00–19.00, (Tues 09.30, Thur 20.00) Sat 09.00–18.00 Sun 12.00–18.00.

Waterstone's 7 Dawson St, Dublin 2, tel 679 1415,
website www.waterstones.co.uk
A recent refurbishment has left Waterstone's none the worse for wear, although some of the books must surely have been jettisoned to make room for the Bewley's café on the second floor. Like the group's flagship in London's Piccadilly the branch seems in danger of reducing stock in favour of style. Chairs on every floor are very welcome, as is the more active promotional effort including frequent (free) readings by current authors in the evening.
Open Mon–Fri 09.00–19.00 (Thur 20.30) Sat 09.00–18.30 Sun 12.00–18.00

AND FOR SPECIAL INTERESTS

Books Upstairs 36 College Green, Dublin 2, tel 679 6687,
website www.booksirish.com

A little cramped, but it manages to fit an astonishing variety of books into
the space available, as well as a slew of magazines not available elsewhere, including such worthy titles as *New Left Review*, *Red Pepper* and
The Internationalist. A sizeable secondhand section at the back of the shop is
worth looking at for slightly obscure bargains.

Open Mon–Fri 10.00–19.00 Sat 10.00–18.00 Sun 13.00–18.00

Celtic Bookshop (An Siopa Leabhar) 6 Harcourt St, Dublin 2, tel 478 3814,
e-mail ansiopaleabhar@eircom.net

The only shop in Dublin specialising in Irish language books. It also has a
good stock of Irish interest books in English.

Open Mon–Fri 09.30–17.30 Sat 10.00–16.00 (closed Sat 13.30–14.00)

Forbidden Planet 5–6 Crampton Quay, Dublin 2, tel 671 0688

A branch of the British chain and your first port of call for comics and graphic
novels—and probably also fantasy and science fiction. Although mainstream
bookshops often have respectable collections, Forbidden Planet's goes beyond
respectable and into the realms of the envy-inducing. On top of that, they sell
all the associated merchandise too: T-shirts, videos, DVDs, action figures (lots
and lots of action figures), posters, and even lunch boxes, though one can't help
wondering if the *Xena Warrior Princess* breakfast cereal was going a little bit far.

Open Mon–Sat 10.00–18.00 (Thur 19.00)

Murder Ink 15 Dawson St, Dublin 2, tel 677 7570,
website www.eclipse.ie/murderink/

Mostly detective novels, crime fiction and US thrillers, but will also order and
provide books from the US that are still in print (given two weeks' notice).

Open Mon–Sat 10.00–18.00 (Thur 19.00) Sun 12.30–17.00

SubCity Comics 2 Exchequer St, Dublin 2, tel 677 1902

Although smaller than Forbidden Planet, SubCity is more focused, selling only comics and role-playing supplies rather than trying to cover every possible base. Their stock of back issues is far larger than Forbidden Planet's, though they seem to focus more on conventional comics than the unusual or the offbeat. Still, there's a lot to be found here, and it's just about the only place in Dublin where you can buy role-playing games when there's no convention on.

Open Mon–Wed 09.30–18.30 Thur, Fri 09.30–20.00 Sat 09.00–18.30 Sun 12.00–18.00

Tower Records 6–8 Wicklow St, Dublin 2, tel 671 3250,
website uk.towerrecords.com.

Tower is mostly a record store, and thus not the place to go for mainstream books, although they do have some; but if you wander upstairs, you'll find a handsome selection of weird, unique and off-centre books like *Start Your Own Country*, *Modern Pagans* and *That's Mr Faggot to You*, not to mention music books and graphic novels.

Open Mon–Sat 09.00–21.00 Sun 11.30–19.30

Veritas 7–8 Lr Abbey St, Dublin 1, tel 878 8177, e-mail sales@veritas.ie, website www.veritas.ie

Big stock of new religious books, mostly Catholic.

Open Mon–Fri 09.00–18.00 Sat 09.00–17.30

SECONDHAND AND ANTIQUARIAN

So many shops sell secondhand paperbacks, that unless you think you can catch an obscure disease from a book someone else has read, or you really *need* a new thriller, these are the places to start for ordinary leisure reading. Look for such shops in slightly out-of-the-way, low-rent areas and where charity shops abound. Unfortunately, you are not going to get many bargains in Dublin's antiquarian bookshops. There are too many knowledgeable buyers out there chasing too few books but some of these shops have bargain shelves.

Cathach Books 10 Duke St, Dublin 2, tel 671 8675
Specialises in antiquarian books and is just the place for a first edition of *Ulysses*, but the bargain basement is worth a quick look.

Dandelion Books 74 Aungier St, Dublin 2, tel 478 4759
Stocks 25,000 or more used paperbacks, many of which come (unread) from the reviewers. Literature, thrillers and a good section on history too.
Open Mon–Sat 11.30–18.30 sometimes on a Sunday 14.00–18.30.

Flying Pages (formerly The Rathmines Bookshop) 211 Rathmines Rd, Dublin 6, tel 496 1064
Lots of cheap books here, both secondhand and budget paperbacks. You will have to wade through a lot of dull, obvious, or just plain irrelevant stuff to find the gems, but they are there. Since the previous edition the stock has been cut right back, though, which is disappointing.

Greene's 16 Clare St, Dublin 2, tel 676 2554
Across the road from Oscar Wilde's parental home on the corner of Merrion Square, this shop has been in the same place since 1843, and some of the books upstairs look as if they were part of the original stock.

Market Arcade off Sth Great George's St, Dublin 2
As well as all the other great stuff here, the Arcade has several stalls offering secondhand paperbacks and lots of them.

Oxfam Bookshop 23 Parliament St, Dublin 2, tel 670 7022
A bright, neat and attractive secondhand bookshop, with a good medium sized stock and not dear—not to mention the high feel-good factor.
Open Mon–Fri 09.30–17.30 Sat 10.00–17.00

Secret Book and Record Store Wicklow St, Dublin 2
Too secret to have a telephone number, this shop is approached down a dim corridor that in any other European city would be the gateway to some serious erotic shenanigans. It has a small but consistently interesting stock. Because they sell secondhand records as well as books, the music is interesting too.

Stokes Books Market Arcade, Sth Great George's St, Dublin 2, tel 671 3584
Here you'll find beautifully cared-for stock, always with some interesting items, mainly Irish interest, but also general. €2–€5 bargain barrow trays for those looking for secondhand algebra textbooks and the like. No credit cards.
Open Mon–Sat 11.00–17.30

The Winding Stair 40 Ormond Quay, Dublin 1, tel 873 3292
Combines a bookshop (20,000 volumes on three floors) and a coffee shop with good value lunches and views of the Liffey.
Open Mon–Sat 09.30–18.00 Sun 13.00–18.00

Due to open after we go to press are the **Grattan Bridge bookstalls** on the specially widened pavement on Grattan Bridge (which runs between Parliament St and Capel St). This looks as though it will be a welcome new development.

Every so often **Dublin Bookbrowsers** (dave@dubbookbrowsers.com or 087 263 6347) have a monster sale with discounts on books under €10 of up to 80 per cent. Worth catching if you happen to be in town while it's on. The venue changes so check the website. Bookbrowsers also hold a book auction in **Herman Wilkinson** of Rathmines, Dublin 6, tel 497 2245, once a quarter.

OUT OF TOWN
Carraig Books 73 Main St, Blackrock, Co. Dublin, tel 288 2575, opposite the public library (just ask anyone) has a very large selection of literature and old-style lit crit; also a whole wall of religious books. If you're making a day of

it, the weekend **Blackrock Market** off the Main Street has a couple of bookstalls, and for new books **Bookstop,** tel 283 2193, in the shopping centre is worth a visit.

• •

More tips for saving money

■ Haggle. This won't cut much ice in big chainstores unless the product in question is damaged, but smaller places are often quite willing to take a few euro off the price if you ask nicely.

■ Always check out the more expensive clothes shops during Sales and watch out for and always browse through sales racks in *all* shops. Real bargains live here.

■ If you have a student card, use it.

■ Walk the extra mile: Dublin is not an especially big city and the centre is highly concentrated. Unless you live in the outer suburbs or plan to visit them often, it shouldn't be necessary to use buses all the time. And since Ireland has the lowest crime rate in the EU, it's safe to walk the streets—no matter what the papers say.

■ Shop in out-of-the-way places. You will waste a lot of money if you spend it all on Grafton St. As a rule, side streets are cheaper than main streets, the northside is cheaper than the southside and market stalls are cheaper than shops.

■ Do research. Given student discounts and the rising price of alcohol, it can be cheaper to spend your evening at the theatre than in a nightclub. Some clubs are free in before a certain time, some offer discounts to students, some wouldn't let students in if they had a million euro in their pockets. Consulting the relevant magazines can save you a lot of hassle.

Music

There's plenty of music available in Dublin, from traditional to hip-hop, in outlets ranging from warehouse-like chain stores to cramped little basement rooms filled with bootlegged tapes. It's all there if you know where to look. As a general rule, larger stores tend to remain open longer than their smaller counterparts, the latter usually opening between 10.00 and 18.00.

The chains

The major music stores in Dublin are **HMV**, **Virgin** and **Tower**, which all have huge ranges of music, videos, DVDs, books and games, and **Golden Discs**, an Irish-owned chain, hard to miss in the city centre as there are seven branches, including Discount Music (see below).

Discount Music ILAC Centre, Henry St, Dublin 1, tel 872 9245
Owned by Golden Discs, this is probably the cheapest new music store in Dublin city centre.

Golden Disks website www.goldendiscs.ie
1&2 Grafton Arcade, Grafton St, Dublin 2, tel 677 1025, 679 2118
Jervis Centre, Dublin 1, tel 878 1063
31 Mary St, Dublin 1, tel 872 4211
8 North Earl St, Dublin 1, tel 874 0417
St Stephen's Green Shopping Centre, Dublin 2, tel 478 2918
Golden Disks concentrates on mainstream and chart music, with a decent enough choice in its Irish section.

HMV

65 Grafton St, Dublin 2, tel 6795334
18 Henry St, Dublin 1, tel 872 2095
Grafton St is the bigger of the two Dublin stores, and has a lot of staff who know their music and aren't shy about recommending anything. They also

have a ticket office (where a booking fee of roughly 10 per cent of the ticket price almost always applies). It's extremely well organised, with every artist and band catalogued alphabetically to help you find what you're looking for. It also has a good selection of music accessories like carrying cases and headphones.

Tower Records

Easons (second floor), 40 O'Connell St, Dublin 1, tel 878 6680
16 Wicklow St, Dublin 2, tel 671 2603

The Wicklow St branch is good if you're interested in picking up unusual mixes and imports, but at a hefty cost. It wouldn't be unusual to find an imported CD single in Tower for €15. It's open late except on Sundays, and has a free monthly magazine *Top*, which is as well-written as any paid publication. It's the kind of store where practically every time you visit there's something unusual playing which you'd like to know more about. The staff are also well informed, and for the most part, helpful. Tower has an excellent range of film and music magazines and books as well, but is consistently more expensive than every other music store in Dublin city centre so you have been warned.

Virgin Records

14–18 Aston Quay, Dublin 2, tel 677 7361
22–23 Henry St, Dublin 1, tel 873 3855

The Aston Quay shop is a lot bigger than its counterpart on Henry St. It's often worth having a look at the left hand wall, just inside the door along the escalator, as this is where special deals are usually displayed. Virgin has a massive range of films on video and DVD, and an equally impressive range of computer games, music, T-shirts, cartoon and cult books.

Irish music

If you've been in a pub and heard Irish ballads you'd to like to hear again, try the following specialist stores.

Celtic Note 12 Nassau St, Dublin 2, tel 670 4157
Sells Irish and Irish-related music and is worth checking out to find a less mainstream selection.

Claddagh Records 2 Cecilia St, Temple Bar, Dublin 2, tel 677 0262
It also sells blues, country and world music.

Dolphin Discs website www.irelandcd.com
56 Moore St, Dublin 1, tel 872 9998
97A Talbot St, Dublin 1, tel 874 7438
Dolphin has its own record label and sell mainstream as well as Irish music.

Other specialist and secondhand
For real bargains and also for the most interesting selection of music you need to check out the smaller independent shops. When you do you'll realise just how many people sell and exchange CDs, tapes and vinyl to stores. Even more noticeable are the numbers of CDs you come across with a 'promotional only—not for re-sale' sticker on the cover. Dublin either has the biggest proportion of DJs per head of population in the world or the most generous record company executives! In secondhand music stores, only exchange or sell music that you are 100 per cent sure you want to part with, as you won't get a particularly good deal, no matter where you go. It's not unusual to receive only one-third or less of what the store will sell your disc or tape for. Practically every market sells music of some sort—it's pot luck, of course, but worth rummaging through what's on offer—you may find just what you've been looking for.

Abbey Discs 19 Liffey St, Dublin 1, tel 873 3733
An excellent shop for dance, hip-hop and related music.

Borderline 17 Temple Bar, Dublin 2, tel 679 9097
Being in Temple Bar, Borderline's prices are slightly higher than average but it does have a large selection of new, used and rare indie and dance music.

Chapters 108–109 Middle Abbey St, Dublin 1, tel 873 0484
A very organised shop, with a large selection of mainstream new and secondhand CDs, tapes, LPs and books. It's never worth exchanging anything here—you'll rarely get more than one CD in return for three or four.

Comet 5 Cope St, Dublin 2, tel 671 8592
Comet has Temple Bar prices but a great range of both new and secondhand indie and dance music.

Final Vinyl, 40A Camden St, Dublin 2, tel 475 8826
Good range of secondhand CDs and LPs.

Freebird Records Eden Quay, (downstairs in Bus Stop newsagents) Dublin 1, tel 873 1250
Freebird sell, buy and exchange tapes, vinyl and CDs at very reasonable prices e.g. secondhand CD albums at no more than €10, secondhand CD singles for 75c–€1 (kept on the main counter in boxes). Also excellent for compilations, dance and indie music, vinyl, flyers for gigs and nightclubs, and they stock *The Event Guide*.

Market Arcade Sth Great George's St, Dublin 2
There are two outlets here, a shop and a stall, which usually have a good range of secondhand vinyl and CDs.

Mojo Records 4 Merchants Arch, Temple Bar, Dublin 2, tel 672 7905
Mojo buy, sell and exchange videos, DVDs, CDs and records.

Record Collector 30 Wicklow St, Dublin 2, tel 679 1909
A basement shop with lots of interesting CDs, vinyl, tapes and videos.

Rhythm Records 1 Aston Quay, Dublin 2, tel 671 9594
Secondhand and rare discs.

Road Records 16B Fade Street, Dublin 2, tel 671 7340,
website www.roadrecs.com
Road Records specialises in indie, electronic and reggae as well as vinyl, CDs
and 7" singles. It also sells concert tickets.

Markets are great places to browse and bargain-hunt with their mixture of 'tat and treasure (and it's in the eye of the beholder after all).

Blackberry Market Rathmines Rd (near the Church), Rathmines, Dublin 6
Sells mainly secondhand (and some new) furniture, bric à brac, secondhand and new clothes, secondhand books, videos, LPs, CDs etc
Open Sat, Sun 11.00–18.00

Blackrock Market 19A Main St, Blackrock, Co. Dublin, tel 283 3522
More upmarket than Blackberry Market with a wider range of stalls including jewellery, clothes, furniture, books, pottery, bric à brac, hot doughnuts, café etc.
Open Sat 11.00–17.30 Sun, bank hols 12.00–17.30

Market Arcade Sth Great George's St, Dublin 2
A marvellous place to browse. As well as some very good clothes shops, a wine shop and a secondhand bookshop, it also has numerous stalls selling jewellery, books, CDs, LPs, clothes, coins, delicious food and various other delights.
Open 10.00–18.00 (Thur 19.00)

Mother Redcaps Market Back Lane, Dublin 8
Across from Christ Church Cathedral, it has the usual mix of stalls and offerings including food.
Open Fri, Sat and Sun 10.00–17.00

Secret Book and Record Store Wicklow St, Dublin 2
Wide range of interesting vinyl and CDs.

Sound Cellar 47 Nassau St, Dublin 2, tel 677 1940
Country, rock and metal. Sound Cellar also sell concert tickets and have comprehensive listings for upcoming music events.

Trinity Records 14 Trinity St, Dublin 2, tel 670 7951
Reasonably priced new and secondhand music, with a particularly good range of jazz and blues.

Shoppers on Grafton Street.

Haircuts and beauty treatments

Getting your hair cut or coloured, or having a facial or massage, are little luxuries that are still affordable if you're prepared to be looked after by a student, and aren't in too much of a hurry. Try the following **beauty colleges:**

Aspens Beauty College 83 Lr Camden St, Dublin 2, tel 475 1940
All the usual treatments (body wraps, massage, waxing, facials, manicure etc) for up to 50 per cent discount, depending on what you want to have have done. No appointments necessary.
Open Mon–Fri 08.00–20.00 Sat 08.00–18.00 Sun 12.00–17.00

Galligan Beauty College 109 Grafton St, Dublin 2, tel 670 3933
Full range of salon treatments available with discounts of around 50 per cent. Appointments necessary.
Open Mon–Thur 09.30–16.30, 18.00–21.00 Fri 09.30–16.30 Sat 09.30–17.00 Sun 09.30–17.00

All student sessions at the **hairdressing colleges and salons** below are fully supervised and models (that's you!) are fully consulted about the styles used.

You can have your hair cut and blow-dried at any **Peter Mark salon** or one of their training centres by a student for just €10. Colour costs €20 for a semi, €20.95 for a tint, €29.90 for bag highlight, €48.95 for meche highlights—all these prices include a cut, shampoo and blowdry. Chaps can have their hair cut for €7.50. These services are available at all Peter Mark salons from 18.00 on Mon, Tues and Wed and for longer hours in the training centres. It's best to make an appointment in advance as—not surprisingly—these sessions are extremely popular. Toni & Guy offer a similar service with supervised cutting and colouring available to anyone who is willing to try a new look or have a change of style. Appointments are necessary.

Peter Mark Salons 7 city centre locations; branches also in the suburbs
Peter Mark Academy Level 3, St Stephen's Green Centre, Dublin 2, tel 475 1126
Peter Mark Training Centre 18 Nth Earl St, Dublin 1, tel 874 3495

Toni & Guy Academy 44 Clarendon St, Dublin 2, tel 670 8749 (answer service)
Open Mon, Tues, Wed, Fri 10.00–12.30 13.30–18.00 Thur 09.00–11.30 12.30–17.00

Apart from the college routes, it is generally cheaper to have hair cuts and beauty treatments in the suburbs than in the city centre so if you live or work outside Dublin 1, 2 or 4, always look locally first for the best deals and you might find an enormous difference in price.

For specialist **African hair styling**, there is not a lot of choice in Dublin yet, despite the recent surge in demand. Other than **Absolute Hair** (below), the best advice is to ask for a recommendation in your local salon or at any reputable high street hairdressers. When having any major treatment like hair extensions, make sure also to check that the stylist is properly qualified and experienced before you arrange an appointment.

Absolute Hair 44a Sth Richmond St, Dublin 2, tel 478 0968
This is the only place to go if you are looking for a girly hair treat. The shop sells the most wonderful range of hair accessories from as little as €6.65. You can browse here at your leisure for beautiful ornaments or book yourself in for **hair extensions or hair relaxing** treatments with a qualified specialist stylist. On request, they will also do other Afro hair styling and they sell a range of products for black/curly hair. Hair styling is by appointment only.
Open Mon–Sat 10.00–17.00

For sharp new men's' looks or a more traditionally masculine beauty treat which won't cost the earth, there is great value to be had in Dublin's many **barber shops**. Some of the best deals in central locations are as follows:

Regent Barbers 2 Lr Fownes St, Dublin 2, tel 677 8719
Even in Temple Bar, you can get a good basic hair cut for very little money. Regent Barbers charge €10–11 for a cut.
Open Mon–Sat 09.00–18.00

Sam's Barbers 5 Dame Ct, Dublin 2, tel 679 5788
Branches in Dorset St, Park SC in Prussia St, Blanchardstown and Cabinteely. The student's favourite (as much because it is conveniently located opposite the Stag's Head Bar as for its ultra-low price deals). Dry cuts €4.50 Mon, Tues €7.50 Wed–Sat; wash and cut €11.50.
Open Mon–Sat 09.30–17.30

The Trinity Barber 9a Trinity St, Dublin 2, tel 679 3595
For a more traditional approach, try this establishment also favoured among the local student and business community. They do a wash and cut for €12.95 and a traditional hot towel shave for €14.95.
Open Mon–Sat 08.00–6.30 (Thur 20.00) Sun 12.30–17.30

Food, wine and serious beer

Eating out is very good fun but can be extremely expensive. More often than not, the best way to eat good food on a budget is to cook for yourself. But where do you go? What do you buy?

In this section, we hope to let you in on some of the secrets to food shopping in Dublin and give you the cheapest and best options for where to get the kind of food you need. We have listed the less expensive shops for buying basic ingredients, but with food you very often have to buy things that are by their nature dearer than you would like. This means that, occasionally, we will have to direct you to some of the most enticing and best-smelling shops in the city; we know temptation, and we know how hard it is to go into Magill's or Sheridan's Cheesemongers and not come out loaded down with goodies, so here are a couple of tips to keep you in good financial health:

- When you go shopping in cheap markets do not go with fixed ideas: buy what looks good and is on offer or in season. *However*, when you are going into the posh expensive shops know exactly what it is you want to buy, and buy only that. If you are browsing, then do that on one occasion, and return on another to actually buy.
- Eat before you shop. If you shop on an empty stomach in tempting places, the smells will be too much to bear, the sights too much of a delight, and your bank balance will be the loser. The trick is to buy small—impossible when ravenous.
- Make sure you don't go in with much more money than you want to spend—again, temptation inside the shop will turn to remorse as soon as you hit the pavement.

Keep to these rules and you will survive some of the best shops, bank balance intact.

KITCHEN EQUIPMENT
Setting up a kitchen can be a very expensive business and although some accommodation comes complete with lots of equipment provided, it can often be completely bare. If you are looking for pots and pans and utensils, the most reliable budget outlet is **Roches Stores** (in the ILAC centre off Henry St, Dublin 1, tel 873 0044). Everything you need is here at reasonable, though not very cheap, prices; most importantly, this store is reliable and comprehensive. You could also try the kitchenware departments of the bigger branches of **Dunnes Stores**.

SUPERMARKETS

Most of the food bought in the city is purchased in supermarkets—by no means the cheapest option when buying fresh food and raw ingredients. However, they are useful for staples of the larder such as pasta, rice, tinned food, cereals, dairy produce, sauces, condiments and so on. Basically, anything that is not specialist food or raw materials (vegetables, meat or fish) should be bought at these stores.

The main supermarket chains are Dunnes Stores, Superquinn and Tesco. Usually, suburban areas have only one supermarket, and you just shop in the one nearest to you. However, in the city centre there are several and two of the main ones are: Dunnes, in the St Stephen's Green Centre, Dublin 2—more expensive than the usual budget Dunnes but not cripplingly so; and Tesco, in the Jervis Centre, Dublin 1—bigger than Dunnes with more variety and better prices.

Also in the city centre is Marks and Spencer (Grafton St, Dublin 2, and Henry St, Dublin 1) which is trying to break into the supermarket scene, prepared foods here are fantastic but very pricey; also watch out for prices on their fresh foods.

LOCAL FOOD SHOPS

Most of the main suburbs of Dublin have local food shops—a butcher or two, a fish shop, a bakery and a couple of general stores. These are very convenient places to shop, and can really make you feel a part of the local area. Generally the quality of fresh food is good and prices average but unless you are lucky, you are not likely to be offered an enormous amount of choice if you are looking for something even a little out of the ordinary. For any kind of specialist foods you will have to travel.

MARKETS AND NEARBY SHOPS

While supermarkets are cheaper for many kinds of foods, and local shops the most convenient, by far the cheapest—and in many ways the most fun—

way of buying raw ingredients is to head for the street markets which sell food in the open air at knock-down prices.

Probably the most famous of these is **Moore St**, Dublin 1 (linking Henry St and Parnell St), which is filled with a series of stalls where women sell fruit and vegetables for a fraction of the usual shop or supermarket price. This is not a quaint market for the well-heeled, or a show put on for the tourists, but a working part of life for the Dubliners who shop and work there. The traders sell mainly fruit and vegetables, but there is a fish stall as well as a couple of stalls selling chocolate and sweets at bargain prices. But do be aware that most of the time the food is cheaper here because it is not quite fresh. Your veggies won't keep for long and so need to be eaten up within two or three days and this means a couple of trips per week to stock up. The prices are extraordinary though and, as they often depend on what the traders happen to have in at the time, don't go with a fixed shopping list—be prepared to buy whatever is on offer.

The shops on Moore St and nearby Henry St also offer great value. The butchers, for example, cater more fully for those on a budget often selling the cheaper parts of the animals such as ox tails and tongues, cornered tail ends, rib mince and hearts and livers.

One advantage of shopping on Moore St is that these shops tend to treat you like the local shops do; the service is more comprehensive and personal than in a supermarket. For instance, for a very small charge, or for free, a fish shop will give you fish bones to make good stock for soup or other dishes. Similarly, butcher's shops will give you meat bones. The range of choice is superior to that in supermarkets, and on the northside of the city, the prices are far more attractive.

On the southside, head for Camden St, Dublin 2, where you will find the best variety of food shops anywhere in the city. The main feature here is a vegetable market, much like that on Moore St. The quality, like the prices, is slightly higher than on the northside and the most significant difference is that there are fewer stalls and less produce. Also note that these stalls stand at the side of a major busy road, so any produce you buy should be washed extremely thoroughly before you use it.

There are a couple of vegetable shops on Camden St which, while more expensive than the stalls, are cheaper than the supermarkets. Their produce is very fresh and among the best available. There are many butchers, which like those on Moore St, offer bags of various meats at fixed prices as well as quality fresh meats of all kinds. Shopping in this area has all the quality and charm of local shops with all the convenience and variety of city-centre shopping.

You'd soon get bored, though, if you only shopped in the markets—you need all those little special ingredients to make your dinner just right. Here are some places to shop if you are looking for those special extras—from national cuisines to simply the best food available. We give our top favourites first, followed by other specialists.

A1 Favourites

There are some kinds of food that are **specialist** not because they are from a certain country but just because they are the very best. Even on a budget, do not discount them—you would spend €5 on lunch in a café, go to any of these shops with €5 and you will come out with an absolute little delight that teaches you why it is you love to eat in the first place. These shops will seem expensive: the trick is to buy in them as a replacement for your other food shopping rather than in addition. Shop in these places first (and with discipline) and then just fill in the gaps at the supermarket and the markets.

Magill's, the delicatessen at 14 Clarendon St, Dublin 2, tel 677 3830, is a treasure. The front of the shop has a large cheese counter selling the best cheeses from Ireland and abroad and a meat/deli counter which is packed with huge salamis hanging all around so that you can barely see the shop assistants. Cured meats are available, and a particular delight is the presence of real, meaty, quality sausages made with all kinds of meat, to all sorts of tastes. The back of the shop has shelves stacked to the ceiling with jars and tins of sauces, mixes and tinned ingredients as well as jars of fresh spices. There are fresh nuts, Indian sauces, olives by the bucketful, and so many sorts of goodies it takes several trips to take in.

Market Arcade

Sth Great George's St, Dublin 2 *Open* Mon–Sat 10.00–18.00 (Thur 19.00)

The charming Market Arcade, connecting Sth Great George's St and Drury St, is an old Victorian covered market and is characterised by the wonderful mix of shops and a variety of stalls which run down its centre. It was built in the 1880s as part of the first purpose-built shopping centre in the city and is worth a visit by itself. There are secondhand shops aplenty here and you can also avail of the opportunity to get your nose pierced or have a cup of tea in between ambling up and down through the market.

The **Big Cheese Company**, St Andrew's Lane, Dublin 2, 671 1399, is a shop which is very hard to leave empty handed. A slick spacious metal-sheened emporium of culinary treats, it sells far more than cheese. It seems to have been designed as your one-stop, quality food-buying experience. Its stock ranges from Italian pastas, oils, sauces and meats, American cookies and pudding mixes to fresh herbs, wine and, of course, cheese. All these things are available at other shops but the sheer excitement of seeing it all under one roof is hard to discount. The distinctive aspects of the shop are its young friendly staff, its very wide range of cooked and cured meats, and its own range of jams, relishes, pickles and sauces.

The cheese selection at The Big Cheese Company is astounding, but—cheese-wise—nothing can beat the dedicated brilliance of **Sheridan's Cheesemongers**, of Sth Anne St, Dublin 2, tel 679 3143. Walking in, you are struck immediately by the lack of fridges—the staff are politely dismissive of all the other shops which refrigerate their cheese. Delightful and super-helpful staff will talk cheese to you all day; they not only know their cheese, they know each individual batch. Amazingly, they can tell you the taste difference between one block and the block they had last week because of the different grass the cows ate. The shop also stocks unpasteurized cheeses—a rare enough occurrence—and the stronger, fuller taste is highly recommended. They look after the cheese and know intimately all of the eighty or so cheeses they have in stock at any given time. An absolute must.

The Temple Bar Food Market, held on Sat, began as a slightly twee project, an experiment in unusual foods at a time when they were still unusual. But now that quality international eating has entered mainstream Irish cuisine, the market offers an opportunity not to marvel at the Mexican, Japanese, Spanish or Belgian food on offer, but simply to enjoy it in a congenial and informal atmosphere. Eating here is like being at a jumble sale of food, flitting from stall to stall, paying for small amounts of this or that and cramming it into a taste-sated mouth. The natural yoghurts, organic vegetables and raw meats are excellent take-home reminders of a gluttonous hour or two. The food is not cheap, but it is very, very good.

African and Afro-Caribbean

The major recent addition to the culinary landscape of Dublin is the arrival of African food. Along with the rise in the African population, there has been an increased availability of African cooking ingredients. The centres of African shopping are Moore St and Parnell St, both in Dublin 1.

The **Indoor Open Market** on Moore St houses not only a reggae record shop and Chinese café, but a small African food shop. A couple of doors down is **Joyceanne**, tel 872 4140, specialists in Afro-Caribbean cosmetics and foods. On Parnell St, **Tropical Afro-European Beauty & Food Store** tel 878 3199, sells African spices, herbs, meats, vegetables and fruit, such as plantains yam, cassava, fufu and gari as well as dried vegetables and many other exotic morsels, all imported from Africa via Britain. It also sells beauty products and videos. **Infinity Ventures**, also on Parnell St, sells a similar range of products.

Chinese

Stuck slap bang in the middle of town is the fabulous **Oriental Emporium** at 25 Sth Great George's St, Dublin 2, tel 677 8985. To get real value out of this shop, you need to buy in bulk the way caterers do. However, if you can contain your spending impulse to a few items per trip, you can grab a handful of things which will make all the difference. This shop sells everything from pickled lettuce to tinned fish, fresh Chinese vegetables to fresh spices, salted egg yokes to rice noodles and dried vegetables to Chinese sausages. It has a wide range of sauces, pickles and flavourings—in short, everything you need for a Chinese feast. It even stocks Chinese newspapers and crockery and also a wide range of ingredients, sauces and preparations for Indian food. Definitely a must, but watch the prices.

Halal

The **Asian Food Store** at 34 Lr Clanbrassil St, Dublin 8, and **Al Tayibat** at 11 Camden St, Dublin 2 sell halal meats as well as spices, vegetables, industrial-sized sacks of rice and massive tins of olives; you will also find pickled mangoes, chick peas, hummus, curry pastes, lentils and much more. **Teko and Sons** of Sth Richmond St, Dublin 6, **The Islamic Centre** at 163 Sth Circular Rd, Dublin 8, tel 453 3242 and **The Islamic Cultural Centre** at 19 Roebuck Rd, Clonskeagh, Dublin 14, tel 260 3740, also sell halal foods.

Indian

Ingredients for Indian dishes are sold in many shops, and the best selections are to be found in the Chinese and Asian establishments listed above. There is one wonderful mystery of a shop, however, again in the Portobello area: on a fork off Sth Richmond St just north of the canal, beside an Indian restaurant is a nameless, addressless shop marked only by its bright red front. In the door, and past the unattended counter, is a ramshackle delight of Indian chefery. Food lies packed up, still in its wholesale crates or stacked neatly on shelves, while spices lie stored in industrial sized tins or in tiny packets. Fresh and unusual vegetables lie in boxes strewn around the shop, and a counter at the back sells meats. This shop is an enigma and a treasure—a hard-to-find must-see of Dublin food shopping.

International

For cuisine of the world under one roof, check out the **Epicurean Food Hall** on Middle Abbey St, Dublin 1. Though not a haven for budget shoppers, it does have international food in stalls and small shops. The bagels sold in It's a Bagel are flown from New York and are unbeatable. The Mexican stand sells all you need to turn your kitchen into a cantina, while another stall sells confectionery and ingredients otherwise available only in the US. There's a wine shop, a patisserie and even an ice cream stall to treat yourself after all that hard work.

Italian

Dunne Crescenzi, on Sth Frederick St (off Nassau St), Dublin 2, tel 677 3815, is the only authentic source of Italian ingredients in the city centre. It is a café and also a shop, and sells proper Italian pasta in all its many forms as well as fresh mozzarella, fresh parmesan, Italian meats, breads and a spectacular array of Italian wines which hog a whole wall of the café. **The Best of Italy** on Dunville Ave in Ranelagh, Dublin 6, is another good stockist of fine Italian food.

Kosher

The Jewish community is dwindling and so are outlets for kosher food. The two Dublin stockists are **The Big Cheese Co.** (see above) in the city centre and the **Supervalu** supermarket, 13 Braemor Rd, Churchtown, Dublin 14, tel 298 4917.

Russian

At 21 Moore St you'll find Alexander Vikayi's **Slavyanskaya Lavka** (Russian delicatessen to you). Don't be put off by the absence of windows, just push through the doors. Inside there are videos in Russian, newspapers and magazines and a fine range of Russian food.

Vegetarian

In the George's St **Market Arcade**, **Mother Redcap's** in Back Lane in Christchurch and the **Powerscourt Townhouse Centre** there are health food stalls and shops which provide everything that is needed for a healthy and nutritious vegetarian diet. These places can be pricey, however, and the most central and comprehensive collection of health foods to be found is at 73 Sth Great George's St, Dublin 2, in **Down To Earth Health Foods,** tel 719 9702. There is everything here to supplement a vegetarian diet: soya and tofu in all shapes and sizes as well as seeds, nuts, dried and prepared fruits, fresh prepared food, nut burgers, lentils, beans, soya beans, honeys, nut roast, vegetarian burger mixes, breads, salt substitutes, vitamins and a massive selection of herbs.

If you're on a really, really tight budget, you could take advantage of retailers by extensive **free sampling** of their food. This is most fun at the Temple Bar Market. However, with less impressive ingredients, but more quantity, the supermarkets can nearly feed you a whole meal at peak times. Get lost in the crowd and eat the sample size portions of cheese, fruit, sausages, desserts and even wine that is on offer. The city-centre stores are less generous than their suburban counterparts, and winners of the most salubrious and plentiful provider of free nosh are Tesco in the Merrion Centre, Dublin 4, and Superquinn in Blackrock. Both have a wealthy local population to impress, they try extra hard—you need not buy a dinner on a Saturday afternoon.

There will be times when you will be caught short, and, thankfully, Dublin has its fair share of **late-night shops**. The two main franchises are Spar and Centra, and you will find one of them on almost every city-centre street corner. You'll pay more though, as these places take advantage of your time of need. However, they do mean that you can get all sorts of groceries at any time of the day or night. While these shops are more expensive, you will be very glad of them when you are stuck.

There will also be times when you are not in any state to cook but are too strapped for a take-away: frozen food is neither particularly healthy nor budget-friendly but it fills a gap and can be got at any supermarket. Pre-prepared meals from Marks and Spencer (at Grafton St and the Jervis Centre) are the easiest and probably the best but are also among the most expensive.

Another option is to look in Dunnes Stores or Tesco for packs of chopped and washed, fresh vegetables which make up the raw materials for soup mixes and various kinds of stir fries. You still have to do the basic cooking, but at least the preparation is out of the way. Pre-prepared vegetables have the advantage of being cheap, and are also fresh ingredients that have not been processed or had chemicals added, which would suit the more health-conscious cook.

But it really doesn't take long to boil some spaghetti, toss it in a little olive oil with freshly ground black pepper and chopped garlic and sprinkle on some freshly grated Parmesan. With a crisp green salad, some crusty bread and your Chilean red for €7–8, who could ask for more?

The best (and cheapest) of wine

Winelovers in Ireland have to put up with high prices because of heavy taxes. However, it is possible to find good-value tasty wines, and if you can buy a few bottles at a time there are often special offers (money off if you buy two, 7 bottles for the price of 6 etc.) available at some chains, especially O'Briens, Dunnes Stores and Tescos. Your best bet is to get hold of the latest edition of *The Wine Guide—The Best of Wine in Ireland* (available from bookshops and many wine merchants and off-licences, who will often have a shop copy for reference). It gives tasting notes on over 1,000 wines available in Ireland; the wines are listed by price so just decide what you are prepared to pay and proceed from there. (*Shoestring* readers who would like to buy a copy for half-price should contact the publishers at afarman@iol.ie or tel 496 3625.)

Where to get serious beer

As everyone knows, beer is often much better than wine with Indian and other Asian cuisines, and in recognition of that there is a growing interest in upmarket beers and ales. Most off-licences have a small stock, but for the real specialist array in the northside you need to go to the Beer Off-licence of the Year 2002, **McHugh's Off-Licence**, Kilbarrack Road, Dublin 5, tel 839 4692, (between Raheny and Sutton just 200 yards off the coast road), which stocks 100+ fancy beers, with a strong presence of German (including three versions of the popular Erdinger Weisbeir at €2.40 per 500ml), Belgian and Czech. They also have an interestingly rotating selection of English ales including the personal favourite Bishop's Finger from Sheperd Neame in Kent.

The southside alternative is **Redmonds** of 25 Ranelagh, Dublin 6, tel 497 1739, just by the Angle. Redmonds actually have a larger array than McHughs, with as many as 150 different beers and ales, including very upmarket jobs designed to be laid down like wines (try the Oude Geuze Boon Mariage Parfait, €4.35 per 500ml, which the brewers say will continue to improve in the bottle until 2020). As well as a fine range of British ales and Continental beers, Redmonds have popular lines in Australian beers, including down-under favourite Carlton Gold (€2.90 per 375ml).

TOURIST OFFICES IN THE CITY

Dublin Tourism Centre: Suffolk St, Dublin 2

Open June–Sept: Mon–Sat, 09.00–17.30, Jul–Aug: Mon–Sat, 08.30–18.30, Sun, 10.30–15.00.

O'Connell St, Dublin 1

Open Mon–Sat, 09.00–17.00 (closed 13.30–14.00)

Baggot St Bridge, Dublin 2

Open Mon–Fri, 09.30–17.00 (closed 12.00–12.30)

Arrivals Hall, Dublin Airport

Open June–Sept: Mon–Sun, 08.00–22.00, Jul–Aug: Mon–Sun, 08.00–22.30

Dún Laoghaire Ferry Terminal

Open Mon–Sat, 10.00–18.00

The Square, Tallaght, Dublin 24

Open Mon–Sat, 09.30–17.00 (closed 12.00–12.30)

Internet access

Getting internet access in Dublin is not difficult, even if you don't have a computer of your own. For brief sessions, there are any number of coin-operated terminals scattered around the city (for example, they can be found in many post offices, in the ILAC Shopping Centre, in the hall of Trinity College's arts block, in Chartbusters video rental stores, and many other places) though it's probably not a good idea to use them for more than about twenty minutes, since minute-for-minute their rates are positively extortionate compared to proper internet access centres, and too much standing around can get uncomfortable. Not to mention that most cybercafés offer services like printing, CD-writing, access to scanners and fax lines, LAN games . . . all without charging an arm and a leg for the basic service of e-mail and Web access.

Absolutely free access can be got at any public library, provided you're a member and can book in advance (sometimes as much as two days in advance, sometimes as little as one hour). Your time online will be limited, however, as there are plenty of others in the queue. See page 213 for more about public libraries.

The internet cafés and access centres named below all provide at least the basics of internet access and the use of black and white printers; additional services (including food and drinks) are listed explicitly.

Central Cybercafé 6 Grafton St, Dublin 2, tel 677 8298,
website www.centralcafe.ie
Owned by the same people who run Global Internet Café (see below).
Scanning, fax, CD-writing, café
Open Mon–Fri 08.00–23.00 Sat 10.00–20.00 Sun 10.00–20.00
Rates €6 per hour non-member €5 student €3 member

Does Not Compute website www.doesnotcompute.ie
Scanning, fax, CD-writing, photocopying, games, webcams.
Branches at:

> The Bleeding Horse pub (upper floor), 25 Upr Camden St, Dublin 2, tel 476 4928
>
> *Open* Mon–Wed 10.00–23.00 Thur 10.00–01.30 Fri 10.00–02.30 Sat 12.00–02.30 Sun 12.00–23.00
>
> *Rates* from €2.60 per hour
>
> Unit 2, Pudding Row, Essex St West, Dublin 2, tel 670 4464
>
> *Open* 24 hours
>
> *Rates* from €2.60 an hour. Special rates for night-time users

Esat Access Centre Upr Fownes St, Dublin 2, tel 670 4743
Open Mon–Fri 08.00–22.00 Sat–Sun 11.00–21.00
Rates €1.50 per 30 min €3.00 per 60 min €4.00 per 90 min €5.00 per 120 min

Global Internet Café 8 Lr O'Connell St, Dublin 1, tel 878 0295
website www.globalcafe.ie
Owned by the same people who run Central Cybercafé. Scanning, fax, CD-writing; café.
Open Mon–Fri 08.00–23.00 Sat 09.00–23.00 Sun–10.00–23.00
Rates €6 per hour non-member €5 student €3 member

Nethouse www.nethousecafes.com
Scanning, fax, photocopying, webcams, DVD drives, games, phones, training.
Open 24 hours
Branches at:

> 9 Lord Edward St, Dublin 2, tel 679 0977
>
> *Rates* €1.60 per 15 min non-member €1.30 per 15 min student €5.00 per hour student €1.30 per 15 min €3.80 per hour member

43–44 Wellington Quay, Dublin 2, tel 677 1301
Rates €1.59 per 15 min non-member €1.27 per 15 min student/member
113 Lr Rathmines Rd, Rathmines, Dublin 6, tel 496 0261
Rates €1.59 per 15 min non-member €1.27 per 15 min student/member
31–33 The Triangle, Ranelagh, Dublin 6, tel 491 1199
Rates €1.59 per 15 min, €6.35 per hour non-member €1.27 per 15 min student/member
28 Upr George's St, Dún Laoghaire, Co. Dublin, tel 230 3085
Rates €1.59 per 15 min non-member €1.27 per 15 min student/member

Planet Cybercafé 13 St Andrew St, Dublin 2, tel 679 0583
website www.irelands-web.ie/café
Scanning, fax, photocopier, Asian language stations.
Open Mon–Wed 08.00–22.00 Thur–Fri 08.00–23.00 Sat–Sun 10.00–22.00
Rates 5c/min 10.00–00.00 10c/min 12.00–19.00 8c/min 19.00–close
Minimum €1.27 for internet sessions.

Right-Click 70 Lr Camden St, Dublin 2, tel 475 9681,
website www.rightclickireland.com
Scanning, fax, CD-writing, webcams, games
Open Mon–Sun 10.00–22.30
Rates from €2.50 per hour

How to find a pub in Dublin

Dublin's life can be measured by its pubs. There are actually over six hundred in the city, and as James Joyce's Leopold Bloom famously said, it would be a fine puzzle to cross Dublin without passing at least one. Recently the streets of the capital have been invaded by new, sleek, out-of-the-box, hip drinking stations trying to express the changes in the nature of the city through interior design and *über*-strict door policies.

Old, quiet pubs still abound, the old pubs where much that is funny, or tragic, or historic in Dublin life has taken place. The literary pubs, the journalists' pubs and the barristers' bars can still be found, and variety is the spice of boozing. However, more than ever, discretion is required: gone are the days when it used to be possible to pop into pretty much any pub and have a quiet pint.

In this edition we have provided a brief guide to the best of the old and the new—those places where the atmosphere is not too painfully, vainly hip, or those where that's the case, but it is a source of entertainment rather than embarrassment.

Drinking

Mostly, pubs sell beer—stout, lager and ale—and spirits. Wine is available in quarter bottles, and the choice is slowly getting better. Stout—Guinness, Murphys, Beamish—is the cheapest drink, and the traditional Irish tipple. Don't expect to get your stout straight away; it is poured, left to settle for a few minutes, and then topped up. You could take a seat while your pint is being poured and keep an eye on the bar for when your pint is ready. Pints are the usual quantity for beer, and a half pint is referred to as a 'glass'.

You order drinks at the bar and pay for them when you get them (many pubs, particularly suburban ones, however, have table service). Sometimes a group of people buy drinks in 'rounds', where each person in turn buys a round of drinks for everyone. If you get into this, you have three choices: either make your excuses and leave after the first drink, team up with one other person and take turns buying each other's drinks, or be prepared to stump up when your turn comes. Failure to buy a round is a breach of etiquette and is not forgotten.

A common misconception about pubs in Dublin is that people will automatically talk to you—this is not true, particularly if you're on your own. If you're with a group, your chances of striking up conversations with strangers are dramatically increased. If they are single or students, you may well be invited to a house-party, a normal post-pub activity in Dublin. House-parties are basically spur of the moment affairs, usually decided upon in the wee hours by someone who doesn't own the house you're heading to. It's a great way of meeting people in a new city. Make sure you bring 'take out' (cans or bottles from behind the bar), but for safety's sake don't go alone—without another member of your group.

On a Friday or Saturday night, don't spend all night looking for a pub with free seats: there won't be one. It is usual for drinkers in Dublin to stand quite happily all night long.

Lunch

Not long ago the best you could get in a Dublin pub at lunch-time was a (very) tired sandwich. Now most places will serve at least something, and occasionally something rather good. Of course the quality varies, and the prices are higher than you'd pay elsewhere, but there is little to beat a simple plate of smoked salmon and freshly baked brown bread washed down with a glass or two of Guinness. The popular pubs tend to fill up quickly at lunch-time, so if you can, get your orders in before one o'clock.

Price

The price of drink tends of course to rise—publicans are after all aware that people are unlikely to give up drinking just because of a price hike. The Government recently tried to deal with the problem by enforcing a six-month ban on price raising. However, once the time had elapsed, the prices increased again.

You can quickly judge the price level of any establishment by the price of a pint of Guinness—the law obliges the publican to list his basic prices in a visible place. In the city centre you will generally pay between €3.40 and €3.80 for a pint. Posher districts will always be more expensive than less salubrious areas, but you can expect the prices in any one area to be more or less the same. In the descriptions of our chosen pubs we have included the price of a pint of Guinness.

Most pubs raise their prices after 23.30 (referred to as 'after hours' here). Where only one price is mentioned, the pub doesn't charge extra after hours.

Opening (and more crucially, closing) hours

Until recently Dublin pubs snapped shut at 23.00 (in theory)—the 'last drinks, gentlemen' call was a signal for frantic multiple pint buying. Now licensing hours have been relaxed, and most Dublin pubs open Mon–Wed 10.30–23.30, Thur–Sat 10.30–00.30, Sun 12.30–23.00. On the eve of public holidays opening is extended to 00.30. An increasing number of bars now operate late licences, and nightclubs all over the city open till as late as 04.00, though not always strictly in accordance with their licences.

To facilitate the traditional mad scramble to neck a last slew of booze before closing time, pubs will flash the lights on and off about five minutes before they stop serving for the night. The panic is not so intense now, given the proliferation of late bars, and Irish publicans will usually give you enough time to actually finish the drink they serve you. Where UK publican's are unpleasantly strict about drinking-up time the Irish landlord is more lenient.

Some advice

An increasing number of pubs are adopting a 'no trainers, no football colours, no groups of lads' etc. policy, and enforcing their rules with bouncers. So you'll probably want to avoid these pubs—then you can wear what you like. Pubs with bouncers nearly always charge more—they have to pay the hard men as well as the normal staff—and at 'drinking up' time at the end of the night, sometimes hardly give you time to finish what you're drinking.

Avoid Leeson St, South William St and Clarendon St where a pint will set you back far more than you bargained for, and any bar with a queue outside. There are hundreds of pubs, so why queue for one?

Traditional pubs

The Brazen Head 20 Lower Bridge St, Dublin 8, tel 679 5186
pint of Guinness €3.40
Tucked away west along the quays, this pub claims to be the oldest in Ireland. Bridge St is so called because for hundreds of years it led to the *only* bridge over the Liffey. The owners assert, and nobody seems interested in challenging them, that there has been an inn or pub there since before the Norman invasion of 1172. Obviously none of that survives, but a part of the building

certainly does look extremely old indeed: low ceilings, dark small bar room: take out the TV and you could be in a medieval world. Well, not really, actually: where others have survived, the Brazen Heads who run the pub have not been as assiduous in keeping out the marches of modernisation. So all in all, not an absolute gem, but a useful and interesting place to have a couple of pints, if for no other reason than to say that you were in the very first pub in Ireland.

Open Mon—Wed 11.00—23.30 Thur—Sun 11.00—00.30

Doheny and Nesbitt's Baggot St, Dublin 2 tel 676 2945
pint of Guinness €3.70

From the north east corner of St Stephen's Green runs Baggot St, and at this end of the street you will find a handful of highly traditional pubs, the finest of which is Doheny and Nesbitt's. It is a favourite with politicians, journalists and civil servants from the nearby Department of Finance. A narrow bar and a small back room are decked out in traditional wooden furnishings but in summer it is equally nice to drink outside in the alley. One of the main attractions is the traditional music. Here there is a real session where the number of musicians playing can expand or contract according to who does or does not show up. The only trouble is the number of people this brings into the already small-ish pub. In look, style and atmosphere this is a true Dublin classic.

Open Mon—Wed 10.30—23.30 Thur—Sat 10.30—00.30 Sun 12.00—23.00

Kavanagh's Prospect Square, Glasnevin, Dublin 9
pint of Guinness €3.45

The words 'original' and 'unspoiled' are two of the most abused in the English language and nowhere more so than in pub guides. Yet they apply to Kavanagh's better than to anywhere else in the city of Dublin. Tucked away in a residential close behind Glasnevin cemetery, this is a real hideaway. Walk into the dark of the bar, through a set of swinging cowboy-style doors and you enter the perfect place to put everything on hold for a pint of contemplation.

The interior is decorated in plain, unassuming wooden slats and the furniture is bare and functional and the pints are tasty. This is very much a local pub, filled with people and whole families from the surrounding area, lending it a friendly, familiar atmosphere. In summer, the untended patch of green in the centre of the close is used as an extended beer garden.

There are two fascinating things about Kavanagh's. One is its nick-name, The Gravedigger's, so called because it was the place where the gravediggers at Glasnevin Cemetery would refresh themselves—poking the blade of a spade through the window to have it returned laden with pints of stout. The other extraordinary thing about this establishment is the unique pub game played there. This is like darts but with a child safety-catch. The game is played using a series of hooks on the wall and a number of small rubber rings. The idea is to score points by throwing the rings so they land on the hooks, each of which is worth a different amount. While it can seem a little embarrassing, don't be shy, give it a go or you'll be sorry you missed out.

While this pub is a little out of the way, it is the perfect spot if you are on a trip to the nearby Botanical Gardens or Glasnevin Cemetery (see Green and silent), or if you need to soothe a hoarse throat after an afternoon of Gaelic games at Croke Park, which is relatively nearby.

Open Mon–Sun 12.00–23.30

Keogh's South Anne St, Dublin 2
pint of Guinness €3.50
Keogh's doesn't quite know what to think of itself. The front main bar is a traditional old pub, with a bar, a corridor, a snug and not much else. At the back is what the generous would call a lounge, but which is little more than a fat corridor with tables. Upstairs was recently renovated to become the most

spacious part of the pub, but the decorators did not change the front room much, so that it still resembles granny's sitting room.

With all its confusing personalities, Keogh's remains a favourite with students and young professionals looking for a haven from sleek modern bars in the heart of the shopping district

Mulligan's 8 Poolbeg St, Dublin 2, tel 677 5582
pint of Guinness €3.55
Mulligan's is included here principally because it serves the best pint of Guinness in the city. This is, of course, a totally subjective judgement and a hotly debated point, but the Guinness at Mulligan's is our winner: the white, white head, the ultra-sharp line between white and black, the cool crisp taste, the full flavour . . . A pint at Mulligan's is Guinness as it should be, served in congenial surroundings.

However, Mulligan's has other charms—the bar is a delightful low-ceilinged den of old-style authenticity with a famous back room for private plotting. The two lounges have for years been a source of curious joy in their dilapidated, uncared-for, rough-edged décor. They stood almost as a deliberate statement of unfashionable-ness. In an age when Dublin is being threatened by a *nouveau* chic that is born of booming business, they represented straight-up, old-time scruffy boozing.

A tasteful lick of paint has left the rooms more slickly decked out in deep colours, but this remains a bustling buzzing treat, at its liveliest in the early evening.
Open Mon–Wed 10.30–23.30 Thur–Sat 10.30–00.30 Sun 12.30–23.00

Nancy Hands Bar & Restaurant 30–32 Parkgate St, Dublin 8, tel 677 0149
pint of Guinness €3.40, €3.50 after hours
Ten minutes' walk from the Four Courts down the north side of the River Liffey Nancy Hands is a beautifully ornate bar and lounge, with highly polished

dark wood and a blazing open fire in cold weather. The sandwich board outside will usually tell you if there will be any musicians playing, as well as the specials for the restaurant upstairs. Being slightly off the main city centre drag, it doesn't tend to attract that many tourists, so its patrons are almost exclusively twenty-something locals. It's particularly worth visiting around Christmas time, when the bar and lounge are almost completely decorated in white and silver, with unusual decorative lighting. There are also plenty of seats, a welcome relief if you've just been for a walk in the nearby Phoenix Park.
Open Sun–Thur 10.30–23.30 Fri/Sat 10.30–00.30

The Palace Bar 21 Fleet St, Dublin 2, tel 677 9290
pint of Guinness €3.60
Empty it is tatty and a little bedraggled looking, but like Dublin's best pubs the Palace comes alive when it fills up with the chattering , nattering punters that cram into this small city centre bar at night. With mini-booths along the bar to allow little groups to gather there, making it impossible to order a drink, and a little parlour room at the back for the more sedate groups, the Palace is charm itself, a good traditional pub for a good traditional pint of black.

It also has perhaps Dublin's tallest barman (Brian), who towers above the bar at 6'8'. Upstairs feels like someone's living room, with couch-type seating and a small bar, and is very cosy indeed when the rain (inevitably) lashes down outside. If Shane McGowan is in town, you might see him here.
Open Sun–Wed 11.00–23.30 Thur–Sat 11.00–00.30

Slattery's 62 Upr Grand Canal St, Dublin 2, tel 668 5481
pint of Guinness €3.55
If one is to indulge for a moment in flattery, then it's fair to say that this establishment could easily be described as a kind of southside Kavanagh's. Like The Gravediggers, Slattery's is a local pub situated near to a major sports ground (Lansdowne Rd) and, when there is no rugby or soccer on, is equally

as friendly a place. It's a stranger to the kind of city-centre posing which can make Dublin drinking such a trial. The bare floorboards and modest furniture of the interior can mislead the eye and while Slattery's is not as furiously scrubbed and polished as some other pubs, it is nonetheless an exhibition of fine craftsmanship—from the mirror-festooned bar to the finely worked ceiling.

One of the main attractions of this place is the live Irish music. The sessions are real, not tourist traps, and the quality of musicianship is often superb; you never know exactly what you'll be getting and when, but when it comes it is invariably excellent. A genuine treat, Slattery's staunch rejection of passing trends and floor polish is all the more remarkable considering its proximity to middle-class suburbia. There are fine pints of Guinness to be had here as well.

Open Mon–Wed 12.00–23.30 Thur–Sat 12.00–00.30 Sun 12.00–23.00

The Stag's Head 1 Dame Court, Dublin 2, tel 679 3701
pint of Guinness €3.45, €3.70 after hours
On a quiet Tuesday afternoon go to the Stag's Head with one friend, order two pints and sit in the plush, red leather seating in the heavily-mirrored, oak-clad back room. Say nothing for a couple of minutes, take a long, careful first draw on your pint and breathe. We defy anybody following the above instructions to find a single fault with the world or their situation in it. The back room is positively regal in its appointments and the hush of a quiet afternoon is a greater spur to contemplation than the tourist-crowded cathedrals up the road.

The Stag's Head is such an institution in Dublin that if you walk up Dame St you will find a mosaic embedded right into the pavement pointing you in its direction.

The back room, as described above, is one of the loveliest rooms in the city while the bar is a long, narrow and more functional space, though its roof is particularly notable. Downstairs there is a basement which opens on weekends to deal with the huge crowds.

The Stag's is at its best during the week: deserted in the mid-afternoon or busy at night. At the weekends it is the busiest set of rooms in the world—prepare to be squashed.

The food here is fantastic—plain pub grub impeccably well done. Students and young business people can be seen coming back time and again to join older regulars to line their stomachs for the night ahead.

In short, The Stag's Head is everything a pub should be—a rare find.
Open Mon–Wed 10.30–23.30 Thur–Sun 10.30–00.30

Literary pubs
Davy Byrne's 21 Duke St, Dublin 2, tel 677 5217
pint of Guinness €3.60
Probably the most famous and self conscious Literary Pub, not because it is mentioned any more than others, more because it chooses to make this its primary selling point. However, in its efforts to attract sophisticated literary types it ruins the original atmosphere described most famously in Joyce's *Ulysses*, though it probably still lives up to its moniker there as 'a moral pub'.

It is an art deco creation of 1941 inside, which is fine if you like that kind of thing. They have a full and adventurous menu by pub standards, though pricey, and it is hard to shake the impression that the oysters and stout are there to attract the more well-heeled breed of tourist.

It remains, though, a pub where the first Irish government celebrated independence, where generations of writers and artists have relaxed—a certain breed of history has been lived out here.
Open Mon–Wed 11.00–23.00 Thur, Fri 11.00–00.30 Sat 10.30–00.30 Sun 12.30–23.00

McDaid's 3 Harry St, Dublin 2, tel 679 4395
pint of Guinness €3.70
McDaid's is a wonderful pub, a high-ceilinged, dark pub whose slightly eerie atmosphere is at least partially explained by its original function as the city morgue. Early in the 20th century it was a centre for republican anarchist activity but, in the 1940s and 1950s, it moved seamlessly away from this to become a centre for the more dissolute, and perhaps less-productive, end of the literary scene. It would be possible to blame McDaid's for actually depriving us of literature: if Kavanagh, Behan, Cronin et al. had paid more attention to pen and less to pub, perhaps we would have more to read; then again, it probably wouldn't be half as good. A wild place in the middle of the last century, McDaid's has settled easily into the city-centre respectability of a thriving business, and instead of fights and republican songs, the entertainment is now jazz and blues music upstairs.
Open Mon–Wed 10.00–23.30 Thur–Sat 10.00–00.30 Sun 10.00–23.00

Neary's 1 Chatham St, Dublin 2 tel 677 8596
pint of Guinness €3.60
Neary's, in its proximity to the back door of the Gaiety Theatre, has been a resting place for actors as well as literary types, a haven of bohemia mid-century which, like McDaid's, has quietened down into a fairly regular city centre pub.

The racing fraternity has also had a history here, adding to its decadent past. This was a hostelry where Kavanagh could keep away from Behan, along with John Ryan, another literary figure of the day. A bizarre Neary's fact is that the publican after whom it is named doubled up as the Honorary Consulate to the Republic of Guatemala. Nowadays the original decoration upstairs has gone, but the downstairs retains the original traditional fittings, with the always welcome added extra of a big sofa.
Open Mon–Thur 10.30–23.30 Fri, Sat 10.30–00.30 Sun 12.30–23.00

The New New Things

Gubu 8 Capel St, Dublin 1, tel 874 0710
pint of Guinness €3.40

Sitting snugly on a Capel St corner, Gubu is slick without being smug, cool without being frosty. There is a wide selection of beers available here, including the incomparable Budwar, and the moulded concrete interior décor adds an edgy feel to the warm atmosphere.

Gubu works hard to please—the pool table downstairs and the excellent Sunday afternoon jazz are testament to that. Incidentally 'Gubu' stands for 'grotesque, unbelievable, bizarre and unprecedented'—the then Taoiseach Charlie Haughey's response to the discovery of a murderer in the then Attorney General's apartment.

Open Sun–Wed 16.00–23.30 Thur–Sat 16.00–00.30

Hogan's 35 South Great George's St, Dublin 2, tel 677 5904
pint of Guinness €3.55

Hogan's is the old new pub, one of the very first to cater for a young, hip clientele and is the father and mother of the pub trends that are currently sweeping the city of Dublin. In keeping with that fine pedigree, it is a little more stately and more refined than the brash upstarts listed here. Always dark and always filled with a relaxed rather than frantic crowd, it's the perfect place for the Sunday afternoon wind down. Hogan's is original and, arguably, best.

Open Sun–Wed 10.30–23.30 Thur 10.30–12.30 Fri–Sat 10.30–02.30

Ocean Charlotte Quay Dock, Ringsend, Dublin 4, tel 668 8862
pint of Guinness €3.80

Ocean is an outpost of urban cool in the rapidly regenerating district of Ringsend. The bottom floor of an exclusive high-rise apartments complex, beside the old canal dock, Ocean serves the burgeoning office market that is fast emerging around it so the bar is to be avoided at all costs between 17.30 and 20.00 on week nights.

At quieter times it affords a delicious view of the docks and is a perfect spot for spacious summer pints outside on the cobblestones at the water's edge.

Open Mon–Wed 12.00–23.30 Thur–Sat 12.00–00.30 Sun 12.30–23.00

The Odeon 57 Harcourt St, Dublin 2, tel 478 2088
pint of Guinness €4.00, €4.25 after hours

It is a mark of the utterly fickle nature of the new pub scene in Dublin that, a year or two after being absolutely in, The Odeon is now decidedly old hat. However, compared to some that followed, it is a classic. Housed in a converted railway station, its high ceilings, long main room, slightly separated bar area and relatively sensitive furnishing make it stand out. It also has a nightclub on Friday and Saturday nights, when the bar stays open until 03.00.

It is airy, yet not cavernous, and has a more relaxed atmosphere now that crowds endlessly seeking the new have moved on. A pioneer of showing movies on a Sunday afternoon, The Odeon looks like it will survive novelty and become a welcome fixture in a relatively 'dry' part of town.

Open Mon–Thurs 12.00–23.30, Fri–Sat 12.00–03.00 Sun 12.00–23.30

Pravda 35 Lr Ormond Quay, Dublin 1, tel 874 0091
pint of Guinness €3.55, €3.90 after hours

Pravda is another bar that was once the new thing but has since moved on to carve its own niche. For comfortable pints in relaxed, modern surroundings—during the day or on a quiet week night—Pravda is the perfect spot. Roomy, full of nooks and crannies and filled with a young but not exclusive crowd, this bar has improved now that the new has worn off.

Open Sun–Wed 11.00–23.30 Thur 12.00–00.30 Fri–Sat 12.00–02.30

Spi 3 Eden Quay, Dublin 1, tel 874 6934
pint of Guinness €3.55
Located about 10 seconds from O'Connell Bridge, beside Murphy's Laughter
Lounge comedy club, Spi's crowd can best be described as 'mixed'. There are
trendy types, with perfect hair and clothes, but these mesh effortlessly with a
young student crowd and, during the week, the shirt-and-tie brigade. The
two great things about Spi are its location and its relaxed feel. The lighting,
low and soothing, certainly adds to this. At weekends, though, if you're over
thirty and look it you might feel slightly out-of-place.
Open Sun—Wed 16.00–23.30 Thurs—Sat 16.00–00.30

Spy Powerscourt Centre, Sth William St, Dublin 2, tel 677 0014
pint of Guinness €4
Spy is a spanking new refurbishment of three mid-sized Georgian rooms
which, in themselves, are glorious. The renovation could not be said to be
sensitive to the rooms' original state or purpose, but the clash of old and new
is invigorating.

   Though there is a members' room, the two public rooms are far more
interesting—full of Celtic cub-types showing off their style and drinking
away the tension of being so painfully hip. The free pool table beside the
unisex toilets is a particularly nice touch, though the door policy, predictably,
isn't in any way nice.
Open Tues, Wed 21.00–02.00 Thur, Fri 18.00–03.00 (cocktail hour 18.00–
20.00) Sat 21.00–03.00 Sun 23.00–03.00

Best first pint
The Flowing Tide 9 Lr Abbey St, Dublin 1, tel 8740842
pint of Guinness €3.45
For that very first pint of Dublin Guinness to count, you need to take the
cheaper, Dublin Bus no. 41 from the airport, rather than the airport shuttle.

Get off the bus at the last stop in town on Abbey St, cross the road, and enter The Flowing Tide. Inside, you will discover a cosmopolitan old pub where theatre types vie with gambling machines and the TV for attention, while hard, bitter old men mutter in the corner. More or less right beside the bus stop, and serving a fine pint of stout, this pub has everything you need to prime you for that most crucial cultural experiment: the pub life of Dublin.

Open Mon–Sun 11.30–23.30

Best sports bars

Frazers Bar & Restaurant Upr O'Connell St, Dublin 1, tel 878 7505
pint of Guinness €3.50
If you're reading this during World Cup 2002, or indeed, any soccer competition, get thee to Frazers Bar. Fanatically pro-football (particularly where Ireland, Celtic and most English premiership sides are concerned), it's difficult not to get caught up in the fervour of a big match in this bar. Downstairs is quite open and airy, while upstairs feels very much like a nightclub at 02.00 even in the middle of the day.

Open Mon–Thur 10.00–23.30 Fri–Sun 10.00 til late

Shooters Café Bar & Restaurant Parnell Centre, Parnell St, Dublin 1
tel 872 9633
pint of Guinness €3.65, €3.95 after hours
If Frazers is the place to go for Ireland, English and Scottish premiership games, Shooters is the bar for Spanish and foreign league matches. For a really big Spanish game such as, for example, Real Madrid *v* Barcelona, you may find yourself amongst an almost 100 per cent Spanish crowd. Which isn't a bad thing at all, what with their boisterous enthusiasm and friendly openness. There's also an R'n'B club on Fridays and a Trance club on Saturdays. On weekdays, on production of a student card, at the time of

writing (March 2002) all pints were priced at €2.60, approximately €1 cheaper
than most city centre pubs. When there are no big football matches on,
though, it's usually pretty quiet.
Open Mon–Thur, Sun 10.00–23.30 Fri, Sat 10.00–2.30

Best view of Dublin
Mssrs Maguire 1–2 Burgh Quay, Dublin 2, tel 670 5777
pint of Guinness €3.80, €4.00 after hours
If there's a problem getting a seat in many Dublin pubs, the opposite can be
said for Mssrs Maguire. There are four huge floors filled with them, the best
of which being the very top floor, where you can have a great view of
Dublin from one of the window seats. They also have a more comprehensive selection of beers and lagers than most other Dublin bars. What the
door-staff don't tend to allow, particularly at weekends, are large groups
of males, and they have a strict 'no trainers' policy. If you're part of a large
group of males, split up! Better still, go somewhere else, there's plenty of
choice.
Open Sun–Wed 11.00–23.30 Thur 11.00–02.00 Fri, Sat 11.00–02.30

Best beer bar
The Porterhouse 16 Parliament St, Dublin 2, 679 8847
pint of plain porter—don't ask for Guinness, they don't like it—€3.60
The best beer bar is undoubtedly The Porterhouse. It specialises in beers, be
they bottled, draught or even their very own brews. On several floors, it has a
warm inviting feel to it with its stout wooden benches and seats, and plenty of
human-size nooks and crannies for that intimate twosome. For the beer
aficionado it is really the only show in town. It also has good pub grub, and live
music every night.
Open Mon–Wed 11.30–23.30 Thur 11.30–00.30 Fri–Sat 11.30–02.00 Sun
12.00–23.00

Best cocktail

The Octagon Bar The Clarence Hotel, Wellington Quay, Dublin 2, tel 670 9000
pint of Guinness €3.90

You'll pay for them all right, but the cocktails in The Octagon are lip-smackingly, sense-numbingly gorgeous. Full-bodied with booze and made with skilled care, they are well worth the price tag of just under €10 if you can spare the cash. Despite being in a trendy hotel with one of Dublin's best restaurants in it, and even though it is part-owned by U2, the bar itself is fairly anonymous, but worth the trip for a real martini.
Open Mon–Fri 10.30–23.30 Sat, Sun 12.20–00.30

The smallest bar in Dublin

The Dawson Lounge 25 Dawson St, Dublin 2, tel 677 5909
pint of Guinness €3.30

At the Stephen's Green end of Dawson St, across from the Mansion House, is Dublin's smallest pub, The Dawson Lounge, where a group of ten people constitutes a crowd. Attracting a mixed, but primarily jovial suit-and-tie clientele, it sometimes even holds (difficult to believe considering its size) impromptu jazz sessions. Seating and stools are few, so be prepared to stand, particularly at weekends. Blink and you'll miss it passing by on the street, as its front consists of a narrow doorway with steps leading down to the bar. It does, however, have a sign above the door with a cartoon drawing of a huge crowd packed into a confined space and the words 'Ron Black's Dawson Lounge'. Worth a visit for a pint or two, if only for novelty value.
Open Sun–Wed 12.00–23.30 Thur–Sat 12.00–00.30

And finally

Here are a few OK pubs in the city centre. They won't win any prizes, but they're fine for when you're tired and don't want to walk too far.

The Bachelor Inn 31 Bachelors Walk, Dublin 1, tel 873 1238
pint of Guinness €3.25
Thirty seconds from O'Connell Bridge, this pub is perfectly located to begin or
end a night out in the city centre. Style-wise it's no-nonsense, with a long bar
downstairs and a very small upstairs room. Clientele are predominantly local
and older Dubs, though occasionally a group of trendy young things make
their appearance. The Guinness is great, and reasonably priced too. Just don't
expect perfectly polished tables and chairs.
Open Mon—Thur 11.00—23.30 Fri, Sat 11.00—00.30 Sun 11.00—23.30

Chaplins 1—2 Hawkins St, Dublin 2, tel 677 5225
pint of Guinness €3.50
Another very relaxed bar is Chaplins, across the road from the Screen cinema
and Trinity College. No matter what night it is, you always seem to be able to
get a seat here. Just inside the door, there are very cool 'High King' type chairs
with a high back, where you feel you can survey all those before you. Mid-
week clientele are suit-and-tie office crowds from the surrounding buildings,
while weekends have no particular rhyme or reason to their patronage. Lovely
Guinness too.
Open Sun—Wed 10.00—23.30 Thur—Sat 10.00—00.30

The Foggy Dew, **The Mercantile**, **O'Brien's**, **Isolde's Tower** all on or around
Dame St, Dublin 2, are all thoroughly unremarkable watering holes that could
be Irish themed bars anywhere in the world. They are, though, very handy if
you find yourself out late looking for somewhere to have a drink and don't need
the swankiest spot in town. They have bouncers on the door but don't be
intimidated—their entry requirements are far from strict.

Eating out

The fact that there is not an empty seat at a restaurant table by 19.30 on a Friday or Saturday night in the capital—anywhere, ever—is a measure of how important eating out has become in boom-time Dublin:

Anyone hoping to eat more than fish and chips has to book, though usually not too far in advance—an afternoon call should enable you to get a slot. This booming business means that restaurants are now often quoting a finishing time for your dinner as well as a starting time. While this is a gross presumption, and a mean-spirited liberty, supply and demand dictate that sometimes you may just have to put up with it.

Eating out in Dublin is a noisy, chatty and entertaining business. The variety of food available—to budget diners and extravagant epicureans—is impressive, though quality can vary wildly from place to place. There are, however, some old reliable places and keen, new eateries that, with luck and a little booking, should see you sated and smiling without making you bankrupt.

In the following listing, we have included restaurants where you can have a starter and main course for €20–€25 or under. However, just in case you need to celebrate, or want to push the boat out a little, at the end of the section we have made a couple of suggestions of places to go that are a little more expensive, but are well worth a splurge if you're in the mood.

As you have to eat throughout the day, we have highlighted some of Dublin's best cafés and snack stops for lunch, or all-day grazing. If you're on a tight budget, check the opening hours of these establishments as many of them are open late enough to be possibilities for dinner as well. We have included here places where you can have a plate of food and a cup of coffee for €10 or under, though most places are considerably cheaper than that.

Where a venue is wheelchair accessible we have indicated this; however, not all such places are fully accessible. On page 15 we list some fully accessible venues recommended by wheelchair users.

> *It is surprising how, in public places, perfect strangers will place their hands, almost tenderly, on your shoulder or even on your waist, in order to move you out of their way or after having jostled you. Physical contacts which, in other countries, would be practically shocking, are here nothing out of the ordinary.*
>
> FROM DUBLIN: LE GUIDE AUTREMENT

Lunch and grazing

Belgo 17–19 Sycamore St, Dublin 2 (beside the Olympia Theatre on Dame St) tel 672 7555
Belgo is a noisy, brash, chain restaurant that adopts a policy of getting punters in and out in the fastest possible time in order to get the turnover they want. Good for a fast snack, not so good for a leisurely dinner.

However, its main saving grace is its €8 lunch. A main course, such as pork and onion sausages, or beef braised in Belgian beer with frites, will cost between €11 and €15. Its beer selection, though excellent, can be expensive. A glass of Stella Artois costs €2.50, while a pint costs €4.80. Beers cost an average of €3.50–€5.
Open Mon–Thur 12.30–15.00 17.30–23.00 Fri 12.30–15.00, 17.30–24.00 Sat 12.30–24.00 Sun 12.30–22.00

Burdocks 2 Werburgh St, Dublin 8, tel 454 0306
Burdocks is still the best chip shop in the city centre even though, in recent times, the portions you get are not always consistent in size or standard; the

latter, however, is generally very high. Fresh cod and chips will set you back a steep €6.50, but you won't eat for a week.

Queues, which often extend out the door are a testament to the quality. As the staff can be cheery or rude, there is also a lottery element to the whole escapade.

Open Mon–Sun 12.00–24.00

Café Fresh Powerscourt Centre, Dublin 2, tel 671 9669

Café Fresh is the perfect spot for the health-conscious or for those who really care what they put into their body. Wholefood, health food and food that suits particular dietary requirements are all on offer here without any compromise on taste. Herbal teas and organic salads and vegetarian meals sit side by side with cakes and fruit juice in a mouth-watering haven of health.

The soup is filling at €2.50, and meals and sandwiches are €8 and €4, respectively. A plate of three salads at €6.35 will fill the most hungry visitor, and leave all consciences clear.

Open Mon–Wed, Fri, Sat 09.00–18.00 Thur 09.00–20.00

Café Irie 11 Fownes St, Temple Bar, Dublin 2, tel 672 5090

Café Irie is arguably the best place to eat in Dublin at lunch-time. It offers the most varied, exciting and adventurous choice of sandwiches and its surroundings scream of things hip, young, urban and chic. The music is sublime, the service charming, the walls luminous and the prices brilliant. Another unusual bonus is that among the newspapers available for free reading, there are trashy tabloids as well as the usual broadsheets—a nice detail.

However, the food is the real star here. Much of it is vegetarian and all of it is ultra-healthy with nuts, brie, humus and pastrami, guacamole, chicken, beans and feta cheese all very much to the fore. The range of breads is superb, and the soup changes daily from one delightful concoction to another. Prices are an average of €4.50 for a sandwich, with tasty desserts and, for some reason, a really good cup of tea. They also have a range of coffees priced from €1.50 to €2.50.

Another amazing thing about Café Irie is its breakfast, which will set you back about €4.50. If you are sick of the only eat-out breakfast being a greasy fry-up, come here for cereals, muffins or the very special fruit and yoghurt bowl.

The only trouble, quite genuinely, is getting in the door. They have seating for only twenty to twenty-five people, which means there is no point even trying unless you arrive a little earlier than one o'clock. Just before an hour change (when people are leaving before the next rush) or about 15.00 are generally the best times to try for a seat. A true delight.

Open Mon–Sat 09.00–20.00 Sun 12.00–17.30

Cooke's at the National Museum Collins Barracks, Benburb St, Dublin 7, tel 677 7599

The barracks courtyard is a spectacular architectural setting for this café which is just a bit off the beaten track. Inside its light and airy interior is decorated with stylish pictures of some of the museum's culinary artefacts. During the summer you can enjoy your food outside under the arcades. The café has its own speciality teas and coffees as well as Italian gourmet sandwiches, a hot lunch menu and delicious fresh pastries. Soup is €3.60, salad €8.75 and a hot meal €8.80. Wheelchair access to café and accessible toilets in museum.

Open Tues–Sat 10.00–17.00 Sun 14.00–17.00

Cornucopia 19 Wicklow St, Dublin 2, tel 677 7583

Cornucopia is a city-centre refuge for hungry coeliacs, vegetarians and anyone who cares as much about their body as their tastebuds. A self-service café, it engenders a communal spirit with table sharing a common practice.

Gluten-free cakes are a speciality, while the salads are both exquisite and cheap. Soup and a salad here is no wimp's option—it'll keep you going until the next morning. A large salad is €3.30, though the small portion, at €1.80, along with a bowl of cockle-warming soup at between €1.85 and €2.40, often suffices. The late opening makes it a perfect choice for an informal late snack.

Open Mon–Wed, Fri, Sat 08.30–20.00 Thur 08.30–21.00

The Epicurean Food Hall Middle Abbey St/Liffey St, Dublin 1

The Epicurean Food Hall is such a good idea it should have happened a long time ago. A godsend for shoppers, the Food Hall is the perfect place for a mid-shopping snack. Here, you will find the world's cuisine collected under one roof in stalls and small shops. As it is a mix of cafés and food shops, you can often take home the ingredients of your lunch. The Mexican, Indian and Turkish outlets are particularly fine, but a couple of Italian cafés, a bagel shop and a patisserie complete a very tasty picture.

Prices vary enormously, but are in the café rather than the restaurant range. A complete Mexican meal, for example , can be had for €8.

Open Mon–Sat 10.00–18.00 Thur 10.00–19.00

Nectar

Epicurean Food Hall, Mid Abbey St/Liffey St, Dublin 1

7–9 Exchequer St, Dublin 2, tel 672 7501

56 Ranelagh Village, Dublin 6, tel 491 0934

If you're looking for a healthy pick-me-up or a revitalising hangover cure after a night on the town, Nectar is definitely the place to go. This great Australian juice bar specialises in what they call 'raw juice therapy', which includes such refreshers as their *green cleanser* or their *vita-C flu buster*. Nectar also has a range of delicious smoothies and lassis to choose from, all for around €3.50. Breakfast, lunch and dinner menus are available, though it is quite expensive (breakfast costs about €9). You'll have a choice of a healthy muesli breakfast or coffee and a pastry (for those in need of stronger fortification).

A lunch wrap costs €8–€9, a burger €10, and main courses in the evening are about €15. They call it 'new world' cooking and it's pretty eclectic, with dishes ranging from Italian pasta and Moroccan casserole to Mexican wraps and Irish stew, all made using organic ingredients wherever possible. Early bird and night owl specials in Ranelagh and Exchequer St are particularly good value. The crowd is cool and the décor is sleek but comfortable. Window seats are great for people-watching.

Open Epicurean Food Hall Mon–Sat 12.00–18.00
Exchequer St Mon–Sat 09.30–late. Sun 10.30–late
Ranelagh Village Mon–Sun 10.00–22.30

Panem 21 Lr Ormond Quay, Dublin 1, tel 872 8510
A tiny bakery and coffee bar serving exquisite breads, brioches, pastries and tarts, as well as light lunch dishes to eat in or take away, Panem combines the finest, authentic Italian cooking with top local ingredients. Take your pick from pasta or hot, filled focaccia with salad for €5.80, Mediterranean sandwiches or soups for €3–€4.50, and coffee (imported from Sicily, no less) with a sweet pastry dessert or croissant for €3–€4. Cappucino costs €2 while hot chocolate is €2.60. There are only a few chairs but you can stand at the counter while you eat or, on a fine day, take your snack outside and eat it on a bench on the Liffey boardwalk.

Open Mon–Fri 08.00–17.00 Sat 09.00–17.00

Queen of Tarts 4 Cork Hill, Upr Dame St, Dublin 2 (opp. Dublin Castle), tel 670 7499
Quite simply, Queen of Tarts serves the best pastry ever; this comes in sausage rolls, baked savoury tarts or any number of simply delicious things, all at wonderfully reasonable prices. They also serve the most exquisite home-baked

cakes and buns, along with divine scones. The café is comfortable but very small, making access for wheelchairs difficult, however, at least it is on the ground floor. Delicious sandwiches are €4.85, while the gorgeous sweet slices are €3.75. And if you're really hungry, don't miss the savoury tarts at €7.45—small but powerful and tasty treats.

Whether it is just a coffee or a hearty lunch you want, the staff are very welcoming. The only problem here is resisting the temptation to go overboard on the wickedly delicious cakes.

Open Mon–Fri 07.30–18.00 Sat 09.00–18.00 Sun 10.00–18.00

Soup Dragon 168 Capel St, Dublin 1, tel 872 3277

First there were wine bars, then came juice bars—but a soup bar? Is there no end to the faddish excesses of Dublin's economic boom? Actually, this is a great place, right beside Capel St bridge—handy for both north- and southsiders. It serves about a dozen different soups on a menu that changes daily. Flavour options range from the simplest tomato and basil, or broccoli and blue cheese to full-on chunky chowders and Thai green curry. Great healthy breakfasts too. Soups come in three sizes (topped off with a portion of bread and a piece of fresh fruit) and cost from €4.10 to €5.15 for the vegetarian variety and €5–€6.55 for soup with meat. Coffees are also available from €1.65 to €1.90.

Open Mon–Fri 08.00–17.30 Sat 11.00–17.00

Steps of Rome 1 Chatham St, Dublin 2, tel 670 5630

Steps of Rome is an extraordinary Italian eatery tucked off Grafton St and is Café Irie's only challenger for the best-place-to-lunch award. On any day you will be lucky to hear any language other than Italian spoken by staff or customers here. Often, when the ten or so seats are taken, the tiny space will be crammed with people standing around slugging the best espressos this side of Paris. Funnily enough, it is pretty much impossible to predict when this diminutive delight will be busy or quiet. It is open until 23.00, and it kind of ticks over all day—never empty, rarely full.

The espresso here is simply amazing, a real chewy treat that will have you buzzing all day. There are pizza slices for €3.40, and pasta dishes for between €9 and €10.

The pizza slices are rectangles cut from massive slabs on the counter and re-heated in a pizza oven. They bear very little resemblance to the doughy round things we are used to this side of Europe, so you may be surprised. Everything here is utterly authentic. The pasta dishes are absolutely superb, but don't expect to be stuffed, they are not the biggest portions in the world.

Going into Steps of Rome, having a coffee and a divine pizza slice, will set you back around €5, you could even then throw in a slice of their fabulous cheesecake and still not worry a €10 note. For one of Dublin's finest eating experiences, it is ridiculously cheap.

Open Mon–Sat 10.00–23.00 Sun 12.00–22.00

Trí D 3 Sráid Dásain, Baile Átha Cliath 2 (otherwise 3 Dawson St, Dublin 2), tel 474 1050

Visitors in search of a cultural phenomenon should try this place—Dublin's Irish language café. Staff speak Irish and so do many of the customers but don't worry, they welcome all comers and won't make you feel bad

The Custom House

for ordering in English. Trí D serves great coffee, delicious gourmet sandwiches at €4.30 or afternoon tea for under €8. It has a bright, modern interior and lively ambience, and is one of the few public places in Dublin where you will hear the Irish language spoken in real life.

Open Mon–Fri 10.00–18.30 Thur 10.00–21.00 Sat 09.00–17.00

Restaurants

Bangkok Café 106 Parnell St, Dublin 1, tel 878 6618

Bangkok Café is an idiosyncratic delight—a rough gem situated right at the epicentre of what little multicultural life Dublin has to offer. In a cramped, disused shop, tables and chairs of varying types, some throws and a couple of pictures combine to make a Thai restaurant with no pretension and no airs. It's a cheap and cheerful treat for people who don't mind eventful dining.

The excellent food started off being ridiculously cheap but, as the crowds gathered, the proprietors put up the prices. However, you can still have a starter for €6.50, a main course for €12 and a dessert for €4.50. The tiny bottled beers are pricey, though everything else is cheap and tasty, and the whole experience is as much an entertainment in itself as it is simply going out for dinner.

Open Mon–Sun 17.30–23.00

Chilli Club 1 Anne's Lane, Dublin 2, tel 677 3721

This quirky Thai restaurant (the first in Dublin) offers a set evening menu for €22 per person. and for €14, a substantial three-course lunch. Lunch appetisers like creamy coconut soup, spring rolls or satay of chicken served with peanut sauce, are followed by green and red curries or Pad Thai noodles for main courses. The dining room is tiny and has seen better days but in this part of town there are very few places to beat this at the price. The door is always

kept closed so you have to knock to enter. Very friendly service but no wheelchair access. Also has a great take-away menu.
Open Mon–Sat 12.30–14.30, 18.00–late Sun 18.00–late

Da Pino 38 Parliament St, Temple Bar, Dublin 2, tel 671 9308
If it's no-nonsense, simple and relatively-cheap Italian food you're after, you could do far worse than Da Pino. Located at the far end of Temple Bar, and away from the stag night crowding that blights that area every weekend, Da Pino offers good, simple value.

You'll only have to add a couple of coins to €20 to secure a starter and main course from the traditional Italian menu of pasta, antipasti, pizza and meat dishes. The décor is comfortable, and the atmosphere very informal. You won't suddenly feel transported to Rome, but you will be well filled with good value, quality food.
Open Mon–Sun 12.00–23.30

Ely Wine Bar and Café 22 Ely Place, Dublin 2, tel 676 8986
Ultra-stylish wine bar off St Stephen's Green that serves a huge selection of great-value wines—by the glass and bottle—as well as delicious food. Elegant but relaxed surroundings on two floors of a converted Georgian building that once housed a notorious gay nightclub. Don't be put off if you are offered a table downstairs—it's even nicer than the ground floor and very well air-conditioned. Most dishes on the dinner menu are under €20 and those in the lunch-time list are generally under €10. The food is cooked using top-quality ingredients (organic where possible) in a limited number of simple, mouth-watering combinations to create great accompaniments to the wine.

Modern versions of such traditional staples as Irish stew, bangers and mash or fish cakes are done alongside lighter dishes like smoked salmon pâté with charcoal biscuits or a wonderful duck salad. Although the menu is small,

there is always at least one vegetarian and one seafood option. The brunch menu matches each dish with a selected glass of complementary wine for an all-in price. During quieter times of the day, this is one of the best places in the area to drop in for a coffee.
Open Mon–Sat 12.00–15.00 for brunch Mon–Wed 18.00–22.00 Thur–Sat 18.00–22.30 for dinner

Govinda's 4 Aungier St, Dublin 2, tel 475 0309
Govinda's is a café-style 'pure vegetarian' restaurant serving great vegetarian curries, kebabs and veggie burgers as well as delicious desserts and healthy drinks. Everything here is superb value: €2.25 for a small salad, €4.05–€7.55 home-made vegetarian burgers and main courses at €4.25 for a small plate and €7.55 for a large. Bright, cheerful décor and very relaxed atmosphere.
Open Mon–Sat 12.00–21.00

Il Baccaro Meeting House Sq, off Eustace St, Temple Bar, Dublin 2,
tel 671 4597
Traditional Italian *osteria* serving evening meals and good-value, tapas-style snacks which feature Italian meats, cheeses and olives. Pasta, risotto, meat and poultry dishes are from €9 to €20, and the delicious authentic Italian desserts are available from €3.38. Wine, which comes straight from the barrel, will set you back €18.40 for the house variety. Il Baccaro is perfect for an evening's civilised drinking or a tasty supper accompanied by live music, all in the cosy atmosphere of an underground vault.
Open Mon–Fri 18.00–23.00 Sat 12.00–15.00, 18.00–23.00 Sun 17.30–22.30

Mao 2–3 Chatham Row, Dublin 2 (also at The Pavilion Centre,
Dún Laoghaire), tel 670 4899
Mao is just at the limit of our *Shoestring* guide's price constraint. However, we had to include it because the food—they call it Asian Fusion—is really

rather fab, and the décor is terribly stylish in a magazine-minimalist kind of way. The main courses are very substantial and the chocolate pot has to be tasted to be believed. The menu has an eclectic selection of main dishes, which range from €10 to €17 in price, and the cocktails are just lovely.

That said, Mao is a bit too brash and noisy for a tête-á-tête, and the wine list is a tad overpriced.

Open Mon–Thur 12.00–23.00 Fri,Sat 12.00–23.30 Sun 12.00–22.00

Milano

19 East Essex St, Temple Bar, Dublin 2, tel 6703384

38 Dawson St, Dublin 2, tel 670 7744

38–39 Lr Ormond Quay, Dublin 2, tel 872 0003 (Pasta Di Milano)

Part of the British Pizza Express chain, Milano offers relatively cheap, fast, Italian food that won't trouble Ar Vicoletto (see below), but will fill a hole at short notice. Main course prices range from €7.45 to €10.50. Cheerful, airy design and fast service make Milano the perfect pit stop if you're on the move.

Open Mon–Sat 12.00–24.00 Sun 12.00–23.00

Monty's of Kathmandu 28 Eustace St, Temple Bar, Dublin 2, tel 670 4911

Nepalese cuisine may not be internationally famous, but Monty's of Kathmandu is doing a sterling job of enhancing its reputation—in Dublin, at least. Here, a menu of light curries and spiced kebabs is served up in an informal and fairly basic setting.

Though some of the ingredients and names are the same as in Indian food, Monty's excels in bringing out a host of subtle, intriguing flavours in the cooking. The kebabs burst with flavour, while mild creamy sauces caress the palate. With a starter and main course at €20, it is an affordable taste of a new cuisine. However, because Monty's is not busy at lunch-time and some of the food seems pre-prepared, it is better to eat there in the evening.

Open Mon–Sat 12.00–14.30, 18.00–23.30 Sun 18.00–23.00

Odessa 13 Dame Court, Dublin 2 tel 670 7634

Odessa—a reasonable though somewhat pricey restaurant—comes into its own at the weekend when brunch is the speciality. It's usually best to book well in advance, then you can anticipate the pleasure of it for a few days safe in the knowledge that you have secured a table. The day-long brunch has been much copied but this is where it originated—in Dublin anyway. Eggs Benedict at €8.95 and all sorts of other eggy dishes are only an excuse to lounge around with the papers, watching the slightly glam set recover from the night before. The average dinner main course price will set you back about €12.

Though your own aim might be recovery, surrendering to temptation with Bloody Marys—or more—from the bar is sheer, wicked pleasure.

Open Sat–Sun 11.30–16.30 for brunch Mon–Fri 18.00–late for dinner

Ristorante Romano's 12 Capel St, Dublin 1, tel 872 6868.

Old-style, pre-boom non-smoking Italian restaurant that serves good versions of all the staple Irish–Italian dishes like pizza, pasta and peppered steak, with house wines from €16 a bottle. Slightly hick, pink-dominated interior but, for a square meal in the city centre, hard to beat at the price. Lunch-time special also available at €9 for three courses including tea or coffee.

Open Mon–Sat 12.30–15.30, 18.00–22.30

101 Talbot Upstairs, 101 Talbot St, Dublin 1, tel 874 5011

Award-winning restaurant that sustains itself on a happy buzz from pre- and post-theatre goers. It serves starters like soup or herring salad, for €4–€6, as well as a selection of pasta dishes for €9.50 each. Their à la carte menu ranges from €13.90 to €17.15, and roast fillet of pork with parmesan and cashew nut crust, pan-fried fish with pesto or char-grilled swordfish, for example, give an idea of the standard of cuisine. The service is always excellent here—perfect when you're really hungry and can't wait for your food. They really excel in the dessert department, with such tempting treats as white chocolate and Baileys cake, fresh fruit pavlova, and pears poached in wine with crème fraiche and shortbread biscuits. Yum! A bottle of wine will cost from €14 and the restaurant also serves a small selection of beers.

Open Tues–Sat 17.00–23.00

Wagammama South King St, Dublin 2, tel 478 2152

Wagammama is a new-age, Asian food chain that serves restaurant food at a fast-food pace. Diners line up at long communal tables as their orders are beamed from electronic waiter pads to the open kitchen. For speedy dining between, or outside, normal lunch or dinner time, Wagammama is perfect.

Its positive-eating meals are excellent value—noodles average €8–€10, but a beer costs a whopping €4.25. There are all kinds of rice and noodle dishes, fresh juices, pickles, and Asian beers on Wagammama's menu which offers quality fast-food with a difference.

Open Mon–Sat 12.00–23.00 Sun 12.00–22.00

Yammamori 71–72 South Great George's St, Dublin 2, tel 475 5001

Long before Japan became the world's trendiest country, Yammamori was serving up noodles and saki to a hungry Dublin public. Others have come and gone, but the original still does a brisk trade.

Yammamori offers all kinds of noodle dishes at between €8 and €9.50 for lunch and €13 for dinner, which are served in an informal atmosphere, in an unpretentious setting. Though not as flashy as some more recent arrivals, Yammamori gets the basics right, and is also conveniently located in the heart of pub-land.

Open Sun–Wed 12.30–23.00 Thur–Sat 12.30–23.30

Bubbling over

Ar Vicoletto 5 Crow St, Temple Bar, Dublin 2, tel 670 8662

Ar Vicoletto is only slightly too expensive for our main criteria, but if you can afford a few extra euro, your taste buds and stomach will thank you for about a week.

Ar Vicoletto is an unpretentious, informal, friendly restaurant—tiny and exceptionally fine. The food is not *like* Italian food, it *is* Italian food. A plate from Ar Vicoletto is indistinguishable from its peer in Rome or Palermo. Staff are exactly like staff in Italy: attentive in patches, always friendly, not always efficient. Two people can eat for around €45, and the wine list is very reasonably priced.

This is not somewhere to rush for a quick bite, it is a place where food is to be enjoyed—however long that takes.

Open Mon–Sat 13.00–16.00 18.00–24.00 Sun 14.00–23.00

Aya 49–52 Clarendon St, Dublin 2, tel 677 1544

Aya is a Japanese restaurant that specialises in Sushi and really comes into its own from Sunday to Tuesday. It offers 55 minutes at the Sushi conveyor belt during which time you can eat whatever passes in front of your eyes.

This *Generation Game* cuisine comes in at €23 for a starter and a main course, €29.90 including dessert. A warning, though: the protein-rich Sushi is very filling and 55 minutes is a long, long time. Take your time in order to avoid pains later on in the evening.

Open Mon–Sat 12.00–16.00 17.30–23.00 Sun 12.00–22.00

Bond 5 Beresford Place, Dublin 1, tel 855 9244

Bond is a new idea for lovers of good wine and good food. It is housed in a very grand building, which forms part of the remaining crescent of magnificent (if somewhat dilapidated) Georgian houses behind Gandon's

Custom House. It sells over 100 wines from around the world at prices comparable to those in the shops. You can either take a bottle away, drink it alone on the spot or match it with great food from the lunch or dinner menu. The corkage charge is €6.35 so you can get some very fine wines at a significantly lower price than in other restaurants.

The cuisine is eclectic in origin, based on serving classic ingredients with an up-to-date twist. The owner likes to term it 'Modern European' cuisine. A main course pasta special costs €15.95, steak €22, fish €22, and if you really feel like splashing out their veal costs €28. The interior has been updated from the original to slick lines with warm wood flooring and minimalist furnishings. Walls are dotted with richly-coloured modern canvases. Friendly, helpful staff and very relaxed atmosphere.

Open Mon–Fri 12.00–15.00 Mon–Sat 18.00–21.00

TOURIST OFFICES IN THE CITY

Dublin Tourism Centre: Suffolk St, Dublin 2

Open June–Sept: Mon–Sat, 09.00–17.30, Jul–Aug: Mon–Sat, 08.30–18.30, Sun, 10.30–15.00.

14 Upr O'Connell St, Dublin 1

Open Mon–Sat, 09.00–17.00 (closed 13.30–14.00)

Baggot St Bridge, Dublin 2

Open Mon–Fri, 09.30–17.00 (closed 12.00–12.30)

Arrivals Hall, Dublin Airport

Open June–Sept: Mon–Sun, 08.00–22.00, Jul–Aug: Mon–Sun, 08.00–22.30

Here we are now—entertain us

Dublin is one of the finest places in which to be entertained in Europe. For a start, the weekend starts on Thursday (some would say Wednesday), which means a whole extra night when the city lets rip. To find out what's on, look up a newspaper—*The Irish Times* entertainment supplement, '**The Ticket'** is issued every Thursday—or ***The Event Guide*** which is available free in many shops and cafés in the city. If you've got Internet access (and see Internet access) look up **Entertainment Ireland** at www.entertainment.ie for very thorough and consistently updated information on what's going on throughout the country. This will help you avoid whiling away endless expensive hours in the pub as is often so tempting. To get entertainment on a strict budget you need to do unusual things which is half the fun. Want to see a movie? Go suburban. A play? Go experimental. Jazz? Catch the free Sunday rhythms. A comedy act? Get in free to Dáil Éireann. It's all in here.

Theatre

Ireland's biggest export may well be words, and Irish playwrights have had a long tradition of success and quality over the years. Theatre is thriving in Dublin and this is reflected in improvements such as the Gate's recent face-lift and the development of the Gaiety Plaza—the pavement area with seats and a glass awning outside the theatre where you can rendezvous before a performance, or have a chat afterwards.

But while Dublin theatre is in a healthy state, with better attendances than in many cities, it is hard to shake off the impression that the theatres of the city tend to plump for safety and box-office security rather than innovation. Do not come to Dublin if you are heavily into your Drama or if you want to see experimentation or theories of theatrical practice tested out.

Do come to the theatre here if you want to see famous plays or traditional new plays put on with aplomb and skill.

Much of the pride surrounding theatre in Dublin rests with the **Abbey** and the **Gate**. An overemphasis on drama which is about being Irish (rather than just Irish drama) and a need to produce highbrow theatre with popular appeal hamstring these theatres' ability to engage in serious experimentation or innovation. Expect to see new drama by playwrights with an already established reputation and lots of Wilde, Beckett, Ibsen, and other traditional, serious theatre.

The Abbey has a baby sister theatre called the **Peacock** which concentrates more on unusual new and Irish drama, and is altogether less formal.

The **Gaiety** makes no pretensions to Serious Theatre. It is Dublin's oldest commercial theatre, and behaves as such: it has no shame about putting on middlebrow and populist shows which often come off better than their serious counterparts. Fans of raw tack should keep an eye out. Another reason to keep a look out for the Gaiety is that it is a theatre for hire and touring companies of international repute will often perform there and completely outshine domestic theatre; it can be the best place in the city to see quality theatre. On Friday and Saturday nights, it is also a nightclub (see **Jazz** below).

If it is pure entertainment you are after then the **Olympia**, Dublin's second-oldest theatre, specialises not so much in plays as in a broader selection of entertainment. It hosts gigs of all kinds, from tribute bands to visiting and local originals, as well as ballet, revue, pantomime, variety and comedy.

The few theatres where you can see experimental drama are usually under-funded, and as with all experimental or innovative work, they can be a bit of a lottery in terms of quality. However, the gamble can also be very rewarding. The **Project**, the **New Theatre**, the **Focus Theatre**, the **Crypt Arts Centre** and the **Tivoli Theatre** constitute this group of low-profile theatres which, by and large, work with new material, much of it from young Irish writers.

The slightly more mainstream **Andrews Lane Theatre** is also worth a visit for its mix of classics and innovation.

Another, different way to see theatre is to visit the **drama societies** of the two universities, **Trinity College** and **UCD**. They are both, of course, amateur, but the standard is always tolerable and can be surprisingly high. The mix of plays runs from traditional Shakespeare to medieval drama to the most experimental and unusual kinds of theatre imaginable. The prices are very attractive, and while UCD is a little far out, Trinity's **Players' Theatre** is one of the most central theatres in the city.

Another tradition which is becoming increasingly popular is that of putting on theatre in places where you are not meant to put on theatre. This is not so much a post-modern experiment in artistic displacement as a faintly touristy gimmick. **Bewley's Café**, on Grafton St, has undergone major renovation and puts on lunch-time drama—the admission fee includes soup and a sandwich. Bewley's also has cabaret on Thursday, Friday and Saturday nights.

For children, there is the **Lambert Puppet Theatre,** near Dún Laoghaire, which puts on versions of well-known fairy tales and children's adventures every Saturday and Sunday. It's also worth checking out **The Ark** cultural centre for children in Temple Bar, who put on all sorts of marvellous events, including theatre.

The Dublin Theatre Festival, in October, is the theatrical highlight of the year. It has a lively fringe element and takes place in all the major theatres across the city.

So, all in all, Dublin is fairly well served theatrically although the emphasis is definitely more on entertainment than on pushing back the boundaries of what is theatrically possible. The major theatres are too cautious so you may want to skip the whole deal, and just go straight to the Gaiety for unashamed brassy entertainment. When looking for serious theatre, hit the smaller venues—you will see some rubbish, but at least you tried, and there is always the possibility that you will hit on some gems.

Performance times: most evening performances start at 20.00 and Saturday matinées at 14.30 but always check: long plays sometimes start at 19.30 or earlier.

A cheaper way to see a show is to get yourself a ticket for a **preview performance**. These are usually staged a few days before the actual opening date. You need to watch the events listings to see what is coming up, but this can be a worthwhile and economic option.

Wheelchair users should be aware that while many of the theatres have access, they generally prefer if you telephone to let them know that you are attending in order that someone can be available to assist. It is also worth noting that of the ones that have wheelchair access, some do not have dedicated toilet facilities.

Abbey Theatre Lr Abbey St, Dublin 1, tel 878 7222
website www.abbeytheatre.ie
Seats range from €15 to €25; matinées and previews €15, concessions and wheelchair seats €7.50. Wheelchair access: level access to ground floor, balcony and bar via lift, drinks also served on ground floor. Wheelchair accessible toilets. Places at the back of the auditorium reserved for wheelchair users, but phone ahead. All balcony seats have induction loop system for hearing aid users. Occasional performances are sign-language interpreted. Guide dogs permitted.

Andrews Lane Theatre 9 St Andrews Lane, Dublin 2, tel 679 7760, website www.andrewslane.com
Prices vary according to the production company but usually range from €15 to €20. Some concessions and previews available, reduced prices Mon–Tues. Wheelchair accessible and wheelchair accessible toilet.

The Ark Children's Cultural Centre, 11A Eustace Street, Dublin 2, tel 670 7788

Bewley's Café 78 Grafton St, Dublin 2, tel 086 878 401
Lunch-time drama €10, price includes bowl of soup and a sandwich. Performances begin at 13.10. Cabaret on Thursday, Friday and Saturday nights. Wheelchair accessible, but phone ahead. Wheelchair accessible toilets.

Crypt Arts Centre Dame St, Dublin 2, tel 671 3387,
website www.cryptartscentre.org
Seats €8–€10. Prices can vary, depending on production company. Concessions also available. Wheelchair accessible but not toilets. Parking can be arranged for wheelchair users if you phone in advance.

Dublin Theatre Festival
For information tel 677 8439, website www.eircomtheatrefestival.com
Festival runs for the first two weeks of October every year.

Focus Theatre 6 Pembroke Place, off Pembroke St, Dublin 2, tel 676 3071
Seats €10–€16.

Gaiety Theatre Sth King St, Dublin, 2 tel 677 1717,
website www.gaietytheatre.com
Seats range from €15 to €29 depending on the production. Some concessions available. Wheelchair access, through a side entrance, must be arranged in advance. Wheelchair accessible toilet. Guide dogs permitted.

Gate Theatre 1 Cavendish Row, Dublin 1, tel 874 4045,
website www.gate-theatre.ie
Seats range from €20 to €22 with reduced matinée, preview and concession prices. Lift for wheelchair but phone ahead so that staff can assist. Wheelchair accessible toilets. Guide dogs permitted.

Lambert Puppet Theatre Clifton Lane, Monkstown, Co. Dublin, tel 280 0974
Seats: children €8.50 adults €9.50. Weekend matinée performances. Wheelchair access but phone ahead.

New Theatre 43 East Essex St, Dublin 2, tel 670 3361
Seats from €10, preview and concession prices available. Wheelchair
accessible seats but no wheelchair accessible toilets.

Olympia Theatre 72 Dame St, Dublin 2, tel 1890 925130,
website www.ticketsonline.ie
Seat prices vary depending on the kind of performance and time of the day.
Wheelchair access with wheelchair accessible toilets.

Peacock Theatre Lr Abbey St, Dublin 2, tel 878 7222,
website www.abbeytheatre.ie
Seats €12.50, €17; matinées and previews €12.50. No specific wheelchair
access, but assistance can be given—best to phone ahead to check. Occasional
performances are sign-language interpreted. Guide dogs permitted.

Players' Theatre Trinity College, Dublin 2 (beside the rugby pitch),
tel 608 2351, website www.csc.tcd.ie/~players
Performances throughout the year but not every week. Phone or see website
for details. Wheelchair accessible.

Project 39 East Essex St, Dublin 2, tel 1850 260027, website www.project.ie
Seat prices vary depending on the production. Evening, matinée and lunch-
time performances. Wheelchair accessible but phone ahead so that staff can
be made available. Wheelchair accessible toilets.

Tivoli Theatre Francis St, Dublin 8, tel 454 4472
Seats range from €15 to €22, depending on the production. Evening and
matinée performances. Wheelchair access and accessible toilets.

UCD Dramsoc (Arts/Commerce Block) Belfield, Dublin 4, tel 706 8545
Performances at 13.00 and 19.00, Mon–Fri. Wheelchair access and accessible toilets.

Cinema

Cinema is one of the great joys of life in Dublin and the city has one of the highest rates of cinema-going public in Europe. The actual cinemas are so individual and different that the same film can become a completely different experience depending on where you watch it. From the out-of-town entertainment multiplexes to intimate suburban relics to the chic city centre ultra-modern dream palaces, every whim is catered for in fine style.

There is one rule that you must obey to see films in Dublin on a shoe-string: **never ever** go to the movies in the evening. In the afternoon, cinemas around the city can be around two-thirds of the usual evening price and the **UGC** (see below) has an even cheaper 'early bird' rate if you go before midday: to go in the evening is just plain daft. This is not about saving money for its own sake—quite simply, you can go to the movies far more often if you behave yourself, and resist the extra night-time charge. Not only that, but all of the cinemas around the city are best when they are empty and in the middle of the afternoon; the feelings of guilt at not doing anything else with your time, and of luxurious gluttony that you don't have to be at work right now, become a massive part of the enjoyment of the whole experience.

The **Dublin Film Festival**, a showcase for Irish and international cinema usually held in the first week of March, didn't take place in 2002—at the time of going to press its future was unclear.

The French Film Festival is held mainly in the **Irish Film Centre**, and is held in the first week in November. Details from the IFC tel 679 5744.

This section is divided not cinema by cinema but experience by experience. Just look at each 'what I want' bit and choose the viewing experience you want that day.

I want Cinema with a capital C: arthouse and quality films.

The Mecca of Irish quality film viewing is the **IFC (Irish Film Centre)** which is housed in the former Friends' (Quakers) Meeting House. It is everything you could ever wish for in an arthouse cinema. It is located in trendy, left-bank Temple Bar, has two screens, a bar/restaurant (great food value), a fantastically-stocked shop selling posters, videos, T-shirts, memorabilia, scripts, biographies and critical material. The IFC shows arthouse movies, occasional uncertified films (as a members' only club it, does not have to submit all its films to the censor for approval), and seasons of films. It is also one of the few cinemas in Dublin to show the usually-ignored genre of documentary.

In the cinemas themselves, the seats are comfortable and the surroundings of each of the two screens are lovely. The first is a large room with wide comfortable seats sloping towards a high screen with good-quality stereo sound. The second screen is in a charming upstairs room where the unusual setting suits most of the movies shown there. The seats are on a wooden slope and the small screen creates an intimate, rather than a claustrophobic, atmosphere.

You can buy drinks and coffee at the bar to take in (but no alcohol in the auditorium). There is only one chocolate machine, so if you need sweeties to enjoy a film, then bring your own.

The IFC can sometimes be painfully obscure in its programming, unlike the wonderful **Screen** cinema on D'Olier St. It has one of the most endearing pieces of street sculpture in Dublin—the little (four foot high) bronze figure of a cinema commissionaire, bushy moustache, peaked cap, elongated arm with torch and all.

The Screen is a commercial cinema showing the commercial end of the arthouse market and the arthouse end of the commercial market—an incredibly delicate balance which it manages with style, aplomb and perfect judgement. It is a small three-screen operation with cheap carpets and out-of-date signs. The sweetie/popcorn/drinks provision is basic at best and the security presence just one friendly fellow. Attendances rarely trouble more than half the seats (but remember a well-reviewed popular movie will attract queues, especially on Friday and Saturday nights). It is, therefore, a cinema-going treat, a piece of esoteric entertainment in itself.

It is also one place which is very definitely at its best in the quiet of the afternoon when you can join the truanting students from nearby Trinity College. There is always something worth seeing showing at The Screen, though one possible drawback is the slow rate at which the programmes change. However, this does mean that the more absent-minded viewer has a better chance of getting round to seeing that movie before it disappears forever. The only other blot on an otherwise super reputation is that the cinema does not serve coffee—if you need caffeine to see movies, better get it elsewhere first.

Another place to look for quality movies is in the **UCI's Director's Chair** season: classic films shown on excellent big screens and in comfort. Not now as regular as in the past, there is usually at least one screening per month, but phone for details (see p 170 for UCI details).

IFC 6 Eustace St, Temple Bar, Dublin 2, tel 677 8788, website www.fii.ie
Annual membership €12.70. Weekly membership €1.27.
Tickets €5.80 for daytime screenings and €6.30 in the evening. Screen One is wheelchair accessible and guide dogs are permitted. Wheelchair accessible toilets.

Screen College St, Dublin 2, tel 672 5500
Tickets €5 before 18.00 €7.50 after 18.00. Screen One is wheelchair accessible.
Wheelchair accessible toilets.

I want blockbusters in the city centre
You have two main choices here: the first is the **Savoy.** This five-screen
picture-house is traditional city centre cinema with few trimmings. Go here
for straight ahead, new release, low-maintenance movie watching. The only
real distinguishing characteristic of this place is the gigantic Screen One—
the biggest screen in Ireland. This makes it the best place to see those just-
out, must-see, special effect blockbusting extravaganzas. Go with popcorn,
sticky juice and sweeties; knowing the crowd, you'll probably throw more
sweets than you'll eat, but that's entertainment.

The other main city-centre mainstream cinema is the **UGC Multiplex** on
Parnell St. This multiplex shows all the new movies—the kind of cinema you
usually only find on the outskirts of cities. The sound systems in the screens
are excellent and the cinemas are comfortable and perfectly good. One of the
major advantages of the UGC is that there are movies being screened all the
time, so if you just turn up there is bound to be a film starting soon—just
check the airport-like display screens for times. Various kinds of snacks are
available upstairs, and places to sit and eat them.

Savoy Upr O'Connell St, Dublin 1, tel 874 6000
Tickets €5.50 before 18.00 €7.50 after 18.00. Screen One wheelchair accessible
once you get past three steps. No accessible toilets.

UGC Multiplex Parnell Centre, Parnell St, Dublin 1, tel 872 8444/8400
Tickets €5 before 18.00 €6.35 after 18.00. UGC also offers special 'Early Bird'
price of €3.75 for screenings before 12.00. Wheelchair access and accessible
toilets.

I want to go to a suburban cinema

The **Stella** serves Rathmines and is a marvellous old, unchanged cinema where movies are shown a week or two after their initial release. The decor and seats are functional at best but the Stella is cheaper in the evening than most other cinemas.

Similarly the one-screen **Classic** in Harold's Cross is cinema-going, old-style. There is a small kiosk in the foyer for ice cream and sweets, and when you get up from your wooden padded seat and leave the cinema, you emerge into a dingy lane which then leads to the street. Again, the films are usually a little out of date and the billboard above the entrance can be anything up to a year old. The most intriguing thing about the Classic is their showing every Friday night at around 23.00 of the cultish *Rocky Horror Picture Show*; for die-hards and first timers, it is, by all accounts, a bit of a riot. Bring your suspenders.

Other suburban options are the **IMC** in Dún Laoghaire and the **Ormonde** in Stillorgan both of which are cinemas of the multi-screen variety.

Classic 314 Harold's Cross Rd, Dublin 6, tel 492 3324
Dublin Bus nos 16, 16A, 49, 49A from city centre.
Tickets €6.35 evening

IMC Bloomfields Shopping Centre, Dún Laoghaire, tel 280 7777
DART or Dublin Bus nos 7, 46A rom city centre to Dún Laoghaire main street.
Tickets €5 before 18.00 €7.30 after 18.00

Ormonde Stillorgan (opposite the Shopping Centre), Co. Dublin
tel 278 0000
Dublin Bus nos 11, 46A from city centre to Stillorgan.
Tickets €5.50 before 18.00 €6.50 after 18.00

Stella Picture Theatre 207 Lr Rathmines Rd, Dublin 6, tel 497 1281
Dublin Buses nos 14, 15 or 83, all from Dame St, Dublin 2.
Tickets €6.35 evening, €4.50 weekend matinées ; wheelchair access but no accessible toilets.

I want to shop, then go ten pin bowling, eat fast food, then maybe see a movie.
There are three **UCI multiplex** cinemas in outer Dublin: in the north, in **Coolock**, in the south, in the Square Shopping Centre at **Tallaght**, and in the west, in **Blanchardstown**. They are situated in large shopping and entertainment complexes. These places are palaces if you want a tasty trashy treat with comfy seats, bright neon, shiny metal and food and drink services in the cinema itself. Like the **UGC**, they have large numbers of screens with excellent visual and sound equipment and show all the latest films. They are the perfect place to make a whole night out of one simple movie.

UCI Blanchardstown Town Centre, Blanchardstown, Dublin 15,
tel 1850 525 354
Dublin Bus no. 39 from Middle Abbey St, Dublin 1, 25-min journey.
Tickets €6 before 17.00 €7.30 after 17.00

UCI Coolock Malahide Rd, Malahide, Dublin 17, tel 848 5122
Dublin Bus no. 27 from Talbot St, Dublin 1, 10–15 min journey.
Tickets €6 before 17.00 €7.30 after 17.00

UCI Tallaght The Square, Town Centre, Tallaght, Dublin 24, tel 459 8400
Dublin Bus no. 54A from Eden Quay, Dublin 1, 30-min journey.
Tickets €6 before 17.00 €7.30 after 17.00

I want to watch a film at home
Sometime you just don't want to go out, or you're nearly but not quite broke—this is where **Laser** video rental comes in.

Laser is brilliant. Why? Because unlike most video stores, Laser don't stock 50 copies of the latest new releases and a cursory sprinkling of others. Laser stock one each of every conceivable film. Do you want to see a foreign film? Go to Laser. A sleazy flick by Russ Meyer or Roger Corman? Go to Laser. A minority interest film? Go to Laser. An obscure arthouse film? Go to Laser. A documentary about extraterrestrials, or flower arranging? Go to Laser. They have it all. And, which is quite rare nowadays, they know about their product.

For the very latest, in up-to-date, mainstream, blockbuster videos **Xtra-vision** is the place to go.

Laser

23 Sth Gt George's St, Dublin 2, tel 671 1466

116 Ranelagh Village, Dublin 6, tel 497 3893.

Videos €2.50 per night, new releases €3.50 or €4.50.

Open 7 days a week 11.00–00.00.

Xtra-vision branches all over the city and county. Two in the city centre are:

Baggot St, Dublin 2, tel 667 1255

Prussia St, Dublin 8, tel 838 0041.

Videos €2.50 per night, new releases €4.00 €4.45 or €4.75.

Open Opening hours vary; larger stores are open 7 days a week, 24 hours, smaller ones are usually open 12.00–00.00.

I want to see a film but I have no money

During the summer there are **free films** in **Meeting House Square** in Temple Bar, Dublin 2, every Saturday night during July and August. A celebrity is invited to introduce a favourite movie and it is shown in the open air on a big screen to an often lively Saturday night crowd. Old classics often get a welcome airing.

Bear in mind that this happens on a Saturday night for free, so if you need silence to concentrate on a film, don't go—you will just get annoyed.

A combination of nightclub beat rumble and boisterous participation by some of the crowd can make the experience unique and fun: it can also ruin some peoples' movies. It is, however, highly recommended and is wheelchair accessible.

Tickets (free, but you do need one) are available at the Temple Bar Information Centre, 18 Eustace St, Dublin 2, tel 671 5717.

Clubs

A good bit of the buzz surrounding Dublin in the past couple of years has centred on the city as a youth capital, and has rested on the strength of its clubs. This reputation is founded on a relatively small number of clubs, but they are truly very good ones.

The trick to clubbing in Dublin is to be careful where you go, and to stick to certain places. There are far too many dives in Dublin which are, technically, nightclubs but in fact are hellholes of lager-fuelled aggression and sleazy middle managers in shiny suits trying as hard as they can to pick up girls or pick a fight with the (large) bouncers. There will be times when you are tempted—mostly, they have no cover charge, and they are open late with loud music. However, don't give in, the whole experience is hauntingly depressing, shockingly expensive and one which few repeat. Just avoid Leeson St and Harcourt St (apart from The PoD, see below).

So where do you go? The big names are **The Kitchen** (U2 owned, attached to the Clarence Hotel), the **PoD**, and **Rí Rá**. Rí Rá is a more studenty, less exclusive club than the other two but this is by no means an indication that the music and feel of the place is any worse. Its more relaxed atmosphere can be welcome. The Kitchen is a subterranean delight of top name DJs and the odd celebrity attendance. Along with Rí Rá, it strives to catch the student market early on in the week, but its door policy is relaxed so you don't have to look like a millionaire to get in, even on Friday and Saturday nights.

PoD, unused to the kind of rivalry The Kitchen has been giving it, is coming back. Because it is bigger it can often attract the very biggest names in guest DJs. Slightly less friendly security staff can make a trip to the PoD a little more daunting than the other two, but still it remains a top place.

There are a large number of other late night bars which call themselves clubs, but these three are the only places you will get assured top clubbing for the reasonable early/midweek price of €6–€10.

The Kitchen East Essex St, Dublin 2, tel 677 6635
website www.the-kitchen.com

The PoD (beside the Odeon), Harcourt St, Dublin 2
tel 478 8581, website www.pod.ie

Rí Rá 8 Sth Great George's St, Dublin 2, tel 671 1220

Wheelchair access: most of these clubs have some steps but staff will usually be able to help, best to ring first though.

FOR MALE READERS
Do not be surprised, when using the toilet, if your neighbour enters into conversation. he is merely being friendly, and intends no ulterior motive. A favourite story tells of the rock star Bono going to the urinal before a performance. A stranger comes in and expeditiously relieves himself. Having made no previous signs that he recognises Bono, who is still standing there quite unproductively, the stranger cheerfully comments: 'Stage fright, is it?'

PETER COSTELLO DUBLIN'S LITERARY PUBS

Gigs and bands

The Event Guide is your bible here. It is a free paper made up of listings of all the gigs going on as well as short articles and ads for bands and gigs. It comes out every two weeks and can be picked up in many shops, cafés, bars, and most of the venues where music is on. *The Irish Times* Thursday supplement, 'The Ticket', also provides a good source of entertainment options as does the website www.entertainment.ie. For a fuller and more unorthodox view of the music scene in Dublin, check out the various fanzines and freesheets—amateur magazines with lots of attitude and no money—available in the smaller record shops.

Dublin is on all the major touring circuits, so your favourite bands will come here eventually. The big venue is **The Point** which stages very big acts on an ongoing basis. Occasional concerts happen at three of the city's outdoor sporting arenas: **Croke Park**, **Lansdowne Road**, and the **RDS** (Royal Dublin Society). Average ticket prices for these venues can range from €27 to €50 and over, depending on the act.

Dublin is blessed with fantastic mid-scale venues, where most acts appear. The **Olympia Theatre**, **Whelan's**, **The Red Box**, **Vicar Street**, and the **Ambassador** are all intimate venues in a wide range of styles from functionalist and modern to old vaudeville theatre to glorified pub back-room.

These are the best venues to visit to see familiar acts. The Olympia, Whelan's, Vicar Street and to a lesser degree the Red Box, are all worth checking out on spec as well. They have constant programmes of acts including unknown or obscure ones, and the quality can be excellent—their very appearance at these venues often (though not always) can be a guarantee of quality.

One of the most intriguing unique aspects of the live scene in Dublin is **Midnight at the Olympia**. While in its heyday it used to attract real acts, the promoters these days plump for tribute bands almost exclusively. But if you get the right crowd, at the right stage of inebriation and the right band in the right mood, you can have a live experience you just couldn't have in any other city.

Vicar Street hosts music and comedy gigs of a similar calibre to that of the Olympia. However, it makes for a different experience. Vicar Street was designed with modern sound in mind and this gives it more a TV-stage kind of feel. It combines a nicely-sized intimate venue with a bar and a smaller performance space called **The Shelter**. There are standing-room tickets available but if you book in time, and pay a bit more, you will be allocated one of the small, round tables that nestle in from of the low stage; here, you can enjoy your drinks in more comfort. Performances at Vicar Street are usually over at around closing time, or sometimes a bit before.

A new venue is the **Ambassador**, which was listed in the cinema section of the last edition of this guide. It has now changed medium and is generally host to bigger acts than appear at the Olympia or Vicar Street. It lies between these and the Point in terms of price, but has the convenience of being located at the top of O'Connell St, in the city centre.

Tickets for almost every venue in Dublin are available from **Ticketmaster** which has booking outlets at the ILAC Centre and the Jervis Centre both in Dublin 1, and also in the St Stephen's Green Shopping Centre, Dublin 2. Bookings can also be made by phoning 1890 925 100 or on the website www.ticketmaster.ie. Telephone and Internet bookings are subject to a €5 per ticket service charge.

If you are feeling adventurous, you can try the numerous pubs around the city which put on live bands. Naturally it is a complete lottery whether you get tomorrow's Beatles or yesterday's Bee Gees, but the prices reflect this. If all you want is live music, then the cheaper and, in many ways, more thrilling option is to trail the pubs looking for music. **Eamon Doran's** in Temple Bar is one of the most popular venues for new acts of the guitar variety. For other pubs with music, like **The International Bar**, check out the aforementioned *Event Guide*, or look in the public libraries for *Hot Press* and *In Dublin* magazines; these are quite pricey, but very useful if you read them for free in the library.

As for other costs, only drink will really cost you any more money. Generally, the pubs will have normal prices (€3.40–€3.80 pint of Guinness), but the bigger venues will charge more. The major venues (The Point, Lansdowne Road, Croke Park, RDS) all have **wheelchair access** but only a selection of the others do.

The Ambassador O'Connell St, Dublin 1, tel 887 4868

Croke Park Jones Rd, Dublin 1
Wheelchair access

Eamon Doran's 3a Crown Alley, Dublin 2, tel 679 9114
Wheelchair access possible with assistance

The International Bar 23 Wicklow St, Dublin 2, tel 677 9250
No wheelchair access.

Lansdowne Road Dublin 4
Wheelchair access

The Olympia 72 Dame St, Dublin 2 tel 1890 925 100
Wheelchair access and accessible toilets

The Point North Wall Quay, Dublin 1, tel 836 3633
Wheelchair access

Red Box Harcourt St, Dublin 2, tel 478 0166
Wheelchair access and accessible toilets

RDS Ballsbridge, Dublin 4, tel 668 0866, e-mail info@rds.ie
website www.rds.ie
Wheelchair access

The Shelter 58–59 Thomas St, Dublin 8, tel 454 5533
Wheelchair access but no accessible toilets (toilet in Vicar Street can be used)

Vicar Street 58–59 Thomas St, Dublin 8, tel 454 5533
Wheelchair access and accessible toilets

Whelan's 25 Wexford St, Dublin 2, tel 478 0766
Wheelchair access and accessible toilets

Traditional music

There are pubs all over Dublin offering regular sessions of Irish traditional music. This music is quite unlike any other folk music in Europe, ranging from the haunting, soulful, solo singing of the *sean nós* singers to the lively vibrant dance tunes of a session. In few other folk cultures can musicians who may never have met before sit down and begin to play tune after tune without reference to sheet music. These sessions can last many hours which makes them ideal forms of pub entertainment. Since the musicians, to all intents and purposes, seem to be playing for their own enjoyment, they don't require the absolute silence that a classical musician would.

The scope of what's called traditional music ranges from ultra-traditional classic instrumentals right through to mawkish collections of rousing rebel songs. Most music pubs will offer something in between, a blend of instrumental music and ballads.

Twenty years ago, the numbers of pubs offering traditional music of any kind was tiny. However, with the explosion of interest in Irish culture in general, and traditional music in particular—both at home and abroad—

the concerned publicans of Dublin have found it in their hearts to sponsor and support an entire generation of traditional musicians. Many pubs offer sessions: the best are listed below.

The Lighthouse Bar 2 Church St, Howth, Co Dublin, tel 832 2827
—has sessions on Fri–Mon
DART or Dublin Bus no. 31B

The Oliver St John Gogarty Temple Bar, Dublin 2, tel 671 1822
—holds regular sessions throughout the weekend. This is also the starting point for a musical pub crawl.

The Pierhouse Bar 4 East Pier, Howth, Co Dublin, tel 832 4510
—has a particularly fine session on Sunday nights.
DART or Dublin Bus no. 31B

The Snug Dorset St, Dublin 1, tel 830 6693
—has a fine session on Tuesday nights.

All these sessions are free. They represent only a handful of the sessions going on throughout the city but these are the places which offer the best balance between the authentic traditional music, beloved of purists, and the exciting vibrant nature of this most accessible of folk musics.

Other venues for traditional music are:

The Brazen Head 20 Lr Bridge St, Dublin 8, tel 679 5186
The Cobblestone 77 North King St, Smithfield, Dublin 7, tel 872 7991
Devitts 78 Lr Camden St, Dublin 2, tel 475 3414
O'Donoghue's 15 Merrion Row, Dublin 2, tel 676 2807
The Temple Bar 47–48 Temple Bar, Dublin 2, tel 672 5287

Jazz

The jazz scene in Dublin is best described as intimate—small, familiar and yet of a refreshingly high standard. The right places are buzzing with talent and the reason for the size of Dublin's jazz circuit is not lack of interest or playing ability, rather a sign that jazz as pub entertainment/background muzak has not yet caught on. This means that when you do go to a gig, you know that it will be a quality session and not some talentless Dixieland scamsters making a quick euro. (Sadly, this does sometimes happen: if you ever see a trumpet player in a straw hat, or if there is a stripey blazer in sight, then you know to run a mile.) The downside is that there are very few casual, free pub jazz gigs. However, there are some to be found, particularly on a Sunday afternoon, and the following can be availed of free of charge:

The Globe, the hang-out for trendy young things, has a session on Sunday evenings from 18.00, where local talent is on display; in Ballsbridge, a short bus ride from the city centre, a more laid-back time can be had at the **Herbert Park Hotel's** afternoon session, book a table first though. **Zanzibar**, on Ormond Quay, also has jazz on Sunday afternoons.

Probably the most well-known jazz venue nowadays is **J. J. Smyth's**, which is home to the jazz club **Pendulum**. J. J.'s has an intimate upstairs room where the gigs take place and these feature regular favourites as well as visiting acts.

Renard's has a jazz and supper club, from 23.00 on Sundays and Wednesdays, showcasing new and established talent in a super-dark club basement.

Top international jazz visits Dublin regularly, and often takes in the larger venues like the **Temple Bar Music Centre**—look for details in the newspapers and *The Event Guide*.

All these gigs bring you very serious jazz—all furrowed brows and middle-aged men. If you are looking for a little more swagger and a little less soul-searching, then there is good quality good-time jazz going on at the weekends. The **Gaiety** has exploited its late-night-drinking theatre licence with its Friday and Saturday night clubs which offer fantastic, but pricey, nights out. They start at between 23.30 and midnight in the theatre and you will find two bands, two DJs, five bars and a cinema all dotted around the various floors of the building. From be-bop to funk, with a little dash of salsa, the entertainment covers a range of styles, mostly made for dancing rather than beard-tugging contemplation. There is no better way to spend a late weekend night, but the entrance of €11 is certainly steep: drinks on top of that can really hurt the wallet.

Velure, which used to be at the Gaiety has now found a new home at **The Shelter** on Saturday nights where it continues to offer funk, soul, jazz and Latin grooves from 23.30 onwards, though in a smaller space. The **Sugar Club**, on the St Stephen's Green end of Leeson St, features live bands (usually of the Latin and swing kind) as well as DJs. Tables can be reserved here for wheelchair users and there is complete wheelchair access.

Gaiety Theatre Night Clubs Sth King St, Dublin 2, tel 677 1717
Wheelchair access only to some areas

The Globe 11 Sth Great George's St, Dublin 2, tel 671 1220
Wheelchair accessible

Herbert Park Hotel Ballsbridge, Dublin 4, tel 667 2200
Dublin Bus nos 7, 45 from city centre or about a 20–25 minute walk.
Wheelchair accessible

J. J. Smyth's 12 Aungier St, Dublin 2, tel 247 2565
Not wheelchair accessible

Renard's 33–35 Sth Frederick St, Dublin 2, tel 677 5876
Wheelchair accessible with assistance

Sugar Club 8 Lr Leeson Street, Dublin 2, tel 678 7188
Wheelchair accessible, takes reservations for wheelchair-designated tables

Temple Bar Music Centre Curved St, Dublin 2, tel 670 9202
Wheelchair accessible

Velure at the Shelter 58–59 Thomas St, Dublin 8, tel 454 5533
Wheelchair accessible

Zanzibar 34–35 Ormond Quay, Dublin 7, tel 878 7212
Wheelchair accessible

Classical music

For classical music lovers on a budget, there is a lot happening in Dublin,
whether you want to listen or participate.

The **National Concert Hall** is Ireland's main classical music venue. It
houses the **National Symphony Orchestra**, which plays most Friday
evenings. Both amateur groups and touring professionals perform throughout the week in the main auditorium, and the RTÉ Concert Orchestra makes
regular appearances also.

In the adjoining **John Field Room** (otherwise used as the bar area) a variety of rock, jazz, country music, traditional Irish music, folk, and world music concerts as well as smaller classical lunch-time recitals are offered. Details in a monthly brochure available at the NCH itself and in some libraries; also listed in *The Irish Times*.

The **Dublin University Orchestral Society,** one of Trinity College's music societies, gives concerts twice a year. Smaller-scale lunch-time recitals featuring duos or soloists are also held, mainly on Fridays. The standard is really very good as these performances provide a platform for talented young musicians.

There are **choral concerts** throughout the year, and a concentration of them around Christmas, all of which have a small entrance fee. This is reduced if you become a member, which you can normally do at the door. Information on all of these performances is posted in the Music Department and in the Trinity Central Societies Committee (CSC, tel 677 2941).

Trinity College is being singled out simply because of its extremely central location, and its well established active music scene but the other colleges around the city are also well worth checking out. **The Dublin Institute of Technology Conservatory of Music and Drama**, Adelaide Rd, Dublin 2, tel 402 3000, and **Royal Irish Academy of Music**, 36 Westland Row, Dublin 2 tel 676 4412 put on many events, some of them free. Both have notice-boards with information on upcoming events, and fliers on musical events.

Free **Music in the Parks** sponsored by Dublin Corporation takes place in various Dublin parks on Sunday afternoons during the summer, with brass and reed bands, brass quintets, youth bands and jazz. Check upcoming concerts at the notice-board in St Stephen's Green.

Check 'What's On Today' column of *The Irish Times* and the Classical listings in *The Event Guide* for information on occasional concerts. The following are some of the more regular venues:

The Bank of Ireland Arts Centre Foster Place, Dublin 2, tel 671 1488
Wheelchair users ring beforehand.

The **Goethe-Institut** Library 37 Merrion Sq, Dublin 2, tel 661 1155

The **Hugh Lane Gallery** (also known as the Municipal Gallery) Parnell Sq,
Dublin 1, tel 874 1903. Free concerts on Sundays at noon. Series of both
classical and contemporary music. Wheelchair access and accessible toilets.

Instituto Cervantes 58 Northumberland Rd, Dublin 2, tel 668 2024

Meeting House Square Temple Bar, Dublin 2, during the summer. For
details contact Temple Bar Information Centre, tel 671 5717.

National Concert Hall Earlsfort Tce, Dublin 2, tel 475 1572,
website www.nch.ie
The cheapest seats are €7.62 and are in the choir balcony if the concert is
non-choral. Bookings up to three months in advance. There are four spaces
for wheelchair users (early booking advisable). Two parking bays reserved for
disabled drivers at the main entrance.

National Gallery of Ireland Merrion Sq, Dublin 2, tel 661 5133
See the *Gallery News* freesheet, available in the Gallery. Wheelchair accessible
and toilets.

RDS Concert Hall RDS, Ballsbridge, Dublin 4, tel 240 7211
Wheelchair accessible.

If you'd like to play or sing
You might consider joining one of the student groups—depending on
your standard they will be glad to have you. Approach the relevant Music

Department. If that feels a bit too studenty, there are other amateur groups in Dublin, though newcomers to the city can find it difficult to get information about them. However, one of the better-known ones is the **Rathmines and Rathgar Musical Society**, 67 Upr Rathmines Rd, Dublin 6. Otherwise known as the 'R&R', this society has a high amateur standard and applicants are always auditioned. For membership information tel 298 9061.

The two principal **amateur orchestra**s are the **Dublin Symphony Orchestra** and the **Dublin Orchestral Players** both of which charge an annual membership fee. They both give a number of public concerts a year. An audition may be required, but generally evidence of your standard and experience is enough. The DSO can be contacted through the secretary, Simone Orr, tel 288 7212, e-mail orrsimone@hotmail.com. Their annual fee is €90.

Church music

Christ Church Cathedral Dublin 8, tel 677 8099
Choral Evensong on Wed and Thur at 18.00 (all year round), and Sat at 17.00 (not July/Aug), Sung Eucharist and sermon Sun 11.00, and Choral Evensong Sun 15.30. €3 donation. Wheelchair access if informed in advance.

St Ann's Church Dawson St, Dublin 2, tel 676 7727
Sun concerts at 15.30. Seats €12.70 concessions €10.15. Tickets available at the door.

St Patrick's Cathedral Patrick St, Dublin 2, tel 475 4817
Sun Matins 08.38 (Choral), Sung Eucharist, 11.15, and Choral Evensong 15.15, known as 'Paddy's Opera' from colourful characters of bygone choirs. Daily services include 09.40 Matins (Choral), and 17.30 Evensong (Choral).

The regularity of sung services may change during the summer months. Wheelchair access through the side door.

The Pro Cathedral Marlborough St, Dublin 1, tel 874 5441
Sung Mass by the Palestrina Choir every Sun at 11.00 except July–August.

Trinity College Chapel Dublin 2
Choral Evensong every Thur at 17.15 p.m. during term time provides a very soothing, uplifting retreat from the bustle of the city centre. Choral Eucharist Sun 10.45 and a Folk Mass at 12.15. All services are free and open to the public. There are often small receptions afterwards to which the congregation is invited. Not wheelchair accessible.

A highlight of the year is the traditional carol service in the chapel held on the first Monday in December, with the best-loved carols in which everyone can join and more esoteric works sung by the Chapel Choir. This is very popular so you need to get there early.

Comedy

Dublin's comedy circuit is well established, packed with talent, and growing at a fierce rate.

TV has helped many young Dublin careers, and now there is a large comedy industry operating out of the city and proving itself, week after week, on an established circuit. Ireland has produced some of the funniest comics there have ever been: from Myles na Gopaleen/Flann O'Brien's literary comedy to Dave Allen's classic stand up, the tradition has run to this day to award winners like Dylan Moran and Ardal O'Hanlon, Ed Byrne and Tommy Teirnan—famous funny men backed up by a regiment of unknown promising talent.

A handful of pubs have, over the past few years, given themselves over as venues for comedy a couple of nights a week, and they have had increasing success lately. The **International Bar** holds improvisation and comedy nights and the **Ha'penny Bridge Inn** has a more varied programme, taking in monologues, poetry and prose readings, a lot of improvisation; it generally has less straight stand up. This is fine if you are looking for something a little more experimental, but if it is plain old belly laughs you are after, stick to the International.

However, the real sign that comedy is now big business and big news is the 400-seater cinema on the north side of the quays, just off O'Connell St, which operates as a full-time dedicated comedy venue, **Murphy's Laughter Lounge**. The trick here is to check the bill carefully—the young Dublin comics can be seen at a number of pubs around the city for €5 or €6. The Laughter Lounge really comes into its own when it brings international talent to play, so save your cash for those nights when you will get three or four Dublin comics plus a major international talent—a night out which would be well worth €15.

The Ha'penny Bridge Inn 42 Wellington Quay, Dublin 2, tel 677 0616
No wheelchair access.

International Bar 23 Wicklow St, Dublin 2, tel 677 9250
Improvisation on Mon; in-house comedy nights Wed and Thur
No wheelchair access.

Murphy's Laughter Lounge Eden Quay, Dublin 1, tel 874 4611
Wed–Sat €19 (€15). Wheelchair accessible.

Other venues, where established comedy acts can be seen, are:
The Olympia Theatre (see p. 164)
Vicar Street (see p. 177)
Whelan's (see p. 177)

Free stuff

ONE MAN'S CRIME . . .

Why not revel in the misery of others, or cheer on a doomed victim of the brutal law? The Four Courts on the quays are a source of constant news and entertainment for anyone who cares to have a look. Potter up and enter any court at all, as is your right, and you might catch an amusing small case or maybe a even a murder, (children's or family cases are not accessible though). It's free and dramatic and not very far away: what more could you want? At the very worst the courts are well heated in the winter time.

Four Courts Inns Quay, Dublin 7, tel 872 5555, wheelchair accessible, hearings 10.30–12.00, 14.00–16.00.

. . . IS ANOTHER MAN'S GOVERNMENT

Some would say you see more criminals in government than in the courts: certainly it contains a similarly large number of men in suits getting all hot under the collar, and you can make it entertainment, for free. The lower house is called Dáil Éireann and the upper house is called the Seanad. You can arrange either tours or just a seat in the public gallery of the seat of government. Just sit back and watch the (usually fairly empty) chamber as the (usually fairly empty) politicians battle out the milk quotas and legal jargon of government.

The Dáil and Seanad Leinster House, Kildare St, Dublin 2, tel 618 3333 (ask for PR), e-mail info@oireachtas.irlgov.ie. Tickets are allocated through your local TD (member of the House). Wheelchair access. Sittings are during the day but can run into the night-time.

. . . OR MISGOVERNMENT

Some of the best free shows in town are the two Tribunals of Enquiry held in Dublin Castle. Here on display is the raw underbelly of Irish political and business life in the 1980s and 1990s—thank goodness things are just not like that nowadays! You'll have to look in the newspapers to check if either Tribunal is sitting in public, or you can ring the numbers below. Like courts, they sit between 10.30 and 16.00 with a lunch break, and access is on a first-come, first served basis. Contact the Planning Tribunal (Flood) tel 633 9833, or Payments (Moriarty) tel 670 5666.

Free tickets from *The Irish Times*

Every two weeks or so *The Irish Times* gives out free tickets to new film screenings, and more often to concerts and other events. The film screenings are usually announced on Fridays, and the first 100 or so to call at the office in D'Olier St on the following Tuesday get lucky. Mind you, this perk is well-known, so there are often queues round the block. For free concerts and CDs and other perks, look out for coupons in the paper (sometimes twice a week), cut them out, send them off with an SAE, and the first few out of the bag get the goodies.

> *A friend of a friend of ours applied for* The Irish Times *weekend ticket offers every week for six weeks and won every single time. At which point they asked him to stop entering. This is really true.*

The Campanile, Trinity College

Green and silent

A good park can really make a difference to your day. Somewhere to sit down for a couple of hours, look at your maps, guidebooks, the newspaper, write a diary, watch the natives at play or even have a quick snooze. As a place to relax, you can't beat a park. They are places of entertainment, rest, recuperation, relaxation, contemplation, study and interest. And crucially they are, of course, free. You can sit around in the parks all day long without anyone bothering you.

But Dublin is not a green place. There is one seriously really big park in the city, the Phoenix Park. It lies on the northern outskirts of the city and is massive (the biggest city park in Europe). But there are many smaller parks and gardens, numerous and small, and dotted all around the city.

Phoenix Park, **St Stephen's Green** and the **Botanic Gardens** are covered here as the main parks. But you will also find some of Dublin's best, most central and most secret parks so that you can get it together in peace. And don't forget **Trinity College**: a green haven from city traffic where you can sit and watch the heartier students playing rugby or cricket, or just peacefully enjoy the passing crowd.

Most parks are open from 09.00 to dusk.

Phoenix Park Dublin 1
Dublin Bus nos 10, 37, 38, 39
Out on the north of the city, this is the place you have to go if you want wide open spaces and lots of grass. This is where Mary Makebelieve met her tall policeman in James Stephens' classic tale *The Charwoman's Daughter*. Watch out for real Polo (May to September) not to mention numerous other sports. Basically the park is just a massive expanse of space, and the only one Dublin has. But over the years privileged citizens have found themselves houses in it. The Park houses the President's residence and that of the US Ambassador as well as Dublin Zoo. Then there's **Farmleigh**, a former Guinness residence which has just been turned into an official hospitality site for visiting big-wigs. Adjoining the Visitor Centre is Ashtown Castle, a real 17th-century tower house.
Ashtown Castle/Phoenix Park Visitor Centre tel 677 009
Open winter 09.30–16.30 summer 09.30–18.00
Admission including a guided tour of the castle €2.50 concessions from €1.20
Farmleigh tel 815 5900.
Open Sun, bank hol Mon 11.00–18.00
Admission free

St Stephen's Green Dublin 2
This is the most popular, most central, best facilitated and most famous of Dublin's parks and gardens. It lies at the top of Grafton St at the hub of Dublin's business and retail centre on the southside. It is an extraordinary and beautiful place, and a joy to have in the centre of a city: its grounds contain a pond, landscaped gardens, a playground for children, a bandstand and large

patches of grass to lounge around on. It also has several wooden shelters looking on to the landscaped gardens so that even in the rain you can sit and take in your lovely surroundings.

There are few greater summer joys than feeding the mallard ducks in the pond, lying in a soporific stupor on the grass and popping over to see some of the summer bands or Shakespeare in the little amphitheatre. For the botanist there are over two hundred varieties of tree to spot, housing a large number of common and rare birds to be seen and heard. And the historian can envisage the lads in 1916 carefully digging trenches across the Green— that is until they realised that all the British soldiers had to do was to climb to the roofs of the surrounding buildings and shoot down.

In the winter wrap up and take advantage of a slightly less busy Green, sit watching the rain and the fountain and enjoy the fact that you can see the grass, for once not obscured by people.

The key to enjoying the Green is recognising how big it is: don't just head for the central landscaped gardens, look all around the edges for the little spots of seclusion, or for the many super spots around the pond where the ducks and the water drown out the nearby traffic.

Gets incredibly busy on weekday lunch-times and in the summer, but even then there are a load of places to sit and sort yourself out.

Botanic Gardens Glasnevin, Dublin 9, tel 837 4388
Dublin Bus nos 19, 19A, 13, 134

The Botanic Gardens lie on the north of the city in Glasnevin. It is a curious place to spend time, and wonderfully entertaining. Botanic gardens are places of science as well as recreation, a haven for obsessive amateurs to mingle with professional scientists. The ones in Glasnevin have all the usual paraphernalia of botanic gardens, funny shaped greenhouses and all.

The sight of rare plants in greenhouses not with a whole exhibition around them but just sitting on a window ledge in plant pots is wonderful, as is a walk round, spotting the places where the gardens are coming apart at the seams. And don't forget to coo admiringly at the magnificently restored 19th-century curvilinear glasshouses designed by Richard Turner.

But still the gardens are of interest to botanists: the 19 ha gardens, dating from 1795, boast an impressive 20,000 species of plants as well as a large number of truly beautiful trees. A 400-year old fern, cacti, a giant Amazon water lily, and a rose raised from a cutting of the one that inspired Thomas Moore to write that 19th-century favourite 'The Last Rose of Summer' are all among the peculiarities of these gardens.

The most exciting aspect, however, is the smells: as soon as you pass the gate from the busy smelly traffic, a clash of pungent plant perfumes hits you and follows you all round the gardens. A walk round the walls is a secluded pleasant stroll, and the glimpses through to the next door cemetery add a sombre touch to it all.

Open summer Mon–Sat 09.00–18.00 Sun 11.00–18.00 (Thur 15.00) winter Mon–Sat 10.00–16.30 (Thur 15.30) Sun 11.00–16.30. Greenhouses closed 12.45–14.00.

Admission free

Glasnevin Cemetery Finglas Rd, Dublin 11, tel 830 1133
Dublin Bus nos 40, 40A, 40B, 40C

Graveyards are fascinating places to stroll, look at the graves and decipher the worn headstones. Glasnevin is really crowded and tightly packed, filled with the ordinary Dubliners who have been buried there for a century and a half. There is also a very high celebrity grave count: all the big names in Irish political history are here. Charles Stewart Parnell, James Stephens, Éamon de Valera, Michael Collins and Daniel O'Connell all rest here. Not to mention Maud Gonne (Yeats' love), Brendan Behan and Gerard Manley Hopkins. Nobody could miss O'Connell: a grotesquely huge tower stands just inside the main gate, a monument to 19th-century overblown pomp, and quite amusing, despite, of course, being in a graveyard. (For cemetery freaks, Vivien Igoe's *A Literary Guide to Dublin* gives 'who's buried where' maps of Glasnevin and Mount Jerome cemeteries.)

And after all that fresh air, you can retire to the highlight of any trip up Glasnevin way: a fine pint of stout at the next door pub the Gravedigger's, as Kavanagh's is known.

Open 08.30–17.00
Admission free

Iveagh Gardens Clonmel St, off Harcourt St, Dublin 2
The lovely Iveagh Gardens are the thinking person's Stephen's Green. The entrance is about forty seconds' walk from the south-west corner of the Green, in a left turn as you go down Harcourt St. Enter a garden as central and convenient as Stephen's Green, but far less well known. This walled garden was restored in the 1990s and its high walls and buildings on all four sides not only give it a secretive, secluded aura, but bring much needed silence as well. It was presented to the state in 1939 by Lord Iveagh (what would Dublin be like without the money earned from Guinness?), then gifted to University College Dublin in 1941.

As you walk in two things strike you: the two beautiful tree-lined avenues and the massive lawns seemingly taking up most of the garden. It feels like there is far more space than in other parks due to these large open lawns, and the park is given a majestic feel by the two fountains perched rather oddly in the middle of one of the lawns. But take the time to wander round the back of the park, and relish the opportunity to find its little idiosyncrasies. Around the wall at the east end of the park there is a great hidden muddy path which takes you to a rose garden and a tiny maze, surely the easiest maze in the world—at least till the hedges grow a bit more. There is also a bizarre fountain made out of big huge lumps of stone mixed in with two or three large Greek statues and even the trunk of a tree thrown in for good measure. Iveagh Gardens is in many ways the most eccentric of the parks of the city, so take the time to seek out its secrets hidden in its corners.

On a more practical note, there is not nearly so much shelter from the rain here as in Stephen's Green, and there are far fewer places to have a seat.

Blessington St Basin Dublin 7

In complete contrast to the big green spaces of Iveagh Gardens is a park with no green at all: Blessington St Basin. This park is truly a secret and if you like water and birds, this is the one for you. It consists of a large pond surrounded by a concrete path and a fence. There is no grass, but there are many bushes, and the basin backs on to a filled-in part of the canal, a straight stretch of green.

The pond, once a reservoir and the source of water for the famous Jameson and Powers whiskeys, is home to rudd, a fish which makes up for its inedibility with its talent for swimming near the surface of water, making it the perfect spectator fish. Loads of ducks and seagulls and a delightful island in the middle of the pond combine with the seclusion provided by the surrounding houses and the lovely view including an impressive big church in the background to make this a marvellously contemplative spot well worth the trot up O'Connell St and into Blessington St.

Merrion Square Dublin 2

Merrion Square is by no means a secret, but is the best kept garden in the city. The flowers, the winding walkways, the smells, the statues all make for a full sensory treat, parked right in the middle of the city, surrounded by the calm self-confidence of Georgian domestic architecture. There are lots of hideaways and secluded spots to rest in and absorb the real stars of this garden: the fantastic flowers and trees. As you stroll around, imagine what it would have been like with an enormous cathedral in the middle, probably in the execrable clerical architectural taste of the day—this was the Catholic Church's plan from 1920 until they finally gave up the idea in 1974. In the houses round the square once lived W. B. Yeats, Daniel O'Connell, and Oscar Wilde who is commemorated by a multi-coloured statue near the railings opposite the American College previously the Wilde family home.

Dubh Linn Garden Dublin 2

Hidden behind Dublin's busiest building, Dublin Castle, and not far from the must-see Chester Beatty museum, is an extraordinary find: a whole street that nobody knows about and a garden to match. It looks like any town street, and is quiet most of the time, and just off the street is a beautiful, refined, minimalist garden, the perfect oasis from bustle and noise, a place of true tranquillity.

The garden is called Dubh Linn Garden. It is a smallish circle of grass with many benches round the perimeter. The grass is interweaved with snakes made out of paving stones in a Celtic pattern which, when viewed from above, is amazing. The gate you enter through (not the one with the name of the gardens written on it: walk another twenty yards and turn left) takes you onto a raised walkway so that you get a super view of the pattern.

Walk all round the circle and face the back walls of the castle complex for a real surprise. The backs of the buildings are not decorated in the sombre browns and greys of their fronts, but have been splashed in bold primary colours as if in a child's painting. The story goes that Dublin Corporation wanted it one bright colour, so painted each building a different colour to see which was best. Then they realised how ridiculous and how great it looked, and kept them in their glorious reds, yellows, blues and greens. As a city centre oasis that no-one realises is there, Dubh Linn gardens are hard to beat.

War Memorial Gardens Islandbridge, Dublin 8 (entrance from Con Colbert Rd and Sth Circular Rd)

Dublin Bus nos 51B, 78A, 79, 206 to IMMA.

A few minutes walk from the Irish Museum of Modern Art in Kilmainham, these gardens were designed by the architect Sir Edwin Lutyens to commemorate the Irish soldiers who died in the First World War. For years they were meanly neglected by successive national governments who thought the soldiers would have been better off fighting against Ireland's ancient enemy, not doing her dirty work in the trenches. All forgotten and forgiven now, more or less. On a mild day, a stroll around these unexpectedly large, formal gardens provides a pleasant break between visits to IMMA and Kilmainham Gaol (see pp 205 and 206). You might even be lucky enough to enjoy the sight of rowing teams killing themselves in the heat on the river. ('Not many people know this' slot: in the mountains near Glencree there is a small graveyard commemorating German airmen from the Second World War who crashed in Ireland.)

St Patrick's Day Parade. The feast is celebrated on 17 March. In Dublin it is now the focus of a week-long festival.

Other highlights and quirks

And other green spaces to look out for: **Broadstone Park** (beside the Blessington St Basin) is just a 1 km long stretch of straight grass, because it is a filled in canal, entertaining in an odd kind of way; **Croppies' Acre** beside the Liffey beyond the Four Courts, is an area of untended grass left uncultivated because it is the grave of United Irishmen killed in the late 18th century (they were called Croppies because many of them cut their hair short in imitation of the revolutionary French); **Sandymount Strand** (take the DART to Sandymount) is not green, but at low tide the sands cover an area as big as a small airport (and in the 1920s they seriously considered siting Dublin's first airport here); in the middle of the strand is a decayed old sea-bath. There used to be a wooden walkway going out to it. **King's Inn Fields**, beside the Four Courts on the north side of the river, has a fascinating tree which has grown around a park bench over the years, so it looks like the tree is hugging the bench. And the world's best cure for a hang-over—take the DART to **Howth**, and walk all round Howth Hill (taking care to walk *into* the wind), the spectacular seascapes will set you up for the evening!

Museums and galleries

Not many people know this, but there is more to Dublin culture than its famous and lively watering holes. As well as Ireland's national museums, which house major exhibitions, there are numerous independent galleries waiting to be explored in Dublin and these can be found in both obvious and out-of-the-way places. Nearly all of Dublin's museums and galleries stock a free leaflet for visitors which has up-to-date information on current exhibitions.

The majority of Dublin's galleries and museums are situated around the city centre on the south bank of the Liffey. However, don't ignore the northside as some of the most enjoyable ones are there—the Hugh Lane Gallery (Municipal Gallery of Modern Art), the James Joyce Centre and the National Museum at Collins Barracks.

The locations of many of those public spaces listed below are interesting in themselves. In addition, if you are exploring on foot, you will be rewarded along the way with a mixture of Dublin's best Georgian streetscapes and historic architecture, as well as some of its finest contemporary public sculpture.

The Dublin Writers' Museum

A good buy to take on your walks is the *City Guide to Sculpture in Dublin* (Sculptors' Society of Ireland). Dividing the city by area it contains easy to follow maps as well as descriptions of each piece of outdoor sculpture, both historical and contemporary. It costs €6.35 and is available in bookshops, some museums and from the Dublin Tourism Centre in Suffolk St and Baggot St Bridge, both in Dublin 2.

This list is far from exhaustive, but brings you some of the most interesting and some of the lesser-known gems of historic and artistic life in Dublin.

Chester Beatty Library The Clock Tower Building, Dublin Castle, Dublin 2, tel 407 0750, e-mail info@cbl.ie, website www.cbl.ie
If you have time to visit only a handful of Dublin's museums or galleries, this one should definitely be on your list. Having spent years tucked away in cramped suburban quarters, this world-class collection has finally been moved to worthier and more accessible surroundings at Dublin Castle. It was bequeathed to the Irish nation in 1956 by Sir Alfred Chester Beatty and comprises a unique selection of manuscripts, rare books and paintings from Oriental and Western culture. Included in the exhibits are over 270 copies of the Koran; Mogul and Persian manuscripts and illuminations; Syrian, Armenian, Ethiopian and Coptic Biblical texts as well as papyri dating from the 2nd and 4th centuries. There are also collections of Chinese furniture, Japanese prints, and early printed books with engravings by Dürer, Bartolozzi and Piranesi.
Open May–Sept Mon–Fri 10.00–17.00 Sat 11.00–17.00 Sun 13.00–17.00 (Oct–Apr closed on Mon)
Admission free. Café.

City Hall Cork Hill, Dublin 2, tel 672 2204
Next door to Dublin Castle, the City Hall building has recently been restored to its former neo-classical glory. It now houses an exhibition which tells the story of the governance of Dublin through the ages. Whatever about the

exhibition, drop in to admire the beautifully proportioned and exquisitely decorated space, as well as the view from the front to the Liffey and Capel St. Also, don't miss the café in the basement which is an offshoot of the much-loved Queen of Tarts across the road and serves most of the same great food.
Open Mon–Sat 10.00–17.15 Sun 14.00–17.00
Admission to exhibition or guided tours €4 students €1.50 (you don't have to pay to see the main building or get into the café). Limited wheelchair access.

Douglas Hyde Gallery (see Trinity College)

Dublin Civic Museum 58 Sth William St, Dublin 2, tel 679 4260
The Dublin Civic Museum houses a collection of exhibits from Dublin's past which outline the story of the city. Unfortunately, as it is neither large nor comprehensive, it is limited in what it can do to bring Dublin's full history to life. It is very central, however, just beside the Powerscourt Townhouse, so if you are in the area it is worth dropping in for half an hour.
Open Tues–Sat 10.00–18.00 Sun 11.00–14.00
Admission free

Dublin Waterways Museum Grand Canal Quay, Dublin 2, tel 677 7510,
e-mail waterwayslreland@ealga.ie
Located in a modern building that relates both to its surroundings and its function, this museum gives information on the construction and workings of Ireland's inland waterways and canals. The tour includes a short video and an exhibit of a model barge going through locks. Walking to and from the museum you'll see the often-neglected but nevertheless attractive area around the Grand Canal.
Open June–Sept Mon–Sun 09.30–17.30 Oct–May Wed–Sun 12.30–17.00
Admission €2.50 senior citizens €1.90 students, children €1.20 family ticket €6.35 Limited wheelchair access

Dublin Writers' Museum 18 Parnell Sq Nth, Dublin 1, tel 872 2077

Dublin is almost pathologically proud of its literary tradition, and many of the sacred artefacts of the cult of literary Dublin can be found in the Dublin Writers' Museum. There are first editions of books, and memorabilia relating to such famous literary names as Swift, Joyce, Kavanagh and Beckett. On the second floor, the main room is hung with portraits of Irish writers, and the adjoining Gorham Library is noteworthy for its ceiling which is decorated with fine plasterwork. And if this isn't enough cultural tourism, a trip to the Writers' Museum can be combined with a visit to the James Joyce Centre in Nth Great George's St (see below).

Open Mon–Sat 10.00–17.00 Sun and public hols 11.00–17.00 June–Aug late opening Mon–Fri 18.00

Admission €5.50 concessions €5.00 family ticket €15

GAA Museum Croke Park, Jones Rd, e-mail museum@gaa.ie

website www.gaa.ie

Dublin Bus nos 3, 11, 11A, 16, 16A, 51A, 123

The GAA has a special place in the sporting and political history of Ireland (see p. 236). This up-to-the-the minute museum brings you the history of the GAA and Gaelic games—there's lots of interactive stuff which should appeal to kids.

Open May–Sept Mon–Sun 10.00–17.00 Oct–April Tues–Sun 10.00–17.00

Admission Museum only €5 students, senior citizens €3.50 Museum and tour €8.50 students, senior citizens €6

Gallery of Photography Meeting House Sq, Temple Bar, Dublin 2,

tel 671 4654, e-mail gallery@irish-photography.com,

website www.irish-photography.com

This gallery is the place to go for groundbreaking, hard-hitting, controversial, high-brow art. It likes to insult and its sleek award winning architecture and prime place in Meeting House Sq. are testaments to its own, often justified, sense of importance. It is the only gallery in Ireland devoted exclusively to the exhibition of photography. It comprises three floors and is well lit though a little cramped. There are seminars and workshops relating to current exhibitions and these can be useful or, depending on the particular exhibition, even just a laugh to see what they say about some of the work on display. The gallery runs a selection of courses in photography and there are also darkroom facilities available for use by members. Wheelchair access.

Open Tues–Sat 11.00–18.00
Admission free

Guinness Storehouse St James's Gate, Dublin 8, tel 408 4800, website www.guinness-storehouse@guinness.com
Located at the brewery where the famous 'black stuff' is made, this is an exceptionally interesting stone building, divided into seven levels. Once you buy your ticket downstairs you can either join a guided tour or wander around and do your own thing. Everything you ever wanted to know about the brewing process is explained interactively through video, displays and sound. This includes a 'waterfall' of water used to make Guinness, barrels where it's stored (where you can watch a video inside each individual one), and an exhibition of Guinness merchandise from the earliest through to the modern day.

After all this, you can relax with a complimentary pint of the famous brew in the Gravity Bar on the top level, with a spectacular 360 degree view of the city. Though not exactly the cheapest experience of its kind, the Storehouse is a must for Guinness lovers.

Open 7 days 09.30–17.00 except Christmas Eve, Christmas Day, St Stephens' Day, New Year's Day and Good Friday.
Admission €12 concessions €2.50–€8 family €26

Heraldic Museum 2 Kildare St, Dublin 2, tel 603 0311 e-mail herald@nli.ie

Part of the Genealogy Office, the Heraldic Museum caters for the legions of people from all over the globe who come here, year-in year-out, to prove that they are Irish. It exhibits, as the name implies, a collection of artefacts relating to genealogies and armorial bearings from Europe and Ireland. The large-scale Ruskinian-style building is imposing and is similar to the Museum Building in nearby Trinity College. The Alliance Française occupies one half of the building and the café there serves delicious quiches and filled baguettes—perfect for lunch after your visit to the museum.

Open Mon–Wed 10.00–21.00 Thur–Fri 10.00–17.00 Sat 10.00–13.00

Admission free

Hugh Lane Gallery Charlemont House, Parnell Sq Nth, Dublin 1, tel 874 1903, website www.hughlane.ie

In many ways, this gallery contains a more impressive collection of art than any other in the city. This may be because it benefits from a more focused brief than that which a national gallery has to fulfil. It grew initially from a private donation and the current content still retains the slightly esoteric feel of the original (Hugh Lane, whose collection this was, died in the famous *Lusitania* sinking). Situated in a late-18th-century townhouse that was designed by William Chambers, the exhibits include 19th-century sculpture and painting by Irish and international artists. The gallery has recently acquired the entire contents of Francis Bacon's studio at 7 Reece Mews, London, where the artist spent his last 30 years living and working. Bacon's rooms have been painstakingly reconstructed on the gallery's premises and are on view to the public. The gallery also rather generously holds free lectures and concerts on Sunday afternoons. Very friendly and helpful staff.

Open Tues–Thur 09.30–18.00 Fri–Sat 09.30–17.00 Sun 11.00–17.00

Admission free. Wheelchair access.

Irish Jewish Museum 3–4 Walworth Rd, (off Victoria St), Sth Circular Rd,
Dublin 8, tel 453 1797
A fascinating if eccentric memorial to a fast vanishing part of Dublin life.
Although there have been Jews in Ireland for centuries, the big influx came
after the Russian pogroms in the late 19th century. At its peak in the 1940s
the community numbered over 5,000. Now there are less than 1,000. The
Museum, housed in two adjoining terraced houses, which were converted
into a synagogue, is in the heart of what was once Dublin's little Jerusalem.
Well worth the hunt. Dublin Bus nos 14, 15, 16, 19, 65, 83, 122.
Open May–Sept Sun, Tues, Thur, 11.00–15.30 Oct–April Sun 10.30–14.30
Admission free but donations gratefully accepted

Irish Museum of Modern Art (IMMA), Royal Hospital, Military Rd,
Kilmainham, Dublin 8, tel 612 9900, website www.modernart.ie
Dublin Bus nos 51B, 78A, 79, 206 from Aston Quay, Dublin 2
The 17th-century building that houses this museum was originally built as a
home for retired soldiers and was styled on the design of Les Invalides in
Paris. The Royal Hospital—as it is known—now provides a bright and airy
backdrop to a range of 20th- and 21st-century art. Exhibitions are on show
throughout the year and there is also a permanent collection of work by top
Irish artists. The building is surrounded by a splendid garden area which is a
lovely place to walk in summer. If you are in the mood for a further wander,
then try a stroll to the nearby War Memorial Gardens (see p. 195).
Open Tues–Sat 10.00–17.30 Sun and bank holidays 12.00–17.00
Admission free. Wheelchair access.

James Joyce Centre 35 Nth Great George's St, Dublin 1, tel 878 8547,
e-mail joycecen@iol.ie, www.jamesjoyce.ie
The James Joyce Centre and the building in which it is housed are both well
worth visiting. The house is a fine example of the kind of Georgian architecture

associated with Dublin and its ceilings feature some of Michael Stapleton's finest plasterwork. The reading room is very pleasant to sit in and there is an abundance of material to browse through. Among the many volumes there, you will find various editions of Joyce's work as well as biographical texts and works by a variety of other Irish writers. It is very easy to relax and take your time in this museum and the staff are particularly helpful. For those in search of a little light instruction there are daily tours through the house, and also through the surrounding north inner city where Joyce spent much of his youth.

Open Mon–Sat 09.30–17.00 Sun 12.30–17.00

Admission €4.50 students/senior citizens €3.50 *Walking tours* €9 students/ senior citizens €6.50

Kilmainham Gaol Inchicore Road, Dublin 8, tel 453 5984

Dublin Bus nos 51B, 78A, 79, 206 from Aston Quay, Dublin 2

Since 1796, generations of Irish revolutionaries were incarcerated here along with the city's criminals. As a vivid and riveting piece of Irish history this place is unbeatable, and all the more shocking because it was in use right up until 1924. Many famous movies have since been filmed here, including the seminal *Italian Job*. For those who want an insight into one of the most important events in Irish history, a collection of documents relating to the Easter Rising of 1916 are on view, with a notable focus on the rôle of women in the revolution. All in all, an informative and moving place to visit, but also very disturbing.

Open Apr–Sept Mon–Sun 09.30–17.00 Oct–Mar Mon–Sat 09.30–16.00 Sun 10.00–17.00

Admission (by guided tour only) €4.40 senior citizen €3.10 students €1.90 family €10.10 Wheelchair access.

Municipal Gallery of Modern Art (see Hugh Lane Gallery)

National Gallery of Ireland Merrion Sq West, Dublin 2, tel 661 5133, website www.nationalgallery.ie

Overlooking some of Dublin's finest Georgian architecture, the National Gallery is as notable for its situation as it is for its contents. Take some time before you go in to walk around the attractive gardens at the centre of Merrion Sq., and enjoy the stylish streetscape created by the elegant, red-brick, 18th-century façades.

You can enter either by Merrion Sq. or by the new Millennium Wing which opens on to Clare St. Once inside the Gallery you will find a small and solid, but not outstanding, collection of work from the 14th to the 20th century, with examples from most of the major European schools of painting. Irish art is well represented, and of great interest is the superb collection of Irish miniature painting which can be seen by special request. A dedicated Yeats room houses the gallery's permanent collection of works by the renowned Irish artist, Jack Yeats. It also contains works by his father, John B. Yeats and a few by the talented, if lesser-known, females of that notable family.

You can have a great lunch or a coffee in the busy restaurant on the ground floor of the gallery (but annoyingly it closes at 16.00), and there is also a well-stocked bookshop. If time is limited, however, at least check out Caravaggio's *Taking of Christ*, and the fine collection of Dutch and Spanish works, all on the second floor. The staff are friendly and give public tours, by arrangement, at weekends as well as on weekdays.

Open Mon–Sat 10.00–17.50 (Thur 20.30) Sun 14.00–17.00

Guided tours Sat 15.00 Sun 14,00, 15.00, 16,00

Admission free. Wheelchair access

National Museum of Ireland

The national museum is divided into three distinct sites across the city. These are as follows:

ARCHAEOLOGY AND HISTORY Kildare St, Dublin 2, tel 677 7444

Varied collection of artefacts dating from 7000 BC to the 20th century. Well worth a visit for the exhibition of prehistoric gold, as well as some outstanding examples of Celtic and mediaeval art.

Open Tues–Sat 10.00–17.00 Sun 14.00–17.00

Admission free. Wheelchair access to ground floor only, where the main exhibits are housed.

DECORATIVE ARTS AND HISTORY Collins Barracks, Benburb St, Dublin 7, tel 677 7444

Dublin Bus nos 90, 25, 25A

Set in the beautifully crisp architecture of a renovated army barracks, the permanent national decorative arts and history collection contains artefacts from Ireland's domestic, social, economic and military history. Here you will find an array of everyday items and curiosities from elegant silver and glassware to weaponry and costumes. Throughout the year, the museum also runs imaginatively-themed lecture and exhibition programmes. Although not situated right in the city centre, an excellent courtyard café and a car park make this a convenient museum to visit.

Open Tues–Sat 10.00–17.00 Sun 14.00–17.00

Admission free. Wheelchair access

NATURAL HISTORY Merrion St, Dublin 2, tel 677 7444

This is an amazing and faintly ghoulish piece of old Victoriana—almost a museum of a museum. It is made up solely of hundreds and hundreds of stuffed animals and features several species that are now extinct. There are many curiosities to be seen here, such as the skeletons of two whales which hang from the ceiling. It is positively freakish how much dead matter resides here. You can gaze on some of the more bizarre animals of the planet while also marvelling at the warped mindset of the museum's Victorian creators, and the odd, but admirable, decision by Dúchas, the Heritage Service, to keep

the place untouched. Children of all ages love it. A treasure.
Open Tues–Sat 10.00–17.00 Sun 14.00–17.00
Admission free. Limited wheelchair access

National Photographic Archive Meeting House Sq, Temple Bar, Dublin 2,
tel 603 0200, e-mail photoarchive@nli.ie, website www.nli.ie
The National Library's newest venture, this chic purpose-built archive houses
around 300,000 photographs, as well as a reading room and exhibition space
for displays of Irish visual culture. The Archive's exhibitions are regular and
themed and, while they are mainly historical in content, some contemporary
material is also shown.
Open Mon–Fri 10.00–17.00
Admission free. Wheelchair access.

National Print Museum Garrison Chapel, Beggars Bush, Haddington Rd,
Dublin 4, tel 660 3770
Dublin Bus nos 7, 45
The National Print Museum is housed in a converted army garrison chapel. The
focus here is on industrial printing and the displays represent the develop-
ment of the craft from its beginnings right up to the use of computers. There
are guided tours and a video which are very interesting and informative. If you
are keen on the subject of printing, this is definitely worth a journey from the
centre of town.
Open May–Sept Mon–Fri 10.00–12.30, 14.30–17.00 Sat, Sun, 12.00–17.00
Oct–Apr Tues, Thur, Sat, Sun 14.00–17.00
Admission €3.17 students, senior citizens €1.90 family €6.35. Wheelchair access

Newman House 85–86 St Stephen's Green, Dublin 2, tel 706 7422
Newman House is actually made up of two houses that were originally built as
private homes for members of the Dublin gentry. While the two buildings are

very different in style, they are both remarkable, principally, because of the extraordinary plasterwork that adorns their interiors. Much of the beautiful plaster decoration is the work of Swiss stuccodores, Paul and Philip Franchini, but the interiors also include plasterwork the Irishman, Robert West. Access is limited to groups who have pre-booked. Guided tours are given and there is also an exhibition on the buildings' restoration scheme.

Open June–Aug for groups only.

Number Twenty-Nine 29 Lower Fitzwilliam Street, Dublin 2, tel 702 6165, e-mail numbertwentynine@mail.esb.ie.

Built in 1794, this Georgian house has been renovated in an attempt to recreate its original, early 18th-century atmosphere and this exercise has been reasonably successful. The building has been preserved by the Electricity Supply Board in an apparent effort to compensate for the fact that most of Fitzwilliam Street Lower was torn down in the 1960s to make way for the company's hideous office block. It's a bizarre but welcome settlement for such large-scale architectural vandalism. Visitors are shown a short video before being given a guided tour. The latter attempts to give insight into the life of the servants and the well-to-do family who would have lived in a house such as this. However, it is a reconstruction and no matter how painstakingly this has been undertaken, the house does have a staged, museum-y feel to it. For a list of other, privately-owned Dublin houses open to the public, contact the Irish Georgian Society at 74 Merrion Sq, Dublin 2, tel 676 7053.

Open Tues–Sat 10.00–17.00 Sun 14.00–17.00. Group visits by arrangement
Admission €3.15 students, senior citizens €1.25 children free

RHA Gallagher Gallery 15 Ely Place, Dublin 2, tel 661 2558, website www.royalhibernianacademy.com

The Royal Hibernian Academy has four galleries—each containing three exhibitions—together with one commercial gallery and an outdoor area for sculpture. The gallery spaces are large and bright, and attract frequent major exhibitions of Irish and international art. Most of these last between one and two months. There is also a permanent collection here which includes work by Louis le Brocquy, Mainie Jellett and Evie Hone.

Open Tues–Sat 11.00–17.00 Thur 13.00–20.00 Sun 14.00–17.00
Admission free. Limited wheelchair access

Solomon Gallery Powerscourt Townhouse Centre, Sth William St, Dublin 2, tel 679 4237

This is a private contemporary gallery focusing mainly on work by new Irish artists and also on that of early 20th-century artists such as Evie Hone, Sir William Orpen and Jack B. Yeats. Unfortunately, the gallery is not accessible to wheelchair users.

Open Mon–Sat 10.00–17.30
Admission free

Tourist Information and Bookings

By phone, e-mail or online from anywhere in the world:

Bord Fáilte
website www.ireland.travel.ie
tel +800 668 668 66 (+ denotes international access codes)
e-mail reservations@gulliver.ie

Dublin Tourism
e-mail information@dublintourism.ie
website www.visitdublin.com

Dublin Bus Head Office ▪

59 Upr O'Connell St, Dublin 1, tel 873 4222, website www.dublinbus.ie

Open Mon–Fri 09.00–17.30, Sat 09.00–14.00 for general information, route maps, timetables, ID cards and information on tours.

The information and customer service line tel 873 4222 is open Mon–Sat 09.00–19.00

The website www.dublinbus.ie is a really comprehensive site with timetables, details of services and fares

Temple Bar Gallery and Studios 5–9 Temple Bar, Dublin 2, tel 671 0073
Painting, sculpture, photography, drawing and film are among the media represented at this gallery. It provides exhibition space as well as studios for working artists, and also holds superb experimental exhibitions such as first shows by promising newcomers. Spacious and attractive and certainly merits a visit.
Open Tues–Sat 10.00–18.00 (Thur 19.00) Sun 14.00–18.00
Admission free. Wheelchair access

Trinity College Dublin Dublin 2, tel 608 2320/2308
Trinity's central location makes it one of Dublin's most easily accessible, artistic and historic showpieces. Between the extraordinary architecture, the sculptures and the contents of some of the buildings, it really is a visual treat from one end to the other. While you're walking around look out for the sculpture by contemporary artists, for example: *Cactus*, by the American artists Alexander Calder, in Fellow's Square, or *Sphere with Sphere*, by Arnaldo Pomodoro, in front of the Berkeley Library. The Long Room in the Old Library (Ireland's oldest library) contains a superb collection of manuscripts and early

printed books, the most famous being the *Book of Kells*. If possible, visit the Long Room early in the day, or you could end up queuing for quite a while.

Also well worth a visit is Trinity's own purpose built contemporary art gallery (entrance from Nassau St), the **Douglas Hyde Gallery**. This has several exhibitions a year, showing the work of contemporary Irish and international artists. The gallery also holds lectures, tours and artists' talks, on which a big emphasis is placed.

Douglas Hyde Gallery tel 6081116
Open Mon–Fri 11.00–18.00 (Thur 19.00) Sat 11.00–16.45
Admission free. Wheelchair access

Old Library/Book of Kells tel 608 2308
Open Jun–Sept Sun 09.30–17.00 Mon–Sat 09.30–17.00 Oct–May
      Sun 12.00–16.30
Admission €7 students, senior citizens, children €6

Libraries

The libraries of Dublin are a great free resource—to start that 'roots' research, to find out about your legal rights, or simply to while away a wet afternoon in warmth and comfort.

The twenty or so public libraries provide free information on a wide range of personal, hobby and welfare issues, as well as being a source of borrowable books and tapes and a place where magazines and newspapers can be read for free. Many public libraries offer free on-line access; you need to be a member and will probably need to book.

The services are free. If you want to borrow books, tapes, etc., you have to get a library ticket and for this you will need proof of residence and photo ID. Public libraries are scattered about the city; find the address of the nearest listed in the 'corporations and councils' section of the current (2002) 01 Area telephone book under Dublin Corporation (recently renamed Dublin City Council).

The reference section of the library will contain the invaluable annual *Administration Yearbook and Diary*, in which you can find the contact number of your local TD, embassy personnel, civil service and local authority departments, educational establishments, charities, social and cultural organisations.

The library will also have telephone directories, the local voting register (a great way to identify your neighbours), reference books such as the *Directory of National Voluntary Organisations, The Irish Writers' Guide*, as well as guides to your legal and financial rights such as Colm Rapple's annual guide to tax *Family Finance*, and Frances Meenan's *Working within the Law*.

Some of the public libraries have specialist libraries or departments. One of the most useful and interesting is:

Central Library, ILAC Centre, Henry St, Dublin 1, tel 873 4333
Large reference library of current business and trade journals; trade reference books; overseas telephone books; multiple filing cabinets of press cuttings of Irish business and news topics; computer access and lessons; music library. It's a great place, but tends to get crowded.
Open Mon–Thur 10.00–20.00 Fri–Sat 10.00–17.00, free

Other state libraries include:

The National Library Kildare St, Dublin 2, tel 603 0200, website www.nli.ie
Over half a million books; manuscripts, prints and Irish newspapers. Enjoy the great domed reading room that has been home to generations of Irish students, from James Joyce on. Ask for the special genealogy service designed to help you in pursuit of your ancestors. You will need a reader's ticket, (bring ID) which can be got on the premises during normal office hours.
Open Mon–Wed 10.00–21.00, Thur, Fri 10.00–17.00 Sat 10.00–13.00, free

The National Archive Bishop St, Dublin 8, tel 407 2300,
website www.nationalarchives.ie
Reader's ticket required, which can be got on the spot. New reading rooms with an interesting high view of the city. The catalogues take a bit of mastering, but you can find everything here, starting with your ancestor's criminal record. Check the website for an overview.
Open Mon–Fri 10.00–17.00, free

And finally, a few favourites:

Central Catholic Library 74 Merrion Sq, Dublin 2, tel 676 1264
OK, the older stock is a bit single-minded, being mainly of Catholic theological interest, though there is an increasing breadth to the buying policy, but the reference library upstairs is quiet, and there is a calming view over the trees

of Merrion Sq. In winter the gas fires hiss contentedly. Very good eclectic selection of broadly religious periodicals.
Open Mon–Fri 11.00–18.30 Sat 11.00–17.30, free

Contemporary Music Centre 19 Fishamble St, Dublin 2, tel 673 1922
Contemporary music recordings and manuscripts as well as a library of books and music publications and a sound studio. Serious stuff for serious fans.
Open Mon–Fri 09.30–13.00, 14.00–17.30, free

Irish Architectural Archive 73 Merrion Sq, Dublin 2, tel 676 3430
For serious researchers only, this little treasure house of information about Irish architecture contains a quarter of a million photographs, as well as models, drawings and printed information.
Open Tues–Fri 10.00–13.00, 14.30–17.00, free but a donation is gratefully accepted.

Marsh's Library St Patrick's Close, Dublin 8, tel 454 3511,
website www.marshlibrary.ie
This library is the only one here that charges an entrance fee. It is fascinating not only because it was the first public library in Ireland and has a valuable collection of early books and manuscripts, but also because you can see the wire cages where they used to lock in readers when reading rare books—who said learning was easy? These, of course, are not in use today.
Open Mon, Wed–Fri 10.00–13.00, 14.00–17.00, Sat 10.30–13.00
Admission €2.50, children free

Churches to visit

Quite apart from their spiritual and historical associations, churches are great places to escape into, away form the crowds, where you can sit in peace and contemplate for a while, or even pray.

If you are really into churches, find a copy of Peter Costello's illustrated guidebook, *Dublin's Churches*, which contains details and descriptions of over 150 (Christian) places of worship.

Christ Church Cathedral

St Patrick's Cathedral Patrick St, Dublin 8, tel 453 9472,
website www.stpatrickscathedral.ie
Ireland's largest church, it was built dangerously outside the safe circuit of the
city walls on the traditional site of St Patrick's well where he baptised
converts to the new religion. It became a cathedral in 1213, but later fell into
decay, being used as a stable by Cromwell's soldiers, who were an iconoclastic
lot. The great figure associated with St Patrick's is the writer, Jonathan Swift,
who was Dean of the Cathedral from 1713 to 1745. Marsh's Library (see p. 215)
is just next door to St Patrick's.
Open Mon–Sat Mar–Oct 09.00–18.00 Nov–Feb 09.00–17.00 Sun 09.00–
10.45, 12.30–14.45, 16.30–18.00
Admission €3.50 concessions €2.50 family €8 unless you come to pray, at the
time of a service. Wheelchair access by arrangement.

Christ Church Cathedral Winetavern St, Dublin 8, tel 677 8099
The original Christ Church was founded by Sitric, the Norse King of Dublin, in
1038. Like St Patrick's, it fell into decay and was substantially rebuilt in the
19th century. (The rebuilding of St Patrick's was financed by a brewer,
Benjamin Guinness, and that of Christ Church by a whiskey distiller, Henry
Roe—is there some message here?) The medieval crypts are worth a visit.
Open Mon–Fri 09.45–17.00 Sat, Sun 10.00–1700
Admission €3 concessions €1.50. Most of the cathedral is wheelchair
accessible.

St Mary's Pro-Cathedral Marlborough St, Dublin 1, tel 874 5441
Called the Pro-Cathedral to emphasise the fact that the other two cathedrals
in the city, having originally been Catholic, are still held by the Church of
Ireland. Originally, the intention was to build the Pro-Cathedral on the
site that is now occupied by the GPO but, in order to avoid irritating
Ascendancy sensitivities, it was decided to locate it on a side street. The

building was commenced in 1816 and completed in 1825. The church has been the focus of many famous national occasions, notably the enormous funerals of Daniel O'Connell and Michael Collins. Many Catholics longed for a grander cathedral, and for years there were plans (thankfully abandoned) to build one on Merrion Square, which the diocese bought in the 1920s.

Open Mon–Sat 08.00–18.30 Sun 19.00 Regular Masses throughout the day, Taizé Mass Sat 20.00 in St Kevin's Oratory (except August). The exquisite singing of the Palestrina Choir can be heard at 11.00 Mass every Sunday, except during July when they are on holiday.

BLACK CHURCHES

Certain Dublin churches are built in the middle of the road, such as St Mary's just off Mountjoy Square and the Presbyterian Church in Church Ave, Rathmines. Tradition had it that if you ran round such a church three times after dark, you would meet the Devil on the third time round.

Other Catholic churches of note in the city centre are:

St Teresa's Church Clarendon St, Dublin 2, tel 671 8466, where the choir from the College of Music sings at the 11.30 Mass on Sunday mornings.

Whitefriar St Carmelite Church 56 Aungier St, Dublin 2, tel 475 8821, which houses the remains of St Valentine which were given to the order by Pope Gregory XVI in 1837.
Open daily 08.00–18.00

Some further historically-interesting **Church of Ireland** places of worship still in use today include:

St Ann's Church Dawson St, tel 676 7727
Open Sun–Fri 10.00–16.00
Handsome 18th-century interior where many of the great and the good of
Protestant Dublin were baptised.

St Audoen's Cornmarket, High St, Dublin 2, tel 677 0088
Dublin's only remaining medieval church.
Open Mon–Fri 10.00–16.00 (Sat closed) Sun services 08.00, 10.45 and
18.30

St Michan's Church Church St, Dublin 7, tel 872 4154
The crypts contain a number of naturally-mummified corpses. Dublin Bus
no. 134 passes it and the open-topped tour buses have a stop at Arran Quay,
100m from the church.
Guided tours mid-Mar–end Oct Mon–Fri 10.00–12.30 14.00–16.30
Sat 10.00–12.30 Nov–mid-Mar 12.30–15.30 Sat 10.00–12.30
Admission €3 students, senior citizens €2.50 children €2

Religious groups

Ireland is well known for being a religious country. Few of its streets are out of sight of a church tower, or beyond the sound of church bells summoning the faithful to prayer. However, the number of Irish 'faithful' has been dwindling considerably in recent years as the influence of the Catholic Church has largely diminished.

The population of Dublin, like the rest of the Republic of Ireland, is predominantly **Roman Catholic** and many of the capital's citizens are regular churchgoers. Attendance at services tends to be higher among the older part of the community, but some members of all age groups will regularly go to Mass, either out of genuine faith or family obligation. (Off-colour jokes about religion are therefore socially risky unless you definitely know your audience.)

Ironically, the two biggest and most famous churches in Dublin are, in fact, **Protestant**: Christ Church and St Patrick's Cathedrals. These are situated a few hundred metres from one another and are both **Church of Ireland** (the Anglican, or Episcopalian, form of Protestantism that was the Established Church in Ireland until 1867). The most important Catholic Church in the city is St Mary's Pro-Cathedral in Marlborough St, off O'Connell St, Dublin 1.

No matter where in the city you are, there will be a Catholic parish church very near by, with the times of masses posted for the public. The *Irish Catholic Directory* (published by Veritas) lists names and contact numbers for parishes, priests, retreat houses and other information.

Contact names of other groups and communities of believers can be found in the *Administration Yearbook and Diary* (published by the Institute of Public Administration), and Saturday's edition of *The Irish Times* lists the times of religious services of some of them.

> *I noticed now a quality of dryness in the air of Paris which I had never experienced in moist Dublin . . . my brain ached, my gritty socks burned my feet and I felt a terrible absence of sea or hills. I longed for that constant view of wistful Dublin mountains and the busy winds which keep Dublin freshly stirred.*
>
> PETER LENNON FOREIGN CORRESPONDENT: PARIS IN THE SIXTIES

The **Jewish** community in Dublin, which once numbered over five thousand, was initially based around the Sth Circular Rd. It later expanded into Terenure as it became more established and successful. Sadly, however, the Jewish population in Dublin has greatly reduced and now numbers only about a thousand. The principal Orthodox synagogue is at Rathfarnham Road, Terenure, Dublin 6. For further information on all services contact the Jewish Community Offices (and office of the Chief Rabbi), tel 492 3751.

The **Moslem** community, by contrast to the Jewish population, has expanded greatly in recent years. This growth is most vividly reflected by the building of the mosque and Islamic Cultural Centre at 19 Roebuck Rd, Clonskeagh, Dublin 14, tel 260 3740. The centre is a large, confident, yellow-brick complex with a great-value restaurant and shop which are both open to visitors. The other mosque in the city is at 163 Sth Circular Rd, Dublin 8, tel 453 3242, which also has a shop, tel 453 8336.

The French-speaking **African** Congregation and Gospel Choir (Irish Assemblies of God) gathers for service every Sunday in St Mark's Church, 42 Pearse St, Dublin 2, tel 671 4276. There is also an African-style service held at 15.00 on the first Sunday of every month in St Catherine's Church, Meath St, Dublin 8, tel 454 3356.

The **Greek Orthodox Church** (which also caters for the Romanian, Russian and Serbian orthodox communities in Dublin) is at 46 Arbour Hill, Dublin 7, tel 677 9020.

There is a **Buddhist** Centre at 56 Inchicore Rd, Dublin 8, tel 453 7427.

The Grace Bible Fellowship at 28a Pearse St, Dublin 2, tel 677 3170, offers two **Baptist** services a week, Sun at 11.00 and Wed at 20.00. There is also a **Baptist** Church at Grosvenor Road in Dublin 6, tel 497 4798, and the **Calvary Bible Baptist** Church can be contacted at 43 Main St, Bray, Co. Wicklow, tel 286 9262.

The **Religious Society of Friends** (Quakers) have their headquarters at Swanbrook House, Morehampton Rd, Dublin 4, tel 668 3684.

The **Mormon Community** in Dublin can be contacted at The Willows, Finglas Rd, Glasnevin, Dublin 11, tel 830 9960, where they have a church and a family history centre. On the southside of the city, they are at 48 Bushy Pk Rd, Terenure, Dublin 6, tel 490 5657.

The **Baha'i** community have their National Assembly of Ireland at 24 Burlington Rd, Ballsbridge, Dublin 4, tel 668 3150.

The **Lutheran Church** in Ireland (which has regular services in German and English) is at 24 Adelaide Rd, Dublin 2, tel 676 6548.

The **Methodist** Dublin Central Mission is based at 9C Lr Abbey St, Dublin 1, tel 260 5766, and also at various locations around the city centre as well as the suburbs.

Newgrange

City walks and tours

Guided walking tours

Dublin is not a big place so the best (and cheapest) way to get a real feel for the city is to see it on foot. There are several publications available in book-shops or through the tourist offices which suggest routes to walk around the city but, as it is such a small area, these are not really necessary unless you have a special interest. Generally, a good map is all you need. People are usually friendly when approached and asked for directions, even if they cannot always help you. And if you're lucky, you won't be told 'Ah now—if I was going there, I wouldn't start from here.'

If you have a particular interest in history or literature or if you just feel like taking a guided walking tour of the city, the following are a few we recommend; they all last about two hours.

Dublin Literary Pub Crawl tel 670 5602, website www.dublinpubcrawl.com
A light-hearted guided tour by two actors who perform humorous extracts
from Dublin's best known writers and, in true style, visit a selection of pubs on
the way.
Times April–Oct Mon–Sat 19.30, Sun 12.00, 19.30 Nov–May Thur–Sat 19.30
Sun 12.00 19.30
Meet upstairs in the Duke pub, Duke St, Dublin 2
Tickets €10 students €8 on the tour or in advance from the Dublin Tourism
Centre in Suffolk St, Dublin 2

Historical Walking Tours of Dublin tel 878 0227,
website www.historicalinsights.ie
These are conducted by history graduates of Trinity College and cover
the main features of Irish history from Dublin's development right up to the
present day, with more specific subjects covered on the 12.00 tours on certain
days (see below).
Times May–Sept Mon–Sun 11.00, 12.00 and 15.00 (12.00 Sat, Sun 'Sex and
the city'; Mon, Fri 'A terrible beauty–the birth of the Irish state 1916–1923';
12.00 Tues 'Dublin architecture and society') Oct–April Fri, Sat, Sun 12.00
Meet at the Front Gate of Trinity College, Dublin 2
Tickets €10 students/senior citizens €8 from the tour guide

Dublin Bus Head Office

59 Upr O'Connell St, Dublin 1, tel 873 4222, website www.dublinbus.ie

Open Mon–Fri 09.00–17.30, Sat 09.00–14.00 for general information, route
maps, timetables, ID cards and information on tours.

The information and customer service line tel 873 4222 is open Mon–Sat
09.00–19.00

The website www.dublinbus.ie is a really comprehensive site with timetables,
details of services and fares

James Joyce Centre 35 Nth Great George's St, Dublin 1, tel 878 8547
Walking tours of Joyce's favourite haunts in the north inner city.
Times Mon, Wed, Fri, 14.15
Tickets€9 students/senior citizens €6.50 (includes a tour of the **house**)

1916 Rebellion Walking Tour tel 676 2493, e-mail 1916@indigo.ie
website www.1916rising.com
Takes in many of the scenes from this dramatic episode in history.
Times May–Sept Mon–Sat 11.30, 14.00, Sun 13.00 Oct–April weekends only
Meet in the International Bar in Wicklow St, Dublin 2
Tickets €10 bought on the day or in advance from the Dublin Tourism Centre,
Suffolk St, Dublin 2

Guided bus tours

If you are only in Dublin for a short stay or if the changeable weather puts
you off walking, there are a number of bus tours which will still give you a
reasonable feel for the city's sites.

Dublin Bus City Tour tel 873 4222, www.dublinbus.ie
This is a hop-on-hop-off trip around the city's main sites, lasting 1 hour 20
minutes. The ticket is valid all day so you have the option to get off at any of
the 16 stops and back on again whenever you please. Some discounts are
available at attractions along the route.
Times and departure point every 15 min from 09.30 to 17.00; every 30 min
from 17.00 to 18.30, from Dublin Bus, 59 Upr O'Connell St, Dublin 1
Tickets €10 children €5 on the bus or from Dublin Bus, 59 Upr O'Connell St,
Dublin 1, and Dublin Tourism Centre, Suffolk St, Dublin 2

Ghost Bus Tour tel 873 4222
Visits haunted houses and sites around the city and shares tales of body-
snatching as well as Dracula's Dublin origins with gullible visitors from all

over the world. A good laugh if you are with a group but not suitable for children. The tour takes about 2 hours.

Times and departure point Tues–Fri 20.00, Sat, Sun 19.00 and 21.30, from Dublin Bus, 59 Upr O'Connell St, Dublin 1

Tickets €20, available from Dublin Bus, 59 Upr O'Connell St, Dublin 1 and Dublin Tourism Centre in Suffolk St, Dublin 2

Guide Friday Tour tel 676 5377

Another hop-on-hop-off style tour, taking the standard tourist route past the main attractions, but it also goes to the Zoo in the Phoenix Park, making it a good choice for anyone with children. Tours last 1½ hours.

Times and joining points every 10–15 minutes from 09.30 to 16.30 (Jul, Aug last tour 19.00) from O'Connell St, Dublin 1, (near the Gresham Hotel), the Provost's House, Lr Grafton St, Dublin 2 (opposite the Molly Malone statue)

Tickets €12 €10 students/senior citizens €4 children; on the bus, at Dublin Tourism, Suffolk St, Dublin 2, and 14 Upr O'Connell St, Dublin 1

Viking Splash Tour tel 855 3000

See historical Dublin by land and water from an amphibious military vehicle.

Times and departure point every day in summer, except Tues, roughly every hour from 10.00 to 17.00; winter schedules vary; from 64 Patrick St, beside the park at St Patrick's Cathedral

Tickets €13.50 children €7.50 on departure or credit card booking tel 453 9185

> *The South Wall, an 18th-century breakwater built to improve navigation of the Liffey, lies west of Ringsend and makes for a spectacular walk on a fine day. You can stroll right out to the red Poolbeg Lighthouse way out in Dublin Bay, from where you can survey the city and its surrounds from a unique perspective.*

Day trips and tours out of Dublin

The choices are wide—from gloomy tombs that predate the Pyramids to the grandeurs of 18th-century ascendancy Ireland. But the simplest is just to run the circuit of Dublin Bay on the DART, from the bleak estates of Roddy Doyle's Kilbarrack to the windy splendours of Killiney Bay. Get someone to point out Sorrento Terrace, where Neil Jordan and Bono live next door to each other. If you have about €8 million stuffed down the sofa, you too can live there too.

Get on the **DART** and travel the length of Dublin Bay, from the seaside towns of Bray and Greystones in the south, to Howth and Malahide in the North. The route takes you through some of the most historically interesting parts of the city, and, on a fine day, with the glittering sea on one side and the leafy stations and historical buildings on the other, makes a great tour. With an all-day ticket for €6, you can drop off at any of the little stations and visit the seaside towns. There are spectacular walks with sea views at **Howth Head**, **Bray** and **Dalkey**.

If the weather permits and you are an experienced hiker, it is well worth taking at least a day to walk part of the **Wicklow Way**, a stunningly beautiful hiking route that stretches from the outskirts of Dublin south across the Wicklow mountains. this. For maps and more information, ask at the Dublin Tourism Centre or at the visitor centre in Glendalough, Co. Wicklow (see below).

We list below just some of the many attractions within easy reach of Dublin, from big houses to monastic remains.

Brú na Bóinne (The Boyne Valley) Co. Meath, tel 041 982 4798, www.heritageireland.ie
Three mighty megalithic barrow tombs called Newgrange, Knowth and Dowth, built before the Egyptian pyramids or Stonehenge, make the Boyne valley, about 30 miles north of Dublin, a very sacred site. These monuments to

the human fascination with death are memorials left by the ancient pre-Celtic inhabitants of Ireland. Surrounded by standing stones, some more than 4 tonnes in weight, and decorated by mysterious spirals, lozenges and lines, these sites were the great public buildings of Stone Age civilisation. At dawn on 21 December, the shortest day of the year, the first rays of sunlight strike into the very heart of the ancient passage tomb of Newgrange, as they have done for 5,000 years For more information, see Henry Boylan's *The Boyne—A Valley of Kings* which also describes the nearby site of the battle of the Boyne (1690) which secured the Protestant ascendancy in Ireland.

Admission to the tombs is only through the visitor centre and with a guided tour. This is a very busy site and visits have been severely curtailed in recent years for conservation reasons so access to the monuments themselves is not even totally guaranteed, particularly in summer, unless you go on one of the tours that guarantee admission. Wheelchair access is restricted in the tombs but the visitor centre with tea rooms is fully accessible, including the toilets

Open visitor centre Mar—April daily 09.30–17.30 May 09.00–18.30 June mid-Sept 09.00–19.00 mid to end Sept 09.00–18.30 Oct 09.30–17.30 Nov—Feb 09.30–17.00

Admission to the visitor centre €1.90 senior citizens €1.20 student/child 70c

How to get there take a suburban train to Drogheda from Connolly Station, Dublin 1, and then a bus to the visitor centre or you could go on an *organised tour* with

Bus Éireann tel 836 6111 website www.buseireann.ie
Tickets €23 children €12.50
Dep Sat—Thur from Busáras, Store St, Dublin 1, 10.00 returning 17.45
or
Mary Gibbons Tours tel 283 9973
This tour includes a visit to the tomb itself, not just the visitor centre.
Tickets €34

Dep Mon–Fri from Royal College of Surgeons, Stephen's Green, Dublin 2, 10.30, Dublin Tourism Centre, Suffolk St, Dublin 2, 10.45, Royal Dublin Hotel, Dublin 1, 10.55, arriving back in Dublin at 17.00

Castletown Celbridge, Co. Kildare, tel 628 8252, www.heritageireland.ie

The largest and most architecturally impressive Palladian style country house in Ireland, at the end of a long avenue in the village of Celbridge about 20 km miles west of the city. Built incidentally by a lawyer—its hard to believe but they were evidently paid even more then than now.

What little remains of its once immense grounds along the banks of the River Liffey can still be explored by visitors for free all year round and makes a lovely walk on a fine day.

Tours of the house are well worth while, as much for the insights into the fascinating family that once inhabited it as for the architecture and interior design. There are also tea rooms in the house and cafés in the nearby village for refreshments.

There is restricted wheelchair access only but toilets for people with disabilities are available.

Open 23 April–Sept Mon–Fri 10.00–18.00 Sat, Sun 13.00–18.00 Oct Mon–Fri 10.00–17.00 Sun, bank hol 13.00–17.00 Nov Sun only 13.00–17.00
Admission €2.50 senior citizens €1.90 students/children €1.20
How to get there Dublin Bus nos 67, 67A

Glendalough Co. Wicklow, tel 0404 45325/0404 45352, website ww.heritageireland.ie

The name means 'glen of the two lakes' and it is a spectacular setting for mountain walks and picnics yet only an hour from Dublin, making it ideal for a day trip. Take in the scenery and fresh air or explore the monastic settlement that lasted in this secluded spot from the 7th to the 16th centuries. The visitor centre, picnic areas, and toilets are wheelchair accessible, as are some of the less rugged areas around the lake, but much of the park, including the monastic settlements, are not

Admission free

How to get there take St Kevin's Bus, tel 281 8119, which leaves St Stephen's Green West, Dublin 2 (outside the College of Surgeons) at 11.30. The last bus returning to Dublin is at 16.15 Mon–Fri and 17.30 Sun and bank holidays. Or you could go on an *organised tour* with

Bus Éireann tel 836 6111 website www.buseireann.ie
Tickets €25 student/senior citizen €23 children €12.50
Depart from Busáras, Store St, Dublin 1 at 10.30 returning 17.45.

Larchill Arcadian Gardens tel 628 7354, website www.gardensireland.com
A few miles north of Kilcock is the sole surviving example in Ireland and Europe of a mid-18th-century *ferme ornée* or arcadian garden. It's wonderful for anyone interested in historic gardens and great fun for children too. As well as a formal walled garden, there is a 1 km walk through landscaped parkland in which there are ten classical and gothic follies and other features, including a lake. Larchill also has one of the largest number of rare farm animal breeds in Ireland in its gothic model farm and a pets' corner and adventure playground for the kids. In June and July there is a maze—grown from maize! The tea-rooms and gift shop in the visitor centre are wheelchair accessible as are the toilets, and the walled garden.

Open May Sat, Sun (groups during the week) June–Aug daily 12.00–18.00
Admission children €5 senior citizens €4
How to get there Unfortunately, you really need a car. Alternatively take Dublin Bus no. 66 to Maynooth and take a taxi the few miles to the gardens.

Newbridge House Donabate, Co. Dublin, tel 843 2184
Newbridge House remains unchanged since it was built in 1737 and has all the original furniture and features, as well as Robert West's intricate

plasterwork. A traditional farm in the grounds, which preserves the older species of farm animals, is perfect for a visit with children or an educational trip for an uninitiated townee. There is a playground, a shop and a café If it's a fine day check out Donabate Beach nearby. Guided tours—last one starts one hour before closing.

Open April–Sept Tues–Sat 10.00–17.00 (closed 13.00–14.00) Sun and bank hol 14.00–18.00 (closed 13.00–14.00) Oct–Mar Sat, Sun, bank hol 14.00–17.00

Guided tour of house €5.50 concessions €5 children €3 family €15

Farm €1.50 family 3child groups €1 (last tour 1 hr before closing)

How to get there Dublin Bus no. 41, 41A, 41B, 41C, from Eden Quay, Dublin 1, to Swords, 33B from Swords suburban train from Connolly Station, Dublin 1

Powerscourt Demesne Enniskerry, Co. Wicklow, tel 204 6000

The demesne contains the remains of the **Palladian house and formal gardens**, an exhibition, a café, an overpriced restaurant and shops; these are often crowded, but undeniably still beautiful. **Powerscourt waterfall**, a couple of km away, is much better value, and is well worth the trip either as well as or as an alternative to the house and gardens. There are toilet and picnic facilities but it is otherwise unspoilt. The 400 ft waterfall is the highest in Ireland and the surrounding hills and forests are great for walks. The picturesque village of Enniskerry offers cosy pubs and cafés to retire to after the day's activity before heading back to town.

Open house and garden daily all year round 09.30–17.30 waterfall 09.30–19.00

Admission house and gardens €8 senior citizen/student €6.50 children €4 Wheelchair accessible, including toilets; waterfall €3.50 children €2.50

How to get there Dublin Bus no. 44 from Hawkins St, Dublin 2 to Enniskerry village. The demesne is about 15 minutes walk from the village and is well signposted. Wild Coach tours (see below) have a tour to Powerscourt.

Victoria's Way—Sculpture and Philosophy Park Roundwood,
Co. Wicklow, tel 281 8505 website www.victoriasway.net
Standing in a field in the Wicklow mountains, this collection of specially
commissioned solid stone statues from India and Ireland makes a remarkable
sight. One of the latest to arrive is a black granite Indian god playing the
uileann pipes. The project of a single benefactor who receives no support
whatsoever from the tourism or heritage authorities, Victoria's Way is one of
the most remarkable, if not the most easily accessible, treasures in Ireland.
The entire phenomenon will take about another four years to complete, if
there's enough support to keep the collection in Ireland. At the moment there
are about 2,000 to 3,000 visitors a year—more will be needed to keep the
place open so make a point of showing your support while visiting Dublin
and you will be richly rewarded!

Victoria's Way is located just under 2 km from Roundwood, Co. Wicklow,
on the Enniskerry to Roundwood road. Remember that the whole thing is out
of doors, so dress appropriately and wear sturdy shoes.
Open daily May–Sept 12.30–18.00
Admission €2.50
How to get there St Kevin's Bus from St Stephen's Green West (outside the
College of Surgeons) Dublin 2 at 11.30 and ask to be dropped off at the Sally
Gap crossroads. Victoria's Way is 300 metres away, on the Roundwood road.

Bus tours of the coast

A number of companies offer excursions to Wicklow, the Boyne Valley and
various points of interest on the outskirts of Dublin: here are just three of them.

Dublin Bus tel 873 4222, website www.dublinbus.ie
The **Coast and Castle Tour** of north Dublin lasts 3 hours and the **South
Coast Tour** which takes in parts of Wicklow lasts 3 hrs 45 min.

Times and departure point Coast and Castle dep 10.00 South Coast dep 11.00 and 14.00, both tours depart from the Dublin Bus office 59 Upr O'Connell St, Dublin 1.

Tickets for both tours €17 children €8.50 from Dublin Bus or Dublin Tourism.

Over the Top Tours tel 838 6128, freephone 1800 424 252 reservations only
A minibus tour which claims to go where large coach tours don't. One of the tours they offer is the Celtic Experience visiting the Hill of Tara, Mellifont Abbey, Monasterboice and the Hill of Slane.

Times and departure points 09.00 from Dublin Tourism, Suffolk St, Dublin 2 and 09.20 from Dublin Tourism, 14 Upr O'Connell St, Dublin 1

Tickets €25 students €23

Wild Coach Tours tel 280 1899, website www.wildcoachtours.com
Full and half day trips with a more casual feel including a Powerscourt Tour and a Castle Tour. The prices include all admission charges.

Times and departure points vary according to the tour

Tickets full day €28, student/child €25 half day €20 student/child €16

The sporting life

Hurling (Irish Press *photo*)

There are three ways to deal with the phenomenon of sport. The first is to hurl yourself headlong, into the fray showing who's boss on the field in your sport of choice and adding to your prowess by learning whole new ones. The second is to sit on the sidelines with a cool drink, eyeing the exertions of others with a haughty yet understanding grin, reading the newspaper. The third is to ignore the phenomenon altogether and skip back to the chapter about eating.

Dublin caters for all three. Indeed, Dublin offers much in the way of sporting activities. If you're tired of the same old round of international sports you can find here a whole new array of ways of hurting yourself and others in the name of fitness. Gaelic games, run by the GAA (Gaelic Athletic Association), add a whole new dimension to the world of sport, with Gaelic football and hurling attracting massive interest both playing and watching.

Add to this the usual round of soccer, rugby, tennis, and swimming and you have a huge range of sporting facilities and spectating opportunities from beginner to professional.

Almost every sport is catered for to some extent, with a slew of boxing clubs in every suburb, and regular bouts at the National Stadium. Swimming pools pepper the city, and golf clubs of both championship and amateur standard pop up all over the place, with regular tournaments of quality on show. Alternatively, if you don't find this exciting enough, there are many and varied opportunities to gamble on the event to add that extra spice. Dublin has a host of sports to offer the visitor if you're brave enough to search them out. The *Evening Herald* and the *Irish Independent* are the best for details of what's on. For details of horse and greyhound racing venues, see **Gambling**, below.

Tourist Information and Bookings

By phone, e-mail or online from anywhere in the world:

Bord Fáilte
website www.ireland.travel.ie
tel +800 668 668 66 (+ denotes international access codes)
e-mail reservations@gulliver.ie

Dublin Tourism
e-mail information@dublintourism.ie
website www.visitdublin.com

Watching sport

Gaelic games

The first stop for any visitor should be a **GAA** game. The GAA was founded in 1884 as part of the movement towards national independence, to encourage the playing of 'Irish' games such as hurling and Gaelic football as opposed to what were described as 'garrison games' i.e. football, rugby and cricket. It was immensely successful, and became a political nursery for the entire nationalist movement. Going to a GAA game is to experience part of history as well as the living Ireland of today.

The characteristic of GAA games is the vivid speed of the play, and the fluidity with which the play switches from one end to another. **Gaelic football** is a cross between rugby and soccer, played with a round ball, encompassing the handling and kicking skills of rugby and the vision and dexterity of soccer. Players are not allowed to pick the ball up directly from the ground.

Hurling is played with long sticks made of ash wood, with players allowed to handle the *sliothar* (pronounced slitter: the ball) but again not to pick it up directly from the ground. The *sliothar* is made of leather and is about the same size as a cricket ball, although a good deal softer. It has a cork on the inside to make it light and to help it to travel at speed. Hurling, when played well, has a phenomenal velocity about it and an inherent grace that makes it one of the most aesthetic and exciting field sports in the world.

Camogie is hurling for women and is similarly as fast, exciting and skilful as games come. A demanding sport to play and a thrilling one to watch, camogie is well worth investigating, especially if you've never seen it before. Goals in all Gaelic games are a cross between rugby and soccer posts—guarded by a net and high posts on either side. Scoring into the goal is worth three points, while scoring above the crossbar is worth one.

The GAA retains its special hold on the nation's attention. Every town, suburb, parish and village in the country has its own pitch and training facilities, complete with club colours and local flavour. The sport is completely amateur and incites high passions, which verge on the tribal at times. For that reason, it is more rewarding to sniff out a club game where the footballers and hurlers who may never feel the glory of representing their county have the chance to revel in the attention of their parish.

The standard of hurling in Dublin is improving rapidly, with the game's popularity on the increase all the time, while Gaelic football at club level is a mainstay of Dublin's social and cultural life. The biggest club games in Dublin are generally played during the summer and autumn months at **Parnell Park**, Dublin 5—this is the place to head to, practically every Saturday evening of the summer months and most Sunday afternoons during the winter. If you decide to forego the club scene then a trip to **Croke Park**, Dublin 3, the showpiece stadium of the GAA is whole-heartedly recommended. Over the past few years major reconstruction has taken place at the stadium, which is now a hugely impressive state-of-the-art affair, complete with corporate boxes and facilities. From mid-March to the end of September the games become quite serious with regular crowds of 25,000–65,000.

The real start of the Croke Park season is St Patrick's Day (17 March) when the All Ireland club finals are played. From then on the élite county teams take centre stage, the skill levels rise and entry fees rise accordingly. Touts have been known to get anything up to €150 for All Ireland finals' tickets, but they are best avoided as high quality forgeries are frequently in circulation. Go during June or July when tickets are cheaper and easier to come by, without any dilution of the atmosphere or intensity. If you have trouble getting tickets for big games, try the ticket booths on match mornings on Lr Drumcondra Rd, about five minutes from Croke Park.

A big game is usually preceded by a Minor (under-18) match, which starts at 13.00–13.30; the Senior games generally start between 15.00 and 16.00, nearly always on Sundays. You can take a bus from O'Connell St in the city centre, but on big match days would probably make more progress walking, where fans mark an obvious route to the stadium.

Croke Park Jones's Rd, Dublin 3
Dublin Bus nos 3, 11, 16, 51A, 123. Get off at the top of Clonliffe Rd then follow the crowds. For details of times and fixtures check the *Evening Herald* or *Irish Independent*.
Admission early summer championship game €15 for standing tickets to €25 for seated ones. As the season progresses, the prices rise—tickets become like gold dust and at face value cost €30–€50.

Parnell Park Collins Ave E, Donnycarney, Dublin 5
Dublin Bus no. 20B from Eden Quay in the city centre. Get off at Donnycarney Church (Our Lady of Consolation).
Admission €4–€15, depending on the level of the game in progress.

Soccer

Soccer underwent something of a boom period in Ireland in the early 1990s, following the international success of the Irish team. However, most of the good Irish players were creamed off by the full-time professional leagues in England. That trend has been somewhat reversed recently with a number of young Irish players returning home to clubs like **St Patrick's Athletic**, **Shelbourne** and **Shamrock Rovers**. These are the only teams worth going to see. While the standard of fare is inconsistent, it can occasionally be good value for money. You are just as likely to be bored senseless at a nil-all draw as you are to be enthralled by an 8- or even 9-goal thriller. The Dublin Derby games are always worth a risk, especially those involving the three teams named above, who all play bright entertaining football.

St Patrick's Athletic play in Inchicore while Shelbourne and Shamrock Rovers share Tolka Park, a small yet impeccable all-seater stadium in Drumcondra. In fact, most League of Ireland grounds are completely seated.

St Patrick's Athletic 125 Emmet Rd, Inchicore, Dublin 8
Dublin Bus no. 78A from Aston Quay, Dublin 1, stops outside the ground.
Admission €7–€10, students half price.

Shelbourne and **Shamrock Rovers** Tolka Park, Dublin 9
Dublin Bus nos 3, 11 or 16. Get off at St Patrick's College; walk down Drumcondra Rd and turn left down Richmond Rd.
Admission €10 students €5

Rugby

Two or three times a year Dublin is invaded for the weekend by hordes of English, Scottish, Welsh, Italian or French fans for rugby internationals in the **Six Nations Championship** (hence, the shortage of hotel beds at these times) played at Lansdowne Road. Tickets for these matches are at an absolute premium, as Lansdowne Road is a relatively small ground, and only the touts ever seem to have any. You can try your luck by contacting the Irish Rugby Football Union (IRFU—see below). Rugby internationals tend to be special occasions—the atmosphere in the city is scarcely equalled through-out the rest of the year, only St Patrick's Day comes close.

The Irish rugby public have become used to their team's unpredicta-bility, and set out to have a good time regardless of the result. If you manage to come across a ticket then consider yourself blessed and enjoy a unique occasion in the Irish sporting calendar.

Irish Rugby Football Union (IRFU) 62 Lansdowne Rd, Dublin 4, tel 647 3800
website www.irfu.ie
Lansdowne Road DART from Connolly Station (Amiens St), Dublin 1, stops just
next to the ground. Dublin Bus nos 2, 3 or 7.
Tickets €20–40.

Club rugby in Dublin is overshadowed somewhat by the strength of Limerick
and Cork rugby, and the regular league games of spring can be somewhat
tepid affairs in the capital. Watch out for the visits of Shannon, Garryowen,
Cork Constitution and Young Munster to see the real strengths of Irish rugby,
but if you want to back a winner make sure you're shouting for the visitors.

The main clubs are Clontarf, the only major northside club, Lansdowne,
St Mary's, Old Wesley, Blackrock and Old Belvedere. The south-side clubs are
based within a stone's throw of each other in Donnybrook and Ballsbridge,
and Blackrock. During the winter the Smithwicks' Old Belvedere Floodlit Cup
serves up an even share of classic encounters and absolute duds. It's potluck,
but worth the small entry fee. (If it's too cold you can even watch the games
from the comfort of the pavilion bar, with a free pint of the sponsor's brew).

Old Belvedere Anglesea Rd, Dublin 4, tel 660 3378
Dublin Bus no. 10 to Donnybrook. Walk past the church down Anglesea Rd, the
ground is half-way down on the right. Dublin Bus nos 7, 45, 46A to Ballsbridge.
Get off at the RDS on Merrion Rd and walk down Anglesea Rd, the club is
halfway down on the left, past the library and the side entrance to the RDS.
Admission €5 (students half price).

Boxing

You can see regular bouts at the National Stadium and the National
Basketball Arena in Tallaght. Check the *Evening Herald* or *Irish Independent*
for details of bouts.

National Basketball Arena Tymon Pk, Tallaght, Dublin 24, tel 459 0211, e-mail info@iba.ie, website www.nala.ie
Dublin Bus nos 49, 50, 54A, 77

National Stadium 145 Sth Circular Rd, Dublin 8, tel 453 3371
e-mail iaba@eircom.net
Dublin Bus nos 16, 16A, 19, 19A, 122 from O'Connell St, Dublin 1

Cricket

The 'garrison' game *par excellence* is still played in Ireland by a hardy minority. During the summer term you can watch it in Trinity College, Dublin 2, and at the weekend there are usually matches in the Phoenix Park, Dublin 1, or **Leinster Cricket Club**, Observatory Lane, Rathmines, Dublin 6, tel 497 2428, website lccsports.net (Dublin bus nos 15A, 15B).

International cricket matches involving Ireland are occasionally played at **Clontarf Rugby & Cricket Club**, Castle Ave, Clontarf, Dublin 3, tel 833 2621. Check the newspapers for details of matches. Dublin Bus no. 130 from Lr Abbey St, Dublin 1.

Playing sport

Gaelic games

Perhaps the easiest sports to play are Gaelic games, with upwards of 60 clubs in the Dublin area which are always on the lookout for new members. One of the latest developments to hit Gaelic games is the mushrooming of ladies' teams, with the All-Ireland Ladies' Football Final attracting bigger and bigger crowds.

Gaelic clubs welcome people of any talent level, and make great efforts to teach the rudiments of the games, so places can always be found for new people. Newcomers' chances of playing for the first team may be slim but the great thing about the reserve teams is their willingness to embrace the social aspects of the game, indeed they are more renowned as drinking clubs than breeding grounds for new talent. All you need is a pair of boots and a willingness to get fit.

The nearest Gaelic football, hurling or camogie club is never more than a few kilometres away; your local pub should be able to tell you where. Failing that, all Dublin clubs are registered with **Parnell Park**, tel 831 2099, the administrative headquarters for hurling and football in the capital. They will be more than willing to answer any inquiries.

There are 36 camogie clubs all around Dublin and they vary enormously in size and scale of facilities. A personal membership for a camogie club only costs €10. The bigger clubs have more teams and probably provide more effective coaching for beginners. The person to contact is Sheila Wallace, **GAA camogie division**, tel 836 4619. She will advise you on who to call and what club will suit you best. You can also contact Marie O'Brien, the **Dublin County Secretary**, at satjud@oceanfree.net. If you're really fanatical about GAA and camogie, the magazines *Hogan Stand* and *Hi-Ball* are for you. You can also check out the **GAA museum** at Croke Park, tel 855 8176 (see p. 201).

Soccer

There is a huge network of soccer clubs throughout the city, ranging from the semi-professional to the outright amateur. If you believe that you have what it takes to make the grade then get on the phone to your local National League Club, they'll gladly have a look at you or put you in touch with one of their feeder clubs. Again if your interest is merely in a weekly run-out, then your nearest pub more than likely has a team which will meet your needs.

The **Leinster Senior League**, 43 Parnell Sq, Dublin 1, tel 872 6267, has a network of clubs, which compete more strenuously than the pub teams, with more regular training sessions and proper 90-minute games. Again, though, this isn't the most serious league in the world and these teams are legendary for their ability to enjoy themselves after their games.

Rugby

Rugby clubs, like their Gaelic counterparts, are also happy to accommodate new members. Again, whatever your level or experience they will gladly take you on, and your start up costs are no more than the purchase of a gumshield and a pair of boots. The easiest way to find your nearest club is through the **IRFU (Irish Rugby Football Union)**, 62 Lansdowne Rd, Dublin 4, tel 647 3800 website www.irfu.ie. Most clubs have at least five or six adult teams, and there are more and more women's teams, although the boom in interest that has taken ladies' football by storm has yet to fully strike the rugby clubs. Whether your interest is in the occasional game of rugby or a more serious approach to getting fit, Dublin's rugby clubs welcome new members.

Golf/pitch 'n' putt

The quality of Irish **golf** courses is world renowned and the sport is booming helped no doubt by the international successes of players such as Padraig

Harrington, Paul McGinley and Darren Clarke. It's not exactly a shoestring sport but if you really want to chase a little white ball around then the par 3, 18-hole course at the **Spawell Leisure Centre** may suit. You can hire whatever equipment you need to tackle their short course. If you haven't quite reached that stage yet then try their driving range to hone your talents, where you can vent your frustrations to your heart's content. (They also have snooker and indoor and outdoor tennis.)

Spawell Leisure Centre Tempelogue Rd, Dublin 6W, tel 490 1826
Dublin Bus nos 15B, 15D, 49, 65.
Prices €5 weekdays €6 weekends.

Pitch 'n' putt is the shorter and much more affordable version of golf, and there are many pitch 'n' putt courses around Dublin's suburbs. It's usually 9 holes, though sometimes you may be lucky and find a 12- or 18-hole course. For beginners, it's usually better to find a course with short distances (60 metres or less) to the flag. One such course is **Deer Park** in Howth, which has a very manageable 18-hole course with breathtaking views of the sea. If you're a U2 fan, Larry Mullen Jnr lives nearby. A 12-hole course in pleasant surrounding is in **St Anne's Park**, Raheny.

Deer Park Howth, Co. Dublin, tel 839 8777
Dublin Bus nos 31 and DART to Howth Station
Prices €2.50–€4.30
Open 06.30 summer, 08.00 winter, till last light.

St Anne's Park Raheny, Dublin 5, tel 833 8898
Dublin Bus nos 29A, 31, 32.
Prices €3.80 €1.50 students, OAPs (no concessions on Sun)
Open 7 days from 10.00. Closing times vary according to weather conditions and light.

Swimming

Dublin is also well serviced with **swimming pools and clubs**. The easiest place to find them is the *Golden Pages* directory and the quality in general is good. Beware of some of the more dilapidated ones which can be lax on hygiene, it is always a good idea to check the pools out before you use them. Here the best bet is a visit to the commercially run pools as they usually have other facilities and are quite relaxed about time limits. The Council-run pools can be strict on time, and relaxed about cleanliness. Whichever pool you decide to swim in, be sure to lock all valuables away safely in the available lockers.

Swimming in the sea is a very different experience from the chlorinated indoor pools. From May to October the Irish Sea is refreshing—or bracing depending on your taste. The seaside spots themselves are worth a visit even if you don't swim—on clear bright days the views are magical.

One of the best sea bathing spots in Dublin is the **Forty Foot** natural pool at Sandycove which is not tide-dependent. For years this was a men only, skinny-dipping area but it is now open to everybody. Do take the warnings about the backwash from the super-ferries seriously. The undertow and waves created can be frightening and dangerous. You could also swim off the sea wall at the little sandy beach at **Sandycove** even when the tide is out. Another lovely place to bathe when the tide is right is **Seapoint**, which is nearer the city. On the northside there are fine strands at **Dollymount**, **Donabate**, **Malahide**, **Portmarnock** and **Portrane**.

Seapoint and Sandycove are on the DART line and are also served by Dublin Bus no. 7. The northside strands are served by Dublin Bus nos 32, 32A, 32B and 130.

Hill-climbing/walking

Another of the joys of Dublin is the city's close proximity to the Dublin and Wicklow mountains. They are stunningly beautiful and very accessible but can also be dangerous: the weather can quickly change from sunny and clear to cold, wet and misty.

An Óige, the Irish Youth Hostel Association, is a great organisation to become involved with if you're interested in hill-climbing and walking. Walkers generally meet at an assigned spot on a weekend morning, and are brought to their (usually very scenic) destination in a mini-bus after an hour or so's journey. Walks are usually classified according to their level of difficulty, so there's always one to suit all ages and fitness levels—despite its name An Óige welcomes members of all ages and joining it is a great way to meet new people.

An Óige 61 Mountjoy Sq, Dublin 1, tel 830 4555, e-mail mailbox@anoige.ie website www.irelandyha.org

Boxing

This is another sport increasing in popularity. Any city-centre gym will give you details of how to get involved.

Cycling

Cycling clubs tend to be a bit harder to track down. The easiest way to contact them is through the bicycle shops as most have constant contact with the clubs. **Cycle-Ways** 185 Parnell St, Dublin 1, tel 873 4748, is your best bet, as they have plenty of expert, friendly, knowledgeable staff.

Tennis

Tennis Ireland have all the information you need to find out about your nearest tennis courts. What is definitely advisable, though, is to check out Dublin City Council tennis courts, which are rarely completely full (except in

June during Wimbledon) and are very inexpensive. You always have to have your own racquets and balls, and any sort of trainers will be allowed on the tarmacadam surface. Nearly every public park has tennis courts, but check out **St Anne's Park** on the northside and **Herbert Park** on the southside for a large number of courts in good condition.

Herbert Park Ballsbridge, Dublin 4, tel 668 4364
St Anne's Park Raheny, Dublin 5, tel 833 8898
Tennis Ireland 105 Morehampton Rd, Dublin 4, tel 668 1841

Ten-pin bowling

Ten-pin bowling has become increasingly popular in Ireland over the past few years, and is a sport literally anyone can play. The **Leisureplex** has four bowling alleys in Dublin. The peak time in bowling alleys is 18.00 to 23.00 at weekends, and prices vary according to the day and time. Be careful with pool, snooker, food, drinks, amusements here, or your visit will cost you a lot more than you bargained for.

    Leisureplex website www.leisureplex.ie
    Blanchardstown Centre, Dublin 15, tel 822 3030, Dublin Bus no. 39
    Malahide Rd, Coolock, Dublin 17, tel 848 5722, Dublin Bus nos 27, 42, 43
    Stillorgan, Co. Dublin, tel 288 1656, Dublin Bus nos 11, 46A
    Village Green, Tallaght, Dublin 24, tel 459 9411, Dublin Bus nos 49, 54A, 77, 77B
Prices €22.90–€33.00 per hour, maximum six people per lane.
Open 24-hours, 7 days a week.

Snooker

If snooker is your thing, there are a number of halls to choose from. As a general rule, city centre snooker halls are more run-down than their suburban counterparts. Expect to pay an average of €7.50 an hour in most places, though during the day on a weekday is always cheaper than at night and at weekends. **Breaks** snooker club even caters for the snooker enthusiast 24-hours a day, 7 days a week, 364 days a year.

In **Jason's** of Ranelagh, on the southside of the city, there is a real sense of a disappearing world in the dusky confines of green baize echoing to the sound of thunking balls. If you're really lucky then their most famous patron may just be racking them up on the table beside you—Ireland's most recent World Champion Ken Doherty made his first break on these very tables.

Breaks Upr Drumcondra Rd, Dublin 9, tel 837 0653
Numerous Dublin Bus routes
Open 7 days, 24-hours, 7 days, 364 days.

Jason's 56 Ranelagh Village, Dublin 6, tel 497 5983
Dublin Bus nos 11, 11A, 13B, 18, 44, 48A, 86
Open 7 days, 24 hours.

Gambling

Staking a large amount of hard cash on one animal being able to jump and run better than a handful of its peers is an age-old tradition in Ireland, and one which still thrives.

Ireland at its most trusting and its most cunning, its cheapest and its most lavish, its most naïve and its most desperate, at its grimiest and its most splendid is all to be found in the bookies' shops and racecourses of Dublin. As a shortcut to the heart of a nation, it's not a bad start.

There are two ways to gamble: at a racecourse (horses or greyhounds) or in a bookmaker's shop (the bookie's). The two are very different experiences and will be treated separately.

Racecourses

A trip to Leopardstown, south Dublin, or Fairyhouse, 25 km north of Dublin, can be the day of a lifetime. A crisp bright day of suspense and excitement will stay in your memory for years, as will substantial losses, or gains.

How it works: between six and eight races are run in a day starting at 12.30 or 13.00 and ending before 18.00. Each race has a different number of horses riding in it either over flat ground or jumping fences— depending on the season—over a variety of distances. Before the race starts the people visiting the track stake money on the horse they think will win, and if it does then the person wins money.

Essentially, the punter (that's you) looks at each horse, figures out which is most likely to win and puts money on that horse either to win, or to win or come second or third ('each way'). The bookies are also figuring that out and offer short odds (e.g. 2–1: put on €1 and get €2) on the good horses, and long odds (30–1: put on €1 and win €30) on what they think will be the poor horses.

For more details hook up with a gambler or just do it by trial and error: the only other thing to note is that some bookies at the course have a €10 minimum bet, and you should bet a couple of euro at one time anyway so as not to look daft. If you're strapped remember you don't have to bet on every race.

As important to some people as the horses is the sense of occasion and the chance to get dressed up; the posh punters take the social aspect if anything more seriously than the horses. Yet by no means everybody there is rich: the difference between horse racing in Ireland and in other countries, notably England, is the extent of the social mix at the races here.

A trip is surprisingly cheap; €10 in to Leopardstown, (€15 into the enclosure). Remember that racing is a whole day's entertainment. Buses to and fro, the odd drink and flutter shouldn't bring the cost too high if you don't go crazy. If you're lucky you'll cover your costs with a couple of wins but the crucial thing is to set yourself a spending limit before you come and absolutely stick to it throughout the day.

Fairyhouse Ratoath, Co. Meath, tel 825 4877
Buses every half hour on race days from Busáras, Dublin 1.

Leopardstown Foxrock, Dublin 18, tel 289 3607,
e-mail info@leopardstown.com website www.leopardstown.com
Dublin Bus no. 63 or 114. Special buses from Busáras, Dublin 1, on race days, departing before the first race. Wheelchair access to some areas and toilets.

Going to the dogs

Greyhound racing, or the dogs is to a respectable horse-racing meeting what a weekly market is to high street chic: cheaper, rougher, smellier but often more exciting. This is certainly because the races are so fast and furious (between 30 seconds and one minute). One advantage is that stakes can be much smaller without the bookies looking upset. Unless you are a seasoned dog expert it is pretty acceptable just to choose a number between one and six, and plump €1 on the dog in question. Now that there are bars at the track many punters even miss the actual races.

At both Shelbourne Park and Harold's Cross there are a multitude of counters at which you can bet inside, and an equal number of television monitors from which to view the races themselves. They have bars on different levels and even serve dinner, taking bets at your table.

Harold's Cross Greyhound Stadium 151 Harold's Cross Rd, Dublin 6,
tel 497 1081
Dublin Bus nos 16, 16A, 19A, 49
Admission €6 (including programme)
Open Mon, Tues, Fri

Shelbourne Park Greyhound Stadium Shelbourne Pk, Ringsend, Dublin 4,
tel 668 3502
Dublin Bus nos 2, 3. (Actually the walk down Pearse St into Ringsend—just over 1 km from Trinity—is interesting in a gritty republican kind of way—past Pearse's birthplace, the Widow Scallan's pub, and Boland's Mills where de Valera defended the city in 1916 from troops coming along the coast from Dún Laoghaire, turn right into South Lotts Rd for the track.)
Admission €6 including programme
Open Wed, Thur, Sat, ten races each night

Bookmakers

In stark contrast to the stylish race courses, the bookie's shop is somewhere that your mother always hoped you would never go. It can seem a little grim, and is certainly mostly a male environment. You can either revel in the slightly seedy ambience, or just place your bet and watch the race in the pub nearby (there will always be a pub near a bookie's).

There are no set rules regarding maximum and minimum amount you can bet at the bookie's. The limits of each individual shop determine how much one person can bet. Placing a bet here is more complex than at the course because the cashiers are not allowed to place the bet for you. You have to write it down on the betting slips provided and hand the bet and the money to them. Just write the time and venue of the race and below it write the name of the horse plus 'to win' or 'each way' or whatever other way you want to bet. You can bet any amount you like, but if it is just a win or each way bet, then don't bet under a euro, you will feel silly. There is a betting tax of 2 per cent.

You can also bet on Wednesday's and Saturday's National Lottery at the bookie's. Most call it 'Lucky Numbers', and there is a range of ways to put money on. You can choose any combination of numbers that might come up, as well as numbers that won't. The odds are quite good too. If, for example, you want to bet on the possibility of one single number coming up out of 42, bookies will offer odds of an average 5/1. This is very good when you consider the chances mathematically work out at 7/1.

The really exciting thing about the bookie's as opposed to course betting is that you can bet on absolutely anything. If the shop doesn't offer odds on which team will win the ski-down-a-mountain-on-a-baking-tray at the Winter Olympics, then a couple of phone calls by them and they will take your bet. Finding obscure things to bet on can be quite amusing in itself (though snow on Christmas Day is the most common of the unusual bets).

But the real fun comes in the placing of accumulator bets. Basically this is where you stake a small amount of money on a series of outcomes in any number or kind of sporting event. You choose a large chain of outcomes and wait for it to unfold: a horse race tomorrow, a football match next week, the general election the following month, a tennis match—any combination you like. You can place a tiny stake—€1 or even 10c and each time you win those winnings become the stake for your next event. So from almost nothing, *if* all your predictions come true, you can end up having a large fortune riding on one obscure sporting event at the end of your chain. Alternatively, the first or second prediction could fail and you lose your money straight away. If the bookie's isn't busy, ask a punter or cashier to explain the following further variations on accumulator bets: double, treble, yankee, super yankee.

Cheap, immediate, thrilling, gambling is not to be knocked, but neither is it to be abused, so you must make sure you're not really spending too much time down the bookie's.

The whole process, whether at either kind of course or at a bookie's, is a particular and intense pursuit. Casinos are still illegal here, so this is the only gambling available apart from the state Lottery (don't touch it, the odds are rubbish—1 in 5.5 million: take your €1 to the bookie's and put it on the first horse you see, that way you've a chance of winning). The random minglings of hope and despair combined with what for most of us is only an illusion of skill in choosing a bet and the immediacy of the result unfolding on a screen before your eyes is a powerful and engaging experiment and one, as said before, which may well take you closer to an understanding of this city and its people than any number of guidebooks ever could.

Bookies: it really doesn't matter which chain or independent betting shop you go to. Finding them is not a problem in the city centre and they are also dotted around the suburbs. Opening hours are irregular: they open when there is something to bet on, usually most of the day from ten in the morning onwards. Summer opening hours are generally 10.00–21.00 and winter 10.00–16.30.

HOWTH
31 31B

HOWTH
SUMMIT
31B

PORTMARNOCK
32A 32B 32X
105 102 230

SUTTON
31 31A 31B

31A

KILBARRACK
17A 29A 31
32A 32 31B
32A 32B

BALDOYLE
32 32A 32B 32X
129 102 105

KINSEALY
42 43

RAHENY
29A 31 31A
31B 32 32A
32B 105

MOUNT PROSPECT
130

TO MALAHIDE
32A 32X 42
102 230 105

DARNDALE
27 27X 42
42A

COOLOCK
17A 27 27X
104 127 129

ARTANE
27 27B 27A
42 42B 43
104 127 129

KILLESTER
29A 31 31A 31B
32 32A 32B 42A
103 105

DOLLYMOUNT
130

CLONTARF
103 104 130

RINGSEND
5 7 7A 7X

TO DONABATE
33B 33C
TO PORTRANE
33B, 33C

TO
SWORDS
33 33B 33X 41 41A
41B 41C 41X 43 230

SANTRY
16 16A 16C 33 33B
41 41B 41C 746
103 104

BEAUMONT
20B 27B 51A
103 104

WHITEHALL
3 16 16A 16C
33 33B 41 41A
41B 41C 103

FAIRVIEW
20B 27 27B
27X 29A 31
31A 31B 32
32A 32X 32X
42 42A 103
104 127 129
130

BALLSBRIDGE
5 7 7A 7X

DUBLIN AIRPORT
16 16A 16C 41
41A 41B 41C 46X
58X 230 746 747
748 AIRLINK

BALLYMUN
13 13A 17A 46X
58X 102 104 220

DUBLIN CITY
UNIVERSITY
11 11A 11B 13
13A 19A 46X
58X 103 105

GLASNEVIN
13 19 134

DRUMCONDRA
3 11 11A 13A
16 33 41A 41B
41C 44 46X
58X 77X 746

PHIBSBORO
10 19 19A
38 38A 120
121 122 134

CITY
CENTRE

DOLPHIN'S BARN

KILMAINHAM
51B 68 69
78A 206

FINGLAS
17A 40 40A
40B 40C 104
134 220

CABRA
120 121 122

ISLANDBRIDGE
25 25A 26 68 69

PHOENIX PARK
10

TO TOBERBURR
DUBBER CROSS
40B

BLANCHARDSTOWN
38 38A 39 39X
70 70X 76A 236
237 238 239 270

ASHTOWN
37 37X 38
38A 39 39A
39B 70 70X

TO DUNBOYNE/CLONEE
70 70X 270

MULHUDDART
38 220 238 270

CASTLEKNOCK
37 37X 38
237 239

CHAPELIZOD
25A 26 66
66A 66B 67 67A

BALLYFERMOT
18 76 76A 76B
78A 79 206

TO
MAYNOOTH
66 66X 67A
66 66A 66B 66X
67 67A 67X

LEIXLIP
CELBRIDGE

PALMERSTOWN
18 25 25A 66
66A 66B 67 67A 67X

LUCAN
25 25A 25X
66 66A
66B 67 67A
67X 239

CHERRY ORCHARD
18 76 76A 76B
78A